THE ORACLES OF APOLLO IN ASIA MINOR

THE H.W. Parke
ORACLES
OF APOLLO
in Asia Minor

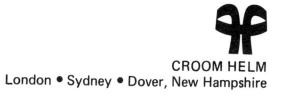

CROOM HELM
London • Sydney • Dover, New Hampshire

© 1985 H.W. Parke
Croom Helm Ltd, Provident House, Burrell Row,
Beckenham, Kent BR3 1AT
Croom Helm Australia Pty Ltd, Suite 4, 6th Floor,
64-76 Kippax Street, Surry Hills, NSW 2010, Australia

British Library Cataloguing in Publication Data

Parke, H.W.
    The oracles of Apollo in Asia Minor.
    1. Oracles, Turkish
    I. Title
    292'.32   BL613
    ISBN 0-7099-4012-2

Croom Helm, 51 Washington Street, Dover,
New Hampshire 03820, USA

Library of Congress Cataloging in Publication Data

Parke, H. W. (Herbert William), 1903-
    The oracles of Apollo in Asia Minor

    Bibliography:p
    Includes index
    1. Apollo (Greek deity) - cult - Turkey
    2. Oracles, Greek - Turkey
    3. Turkey - religious life and customs
    I. Title
BL820.A7P37 1985   292'.32'09392   85-24260
ISBN 0-7099-4012-2

Printed and bound in Great Britain
by Billing & Sons Limited, Worcester.

CONTENTS

Contents

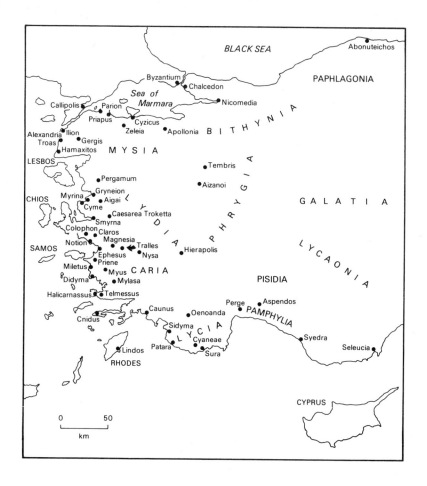

BLACK SEA

Abonuteichos

PAPHLAGONIA

Byzantium
Chalcedon

Sea of
Marmara

Nicomedia

Callipolis
Parion
Priapus
Cyzicus

B I T H Y N I A

Zeleia
Apollonia

Alexandria Ilion
Troas
Gergis
Hamaxitos

MYSIA

LESBOS

Tembris

P H R Y G I A

Aizanoi

GALATIA

Pergamum

CHIOS
Myrina
Gryneion
Aigai
Cyme

Caesarea Trocketta

L
Y
D
I
A

L Y C A O N I A

Smyrna
Colophon
Claros
Notion
Magnesia
Tralles
Nysa

Hierapolis

Ephesus
Priene

SAMOS
Miletus
Myus
CARIA

PISIDIA

Didyma
Mylasa

Halicarnassus
Telmessus

Perge
Aspendos

Caunus

Oenoanda

PAMPHYLIA

Cnidus
Sidyma
L
Y
C
I
A
Cyaneae

Syedra

Patara
Sura

Seleucia

Lindos

RHODES

CYPRUS

0   50

km

PART I

THE APOLLINE ORACLES OF ASIA MINOR
BRANCHIDAE - DIDYMA

Chapter One

THE ARCHAIC PERIOD FROM THE LITERARY SOURCES

The modern tourist who sets out to see the temple of
Apollo at Didyma usually approaches it by road after
a visit to Miletus. The remains of that ancient city
give a deep impression of wealth and importance. The
vast theatre with its corridors and staircases, the
Roman baths now surrounded by fields, the less iden-
tifiable remains scattered thickly over an area roughly
two kilometres by one in extent, all impress the
onlooker with its historic greatness. On leaving
Miletus and its surrounding hills the road to Didyma
takes the traveller to the sea coast where it skirts
a low shingly shore on his right for some eight miles;
on his left are successsions of small featureless
ridges. Then he comes to a little curving bay, protected by the headland - Panormus, "the anchorage for
all weathers". There the road turns inland rising
gently for two miles up a shallow valley. At last
when the ridge is nearly surmounted the tops of a few
huge columns are seen ahead peeping over the crest.
But the full vastness of the temple is not seen until
one is within a few hundred yards of its great facade.
Then is disclosed in a hollow at the top of the ridge
one of the largest religious buildings erected in antiquity.
      The setting, as has been already suggested, is
curiously lacking in beauty and impressiveness compared with those of the other famous Greek shrines. It
has none of the numinous quality which strikes every
traveller at Delphi. Olympia surpasses it in charm
and beauty. Even the great temples of Hera on Samos
and Artemis at Ephesus, its chief rivals in Ionia,
were set in flat plains which exhibited to those who
approached them the full bulk of their great buildings. As often in the Greco-Roman world the reason
for the choice of site was the presence of water. In
a stretch of barren and waterless country this hollow

1

on the hill top contained a spring, which, though it
must have yielded at the best a poor supply, was important through its isolation. It was to be expected
that such a place would in primitive times possess
some sanctity. That it would be for some periods the
most important oracle in Asia Minor was one of those
historic facts which cannot be fully accounted for by
logical explanations.

Pausanias the guide-book writer, in an excursus
on the Greek settlements in Asia Minor remarks in one
tantalizing sentence: "the sanctuary of Apollo at
Didyma and the oracle are older than the settlement of
the Ionians". (1) It is most likely that this statement
is true, but it would be helpful if we knew exactly
what evidence Pausanias relied on in making this assertion. All we possess are legendary accounts and
allusions concerning Branchus, the founder, which suggest a later date for the foundation. They are of
special significance because of the peculiar importance of Branchus as the eponymous ancestor of an
oracular family.

The oracle at Didyma in the archaic period was
managed by the family of the Branchidae. This
arrangement was somewhat unusual. The Apolline oracles of the Greek mainland, and also elsewhere in Ionia,
so far as our evidence goes, were not under the control of particular families. Hereditary priesthoods
were common in Greek states and had survived even in
cults which had become part of the state religion of
a polis. Also families of diviners were known in which
the gift of prophecy was hereditary. But in historic
times Olympia was the only oracular centre where the
position of prophet was confined to the members of
families - the Iamids and the Clytiads, and there at
an early date the practice of divination had become
almost restricted to forecasts of success in the games
obtained by omens from sacrifices. (2)

The Branchidae of Didyma were in a much more conspicuous position. Not only were they the hereditary
controllers of a most important oracle, but their position was so dominant that they even gave their name
to the place. Unlike any other Greek sanctuary the
family name was used to designate the site. Though
Didyma was apparently the actual name of the locality,
Herodotus when using his own words always refers to it
as "Branchidae". (3) This fact suggests that the origin of the sanctuary was, as Pausanias believed, pre-
hellenic and that it was therefore, as may be conjectured, one of those communities centred on the temple
of a local deity such as were typical of other parts
of Asia Minor, before it was hellenized, and which

survived in places throughout classical times.

Branchus himself, the ancestor of the family, is only known to us from Hellenistic sources, but this is just one of the accidents of tradition. The legends told of him are evidently early in origin, even if they are only preserved in later sophisticated forms. Significantly enough, Branchus has a name almost unique in Greek mythology. It was not used as a personal name in the classical period; which was not surprising as it was the same as the Greek word for "sore throat" or "hoarseness". There was, of course, a legend to explain this curious nomenclature. It was said that his mother while pregnant saw a vision that the sun entered her mouth and emerged from her womb. Hence the child born to her was called Branchus because the sun had passed through her throat. The legend in its crudely exaggerated and obvious symbolism is of a type which recurs in the oriental tales of Herodotus. It is clearly primitive and eastern in origin. But one may doubt whether it was originally invented to explain the name Branchus, which as we have pointed out did not literally mean "throat" but "sore throat". The vision was a prophecy that Branchus was the son of the Sun God, but the Greeks re-adapted it to provide, however inadequately, an explanation of his name. Actually the most likely hypothesis is that the derivation of the name is from some non-Greek language of Asia Minor, and that its origin and the foundation of the oracle both dated back before the arrival of the Ionians. (4)

If Branchus was a legendary founder of a cult which preceded the Ionian colonization, it is not surprising that an attempt was made to integrate him into the pattern of Greek legend. Since this involved a link with Delphi it is reasonable to suppose that in its present form, which comes to us from Hellenistic and later authors, it represents a creation from the period after the Hellenistic restoration of the temple. That was a time when Didyma would be happy to earn prestige from a claim to be derived from Delphi. One cannot imagine that the original Branchidae would have tolerated such a legend. In the archaic period the temple and its traditions would need no such support, and historically it is not to be believed that it had any foundation in fact. The story ran that Democlos the Delphian had a son of exceptional beauty named Smikros ("Tiny"). In accordance with an oracle Democlos sailed to Miletus bringing with him his son aged thirteen. "In haste to sail away and in unawareness", as the simple story goes, he left Smikros behind. The boy was discovered in a state of despair by

the goatherd son of Epitharses, and when he heard of
Smikros's misfortune and his origin, Epitharses treated him with no less care than his own son. The legend
continued with an episode which occurred to the boys
when they were herding their goats. They captured a swan
and covered it in a cloak while they argued which of
them should bring it as a gift to their father. The
argument developed into a fight, and when they were
tired with the struggle, they threw back the cloak
and found instead of the swan a woman. The boys fled at
the sight, but she called them back and warned them
that she was Leucothea - the White Goddess. They were
to tell the Milesians that she had been pleased at the
boys' fight and they were to honour her by performing
an athletic contest of boys dedicated to her. The
Milesians accepted this intimation and instituted the
festival. Also Smikros was so respected after the
incident that he married the daughter of a distinguished citizen. Their son was Branchus whose birth was
forecast by the dream of the sun issuing from his mother's womb. (5)

     Evidently this story is put together out of two
or three different elements. The father of Branchus
is brought from Delphi in a rather unconvincing manner.
He is then called to public notice by an episode which
is clearly the aition for the founding of some religious games dedicated to a rather obscure deity,
Leucothea. Finally his marriage to a prominent Milesian links him and the sanctuary at Didyma conveniently with the neighbouring city. The implication of
the legend is that Branchus belonged to the period
after the foundation of Miletus. In fact it was said
that he was descended from Machaereus, the Delphian
who slew Neoptolemus in the sanctuary. This would date
the foundation of the oracle, not before, but after
the Ionian migration.

     The story of Branchus' ancestry did not give any
explanation of his prophetic gifts, unless one were to
suppose that a descendant of a Delphian must be a diviner. The vision of his birth as the sun might have
implied that he was of supernatural origin, but is not
followed up in legend. Instead according to the usual
tradition the gift of prophecy was not his from birth,
but was bestowed on him as a youth. As the story goes,
he was of exceptional beauty, and Apollo seeing him
herding in the country fell in love with him and kissed
him. The god's act was said to be commemorated in his
traditional cult-title at Didyma, where he was called
Apollo Philesios. The Greek name could correctly mean
"loving" or "kissing", and for once it is unnecessary
to suppose a false etymology. The god further demon-

strated his love by bestowing on Branchus the power of prophecy. This was accompanied by the gift of a crown and a rod of bay wood - the tree associated in legend with Apollo. After receiving these bounties Branchus proceeded to utter oracles, and the gift apparently descended in the family until the Persian destruction of the temple in the early fifth century. (6)

The scene of Apollo's encounter with the goatherd Branchus was evidently set on the site of the later oracle-centre. Callimachus in a poem "Branchus" beautifully describes it: (7)

> --"The fair precinct in the wood where first,
> Apollo, you were seen near the twin springs
> when you had fixed in the ground a bough of
> bay."

Callimachus evidently supplied by this description a derivation for the place-name Didyma, which he took to mean "twin" and to refer to the existence of two springs. The importance of the sacred fountain at the oracle-centre is a notion which recurs throughout its history, but the double springs are not mentioned elsewhere. The bough of bay which Apollo fixed in the ground was the origin of the sacred trees within the precinct, which appear in later narratives. The legend of Apollo's love for the goatherd Branchus conveniently explained the location of the temple in the country and his hereditary gift of prophecy. There is a latent inconsistency between it and the story of Branchus, the son of Smikros and a prominent Milesian mother. It is essentially timeless and without any necessary connection with a Greek city.

One other episode is traditionally associated with Branchus. Apollo was wroth with the Ionians and sent a plague. Only Branchus was able to purify them. Callimachus again is the earliest extant author to tell how the purification was accomplished, and he puts the reference rather allusively into the mouth of the Bay when it is defending its precedence against the Olive Tree in a contest which he places on Mount Tmolus in Lydia. (8)

> "O foolish Olive, did not Branchus by striking
> them with a bay and uttering twice or thrice an
> unshortened phrase make whole the sons of the
> Ionians with whom Phoebus was wroth?"

Four hundred years after Callimachus Clement of Alexandria reproduced from a Hellenistic source and with a reference to the poet some further details (9):

5

"The following verses were uttered by the prophet Branchus when purifying the Milesians from plague. Sprinkling the multitude with boughs of bay he led them in the words of a hymn thus:-

> "Sing, children, in honour of the Far-Darter and his sister."

The populace chanted in response:

> "BEDY, ZAPS, CHTHOM, PLEKTRON, SPHINX. KNAXZBICH, THYPTES, PHLEGMO, DROPS."

These strange words sound almost as much gibberish in Greek as in English. Clement of Alexandria reproduced various conflicting explanations of their meaning supplied by Hellenistic scholars, but also recognised that they were like the sentences used to teach children their letters. For the two lines each contain precisely the twenty four letters of the ancient Ionic alphabet. Otherwise, they are a classical equivalent of "The quick brown fox jumps over the lazy dog". Of modern scholars Bentley was the first to recognise properly this alphabetic source and to draw the evident conclusion that so far from being an ancient ritual formula these lines could only have been evolved after the Greek alphabet had reached its fully developed form. This is true, but also it must be recognised that the words were not merely a handy mnemonic for teaching children or an amusing kind of anagram. There was to the Greek mind something magical in such verbal formulae, and there was therefore nothing absurd in supposing that they could be effectively used to exorcise a plague. All one can say is that they would be more typical of the quasi-magical ritual used by some unofficial minister rather than the regular liturgy of an established Greek priesthood.

One further legend is worth discussing here, because if it were to be accepted as historically founded, it would place Branchus in the archaic period and alter one's views on the family of the Branchidae. Leodamas, who was traditionally the last hereditary king of Miletus, had distinguished himself in war against Carystus. He captured the city and in accordance with an oracular command dedicated a tithe of the spoils to Apollo at Branchidae. Among these was a woman of Carystus with an infant at her breast. Branchus "who at that time presided over the shrine took the woman for his wife and adopted the child, who grew in a miraculous way and exhibited an intelligence beyond his years. So Branchus made him herald (_angelos_)

of the prophetic responses and named him Evangelos.
When he was of age he inherited the oracle of Branchus
and became the origin of the family of the Evangelidae
among Milesians." (10) The reign of Leodamas has no
precise dating. On general probability one might guess
that the institution of kingship probably survived till
the 8th century. The war with Carystus is not otherwise known. It is possible that Miletus engaged in
overseas campaigns of this sort, but the almost total
extinction of the early history of the Ionian cities
leaves the matter quite doubtful. Otherwise the legend is of a typical enough pattern - the captive woman
dedicated at a temple who in the end achieves an hon-
ourable position. We shall find another occurrence of
the motive in the legendary traditions of Claros.
Evidently the whole purpose of the story is to provide
an origin for a family of Milesian nobles. This would
furnish a clue to the shaping of the legend if we knew
anything about the family. But extraordinarily enough
it does not appear again in our literary sources and
there is nothing in the inscriptions of Didyma to elucidate it. Only the name Evangelos appears twice in
quite unimportant connections.
　　It is impossible to accept the legend's main
thesis, which is that Branchus had no children of his
own who inherited the oracle, but that it was taken
over by Evangelos and his descendants, called the
Evangelidae. If so, the name of Didyma should not have
been Branchidae, but Evangelidae. It will not be
sufficient to explain away the anomaly by supposing
two families, the Branchidae and the Evangelidae, of
whom the latter held a subordinate role as heralds
announcing prophecies produced by the divination of the
Branchidae. Conon, the author of the legend as transmitted, is quite explicit that Evangelos took over the
oracle by inheritance. The only way out of the problem is to suppose that it is a Hellenistic legend invented to explain the family name Evangelos. By the
time it was concocted the oracle had been revived, but
under state control. So it was possible to allege
that ancestors had once acted as prophets without lay-
ing oneself open to immediate confutation. Wilamowitz
was surprised that an aristocratic family of Miletus
would trace its origin from a Carystian slave woman.
But presumably the distance in the past gave a suitably romantic flavour to the legend, which was in
keeping with the sentimental imaginings of the New
Comedy, and the convenient transfer of Branchus from
the far past to the end of the kingship was only part
of the process of family glorification.
　　Out of this jumble of legends transmitted to us

in late and abbreviated forms what conclusions can be drawn? Branchus appears to be in origin an unhellenic figure, with no original connection with Greek mythology. Hence he is the appropriate ancestor of a family of hereditary priests in a shrine which was originally unconnected with any Greek city-state. Later efforts of myth-making linked him with Miletus and Delphi, but these were only the rationalising attempts of scholars. In the most primitive tradition he may have been simply the son of a sun-god. But the Greeks preferred to this legend the myth that he was the beloved of Apollo - a more fortunate and better endowed Hyacinthus. Even so he retained some features which are untypical of a Greek priest. His use of magic formulae and his possession of something like a magic wand are probably derived from his non-Hellenic origin. But the Apollo whom he worshipped has the typical features of the god known to the early Greeks. He is to some extent a god of the shepherds rather than the farmers, he can send plague as readily as blessing, and he is a source of ecstatic prophecy.

There is one further story about King Leodamas which may be recorded here, though, in so far as it concerns Branchidae, it is not likely to be historic. It is perhaps an illustration of the dearth of surviving material on early Milesian history that the only stories of the period of the kingship are all connected with this last king. Nicolaus of Damascus tells us that Leodamas was a just and popular ruler in the city of Miletus. But when on the festival of Apollo he was leading the procession with the sacrificial animals on the road to Branchidae he was attacked by one Amphitres and his fellow-conspirators. The king was killed, and Amphitres seized power and ruled as tyrant. The sons of Leodamas and their friends retired to Assesos, a town in Milesian territory which was under a governor, installed by the late king, who eagerly welcomed the royal party. (Wilamowitz has plausibly identified the place with strategically placed ruins on the Maeander at Sakys-burnu, where the road turns north from the Carian mountains. Assesos occurs again in the wars of Alyattes of Lydia against Miletus in the early 6th century.) (11)

Amphitres soon besieged the town, and the inhabitants, after resisting with distress for some time, sent to the oracle (evidently Branchidae) to enquire concerning the war. The god replied that helpers would come to them from Phrygia who would exact vengeance for the murder of Leodamas and would free them and the Milesians from trouble. The siege was prolonged until there arrived two young men called Tottes

and Onnes from Phrygia. They approached the wall at
night carrying between them the sacred objects of the
Kabeiroi concealed in a chest, and asked for admit-
tance. The watchmen demanded who they were and received for answer that by the command of a god they
were bringing sacred things for the blessing of the
men of Miletus and of Assesos. Calling the oracle
to mind the watchmen admitted them. At dawn there was
a meeting of the people, to which the young men explained that they had been commanded by a god to go to
Assesos with sacred things as avengers of the murder
of Leodamas (whoever he was, for they did not know)
and to rescue from trouble Miletus and Assesos. They
further explained that to accomplish these purposes
they must make their customary sacrifices. The people
were delighted at the coincidence of the prophecies
and promised to establish the sacred things in a sanctuary among them and hold them in honour if the prophecies were fulfilled. It is not surprising after this
to read that the besiegers were promptly routed,
Amphitres was slain, and the tyranny was abolished.
Its place was taken not by an hereditary kingship, but
by an elected magistrate.

The story of sacred rites and oracles which is
attached to the fall of the Milesian kingship is of a
familiar pattern:- the stranger bearing the cult objects of a foreign god who comes in fulfilment of a
prophecy and rescues from trouble the people who
receive him by the introduction of a religious rite
which is then adopted widely. In this instance the
cult was that of the Kabeiroi, the mystery deities of
Thracian or Phrygian origin, who were accepted in many
Greek cities, particularly in the Northern and Eastern
Aegean. Miletus and Didyma have supplied plenty of
evidence for their worship in the imperial period, but
it would be most unlikely that the introduction took
place as early as the eighth century. A more plausible time would be in the fourth century B.C., or a
little earlier. By the first century A.D., shortly
after Nicolaus of Damascus reproduced the story of
Tottes and Onnes, a Roman proconsul, Caecina Paetus,
confirmed by edict what were described as "the ancestral rights" of "the sacrifices and ceremonies" of the
Kabeiroi. So the legend can be regarded as a pious
fiction. It is, however, obviously well constructed.
The cult probably came from Phrygia, and the names of
Tottes and Onnes appear to be philologically plausible
and may have had religious significance. It is even
possible, if it came in the archaic period, that the
Branchidae took an interest in the cult and helped to
shape the legend. Certainly by the 1st century A.D.

9

at a date somewhat later than our literary sources the worships of Apollo and of the Kabeiroi had become so closely associated that it is usual for the prophet of Didyma on official inscriptions to describe himself as "also at the same time Kotarches" (priest of the Kabeiroi). (12)

The literary traditions which we have so far considered have not contained any genuine record of the oracular activities of Apollo at Branchidae. But one type of enquiry is mentioned in general terms by our sources which must certainly be authentic. This was the sanctioning of colonial foundations. It was a function for which Delphi in particular had a famous reputation. In fact it is clear that it was largely by this activity that the Pythia acquired international prestige. Situated within reach of the sea, but in central Greece, it was easy of access to most of the mother-cities from which early colonies were dispatched, and it appears to have been fortunate in being associated from the beginning with this great movement of Greek population.

The settlement of a Greek colony involved much religious as well as political and economic activity. The mother-city and her daughter continued to be bound usually by ritual, not by constitutional ties. In the colony itself there were cults to be introduced from the mother-city or adopted from the natives. All these activities required religious sanctions. But also founding a colony was a daring speculation, and some encouragement from Apollo would be a great help to morale in the difficult days before and immediately after the foundation.

Branchidae was in a particularly significantly uation for this purpose. It was within ten miles of a great Greek trading city, and we may suppose that by the time when the movement of colonisation started it was already under the political control of Miletus. Traditionally that city had founded colonies in the Black Sea region as early as the first half of the eighth century B.C. But even if this date is regarded as rather too early, at least by the end of the seventh century a string of colonies were spaced out along the trade-routes, and these continued to multiply as far as the Caucasus, the Crimea, and the strait of Kerch, until at last Miletus had upwards of a hundred such settlements established directly or by her daughter cities. Many of these show evidence of the cult of Apollo, but in only one instance was the founder traditionally guided by a Delphic response, and significantly he was an exile from Miletus. In none of the other instances is any individual foundation oracle recorded. But the natural supposition is not that no oracle was consulted, but that it was the local prophetic centre of Branchidae.

The belief that Apollo of Didyma had generally been consulted on the foundation of Milesian colonies is confirmed in a rather quaint document produced generations later. In the mid-second century B.C. Apollonia on the river Rhyndacus, a minor Milesian colony in eastern Mysia, renewed relations with its mother-city. As the contemporary decree from Apollonia records, "the Milesians listened to the ambassadors with every good will, and after they had investigated the histories on the subject and other written records they replied that our city in truth had been founded as a colony of their own city. Their ancestors had accomplished this, at the time when they sent out a military expedition to the regions in the neighbourhood of the Hellespont and the sea of Marmara. They had conquered in war the barbarian inhabitants and had settled our city among the other Greek cities. Apollo of Didyma had been the guide in the campaign." (13) It is curious to find that some four centuries after the foundation of the colony relations with the mother-city had lapsed so that the connection was only recognised after some historic and documentary research by the Milesians. There is no reason to doubt that evidence was found and that it included references to the oracular authority of Didyma. Neither Miletus nor Didyma has supplied any further evidence. There would be more hope of finding inscriptional record in other of the Milesian colonies, and none of these has as yet been thoroughly excavated. On the other hand our literary sources never assigned any other city's colonies to the command of Apollo of Branchidae. This also may represent the historic facts. Delphi was not directly associated with any one great colonising city, and so its responses on this subject could be regarded by any enquirer as disinterested. But Branchidae was so much the oracle of Miletus that one could well suppose that other prospective mother-cities could scarcely consult it, unless they intended to associate Miletus itself with their colonial venture: which so far as our evidence goes, no one chose to do. So it is probably right to suppose that for a couple of centuries from the late eighth to the late sixth century, Branchidae may have been issuing frequent responses in support of the foundation of Milesian colonies, but this activity was somewhat introspective and did not bring the oracle into contact with the rest of the Greek world.

Tradition also associated Delphi and Branchidae

in a quaint legend which was connected with another
aspect of Apollo: his reputation as the source of human wisdom. The motive of the legend was linked with
the Seven Sages who were supposed to be seven contemporaries of great wisdom who knew and recognised each
other's intellect. They were combined in a contest of
humility in which each in turn refused the prize for
being the wisest man. Various versions of the legend
existed which all embodied this same theme. The favourite was that fishermen when hauling in a catch sold
it to some foreigners, but when the nets proved to
contain a golden tripod, the fishermen rejected their
bargain on the ground that this was no normal catch.
The question was ultimately referred to Delphi where
the Pythia declared that it must be given to the
wisest. So it was first offered to Thales of Miletus,
who refused to accept it as undeserved and sent it on
to Bias of Priene, and so it passed through the rest
of the traditional list of the Seven Sages, until at
last it returned to Thales again, who according to the
usual version ended by dedicating it to Apollo on the
ground that he alone possessed true wisdom. Other
accounts cut out the oracle by describing the tripod
itself as being inscribed "For the wisest". An entirely different version with the same motif started off
the contest by telling that one Bathycles of Arcadia
bequeathed a gold bowl with instructions that it was
to be given to the wisest, or Croesus bestowed a cup
with the same command. (14)
    Our sources for these stories are only extant in
late authors, Hellenistic and after, and it is probably out of the question to trace the legend back
precisely to its original form. But certain general
features can be detected. The scene is normally set
in Asia Minor: for instance, the fishermen are from
Cos and the purchasers from Lebedos, or the fishermen
are from Miletus and the purchasers Ionian youths.
Again the transference of the prize usually starts with
Thales of Miletus and the typical narrative ends with
its dedication to Apollo of Didyma even though the
oracular responses are attributed to the Pythia. The
earliest version of the story of Bathycles' bowl described it as dedicated to the Delphinian Apollo in his
local shrine beside the harbour of Miletus. This came
from the Milesian author, probably of the fourth century B.C., and may reflect the claim of that temple to
exhibit such a dedication. Alternatively, the prize
was strangely said to be in the temple of the Ismenian
Apollo of Thebes. This tradition is indicated by
Plutarch, who may have been influenced by Boeotian
patriotism and another local claim to possess the leg-

endary tripod. But behind these divergencies an original connection with Miletus seems clear.

Also the legend cannot be dissociated from the
tradition of the Seven Wise Men, which also has significant signs of originating in Asia Minor. Of the
earliest list Thales of Miletus, Bias of Priene,
Pittacus of Mitylene and Cleobulus of Lindos all belong to that coast or its adjacent islands. Of the
others Solon and Periander both figure prominently in
Asian legends. Chilon of Sparta is the only one without any local connection there. His presence in the
list, apart from his general reputation, may have
been due to the strong involvement of Sparta with
Asian affairs in the sixth century. For it is likely
that the roots of the concept of the Seven Sages go
back to that period. The first list occurs in Plato,
but Herodotus, even though he does not mention them
explicitly as a group, seems to know of them and their
wise sayings individually. Also apart from the local
connections of the Sages the presence of some of them
in the early lists would seem only explicable on the
basis of a choice made in the archaic period. For
instance later Greeks were rather shocked at the in-
clusion of Periander of Corinth. As a tyrant about
whom the Corinthians had horrible stories to tell, he
seemed a most unsuitable selection. But while Herodotus in places reproduces this unfavourable view of
him, he also knew from the Milesians a story in which
he was a helpful ally of their city through his
friendship with their tyrant, Thrasybulus. At a later
stage when Delphi had insinuated itself into the legend of the tripod, the obscure Oetean, Myson of Chen,
who was a figure in the moralising traditions of the
Pythia, was substituted for Periander in the list of
the Seven Sages.

These considerations suggest that the legend and
the concept of the Sages originated in Miletus in the
late sixth century. It was probably connected in its
invention with the sanctuary of Branchidae, which
according to some versions was the ultimate resting
place of the tripod. The ideas which it embodied were
appropriate to the new age of classical Greece which
was to emerge. Instead of the old conception of the
heroic virtues of competition and emulation a new
feeling of human limitations was developing and was
fostered by the oracular shrines. This found its most
typical expression at Delphi in the maxims "Know
thyself" and "Nothing in excess" which were prominently inscribed on the temple of Apollo. By the late
fifth century it was believed that they had been con-
tributed to the Pythian Apollo as an offering of wis-

dom from the Seven Sages. If this had been literally
true they would have had to be inscribed on the earlier temple before it was burnt down in 548/7 B.C.
But it is more probable that they were first inscribed
on the restored Alcmeonid temple about 510 B.C., and
had no original connection with the Sages, but were
associated with them when their legend reached Delphi
from Ionia. (15)

There is no suggestion that the temple of Branchidae ever contained moralising inscriptions. But it
is not surprising, if it took a part also in the new
movement toward humility by developing the legend of
the wise men who modestly disclaimed the title of
"Wisest" and assigned true wisdom to God alone.

With the end of the seventh century Herodotus is
available for the first time as a source of evidence
on Branchidae. He mentions it only casually in connection
with other subjects, but his allusions are historically important. When describing the reign of the
Pharaoh, Necho, he records his campaign into Syria
against Babylon. At Megiddo (609 B.C.) he was inter-
cepted by Josiah, king of Judah, and a battle followed
in which Josiah was killed. The Pharaoh, as Herodotus
records, sent as a dedication to Apollo at Branchidae
the royal garment which he himself had worn in the
battle. Though in Herodotus' day it will not have been
preserved at Didyma there is no ground for doubting
the historic accuracy of the tradition. Dedications
of Pharaohs are recorded from other temples such as
that of Athena of Lindos on Rhodes. Miletus had early
connections with the opening up of Egypt under the
Saite dynasty. So one can understand that Necho would
be aware of this important Greek city. But one is also
inclined to suppose that there might be some special
occasion for the gift. Since the first Saite Pharaoh,
Psammetichus, the Egyptians had employed as soldiers
Greek and Carian mercenaries settled in Egypt. It may
have been in acknowledgement of their part in the battle that Necho chose to send a personal dedication
connected with the victory to the great shrine of one
of the mercenaries' gods. At least it is the earliest
evidence for international recognition of the importance of Branchidae. (16)

A nearer foreign monarchy was the kingdom of
Lydia, whose relations with Miletus had undergone a
complete revolution. Since the accession of a new
dynasty under Gyges before the mid-seventh century,
the Lydians had begun to press the Ionian cities.
Miletus had been subject to annual invasions of its
territory for eleven years when king Alyattes reversed the policy and made terms with the Milesians.

This exceptional treatment of them, while the aggressive policy was further developed against the other Greeks, continued under his son, Croesus. Branchidae appears twice in Herodotus' account of Croesus' reign, and the references are notably inconsistent. It figures in the list of the oracles from all over the Greek world whom the Lydian king was said to have tested before enquiring about his intended war with Persia. The present writer believes that the picturesque story of the simultaneous interrogation of the oracles is a Delphic legend concocted to glorify the Pythian Apollo over his prophetic rivals and to explain the rather embarrassing presence of the vast dedications from Croesus, whose ambition had come to a bad end. Traditionally Branchidae had completely failed the test. But this poor result is very inconsistent with the fact which Herodotus mentions several times that there had been in that temple dedications of Croesus "equal in weight and similar to those in Delphi". Of course, by Herodotus' day after the Persian sack, as Herodotus himself points out, they were no longer there. But he is evidently convinced of their earlier existence. The description of them with its strong comparisons with the dedications at Delphi suggests a Milesian source, hankering after lost treasures, but, even if one allows for some exaggeration, which could not be controlled by reference to the surviving objects, it is clear that Croesus must have greatly enriched the sanctuary at Branchidae in a manner that can scarcely be explained if he regarded the oracle as untruthful. The only way out of the inconsistency, if one is to keep both accounts, would be to suppose that the gifts to Branchidae were made early in his reign, as is suggested by our evidence, and that the subsequent test with its adverse result was applied later. But in the present writer's view the rejection of the legend of the oracular test is the correct solution. Instead one may suppose that the Branchidae had benefited richly by the generosity of Croesus. (17)

On the fall of Lydia, the Milesians succeeded in negotiating with Cyrus a similar state of amity to that which they had maintained with Croesus. This may explain the motives behind the only consultation of Apollo Didymeus, which Herodotus records. Soon after the capture of Sardis Pactyes, a Lydian, led a native revolt against the Persians. His attempt failed, and he took refuge in Cyme. The Persians sent to demand his surrender, and the men of Cyme in perplexity dispatched a sacred embassy to Branchidae to ask Apollo what act of theirs would be pleasing to the gods.

(Herodotus adds the general comment that this oracle-centre had been founded of old and was the one which all the Ionians and Aeolians were accustomed to use.) The response to their enquiry was to surrender Pactyes to the Persians. When the men of Cyme heard this advice they were proceeding to act on it, but a prominent citizen, Aristodicus, the son of Heraclides, opposed the surrender, asserting that he did not believe the response and thought the sacred ambassadors were not reporting the truth. So a second embassy of other citizens, including Aristodicus himself, was sent. He acted as spokesman and, as Herodotus reports it, put the enquiry in a very loaded form: "Lord Apollo, Pactyes the Lydian has come to us as a suppliant, fleeing from a violent death at the hands of the Persians. They are demanding his surrender bidding the men of Cyme let him go. But though in fear of the power of Persia, we have not had the effrontery to surrender a suppliant until first it has been revealed on your part which alternative we should choose." The response given was the same: to surrender Pactyes to the Persians. But Aristodicus acted further on his own. "He went round the temple pulling out the sparrows and all the other kinds of birds which had nested in the temple. While he was doing this it is said that a voice came to Aristodicus from the innermost sanctuary saying: "Most impious of men, why have you the effrontery to act thus? Are you ravaging my suppliants from the precinct?" But Aristodicus was not at a loss and answered: "Lord Apollo, do you come to the help of your suppliants thus, while you are bidding the Cymaeans surrender their suppliant?". But the god spoke again in reply "Yes indeed, I bid you surrender him, that after committing impiety you may the more speedily perish, in order that in future you will not come to an oracle-centre enquiring on the subject of surrendering suppliants". The Cymaeans received the report of this second embassy and did not wish either of the alternatives, to surrender Pactyes and perish or to retain him and be besieged by the Persians. So they escaped the dilemma temporarily by sending him to Mitylene. The Mitylenians, when a message from the Persian commander about Pactyes was being delivered, were preparing to surrender him for some kind of bribe. But, as Herodotus says "I cannot name it precisely: for the business was never settled". The men of Cyme when they heard that these negotiations had been begun by the Mitylenaeans, sent a boat to Lesbos and fetched Pactyes away to Chios. But in the end the Chians dragged him from the sanctuary and surrendered him to the Persians, bribed by the offer of territory on the mainland. Herodotus' narrative ends with a description how the Chians treated this land as the price of blood and would not make offerings to the gods from its produce. (19)

The whole story is among the most vivid and detailed in Herodotus. He evidently based it on some precise information, for he knows such items as the full name of Aristodicus, but on the other hand calls careful attention to his failure to hear what bribe was offered to the Mitylenians. So the basic facts can be taken as historic - the flight of Pactyes to Cyme, the two embassies to Branchidae, and Pactyes' subsequent transfer to Lesbos and Chios. Also clearly the oracle must twice have ordered the surrender. The circumstances of Aristodicus' symbolic protest to Apollo are evidently worked up with pietistic intent. Herodotus himself, significantly enough, sounds a faint note of caution by inserting the qualification "it is said". But it is likely to be not entirely fantasy. Either of two possible explanations can be suggested. Aristodicus, as one may suppose, actually performed his demonstration of driving out the nesting birds, but it may have happened in a more matter-of-fact way that the priests themselves protested with an argument on the lines of the story. Then the episode was worked up for dramatic effect, so that the protesting voice became that of Apollo himself from his sanctuary. Alternatively, the whole story may have rested on the testimony of Aristodicus. His conduct in calling for a second embassy shows how convinced he was that the proposed surrender of the suppliant was impious. When he had attacked the nests he either invented Apollo's protest or convinced himself that he had heard it. The fantasy, whether deliberate or subconscious, exactly fulfilled Aristodicus' purpose, for it was excellently calculated to convince his fellow citizens that the literal meaning of the oracular command, though twice uttered, must not be accepted. The Cymaeans' conduct in finding a compromise short of surrendering Pactyes shows how they had been convinced to abandon their earlier decision in favour of it.

We need not then attribute to the prophet at Branchidae the elaborate sophistication which Herodotus puts into Apollo's mouth. Probably the oracular reply, though at variance with the most obvious rules of Greek piety, represented a realistic piece of advice. Those who originally proposed the sending of the sacred embassy must have foreseen the possibility that Apollo might be ·induced to provide a dispensation which would free Cyme from Persian retribution. Here

17

it is significant to notice that the position of the
Milesians in relation to Persia was different from that
of all the other Greek states. As soon as Cyrus had
conquered Lydia, he agreed with Miletus that they
could remain on the same friendly terms with him as
previously with Croesus. If one believes that the
oracle of Branchidae was at this time completely dominated by Miletus, it would not be surprising to find
that its advice to enquirers on political questions
kept closely in step with the city's pro-Persian
policy. (19)

One must not suppose, however, that the Branchidae
at all times simply echoed the sentiments of the ruling party in Miletus. There are in our literary
sources two verse responses attributed to them in the
6th century. Both come from authors writing at least
two centuries later and are probably not authentic,
but it is perhaps significant that in each context
independently the Branchidae are represented as at
variance with the establishment in Miletus. In one
instance according to Heraclides Ponticus, during a
period of bitter civil strife, the wealthy had avenged
themselves atrociously on the party of the poor who
had previously committed outrages against them. When
the oracle was consulted about evil omens which followed, "the god for a long time kept driving them away
from his oracle-centre", and ultimately justified his
refusal to prophecy by two lines of hexameter verse,
referring to the atrocities of the wealthy. Actually
these verses by their style, which seems inappropriate
to a date in the archaic period, cast grave doubts
on the authenticity of Heraclides' account. He was
an author given to introducing highly imaginative and
sensational episodes into his moralising dialogues.
So he can only be regarded as very unsound evidence
for these happenings. Still one cannot be sure that
he did not build a historical romance round some material derived from local chronicles. Even if one must
reject the hexameter verses of the response as a later
fiction and even the details of the outrages as perhaps invented for the sake of their horror, the civil
strife is probably historic, and the attitude of the
Branchidae to it may be authentically reproduced. (20)

Similarly, Demon, an early Hellenistic writer on
proverbs, explained one by a story which alleged that
at the time of the Ionian revolt, the oracle at Didyma
had discouraged the Carians from allying with Miletus
against the Persians. This had led to a charge that
the oracle had been bribed by the pro-Persian party.
Again one detail in the story is anachronistic, and
the evidence points against the proverb originating

at this time. But one may ask whether Demon is likely
to have invented the idea that the Branchidae might
have been discouraging of the attempt to revolt against
Persia.(21) It might be true that in 500 B.C. the
oracle was slow to follow the new line of policy?
They had much to lose by a large-scale war. Herodotus
tells how Hecataeus the historian, when the Milesian
conspirators met to plot the Ionian revolt, began by
advising them against the attempt, arguing from his
superior knowledge of the extent and resources of the
Persian empire. When this argument failed, he advised
them alternatively to obtain command of the seas and
for this purpose to seize the treasures from the temple at Branchidae which Croesus had dedicated. For
as he explained "thus they would have the treasures
and the enemy would not plunder them". This alternative was also rejected by the conspirators. So for
the moment the sanctuary of Didyma remained unravaged,
but Herodotus' account is a reminder that in time
of war the treasuries of the Greek city's gods were
liable to danger from both directions. A victorious
enemy might loot them, but also it would seem to the
Greeks to be perfectly correct for the city itself to
take over the dedications of their deities and convert
the precious metal into coin in order to meet the
costs of hostilities. There would be an implicit understanding that the treasures should be made good
later after the successful end of the war. But the
fact that this repayment was hypothetical and in the
distant future did not discourage the Greeks from
requisitioning their treasures for immediate need.(22)
Apart from such interested motives, the Branchidae may
have been influenced too by more generous feelings,
for they had reason to be grateful to King Darius.
The evidence for his patronage of Apollo of Didyma is
late and slight, but must have some foundation in
fact. Five hundred years after the Ionian revolt, in
27 A.D., the Roman senate called on the cities of
Asia to justify individually the rights of asylum
claimed by their sanctuaries. The embassies sent to
Rome evidently used the occasion not only to prove
their legal cases, but also to assert the glory of
their antiquity. Tacitus records in one sentence that
the case for Didyma presented by Miletus was based on
King Darius as founder of its asylum. No details of
the circumstances are given, nor is the strange para-
dox noted that the temple was also destroyed under
Darius. But this is not a unique example of the Persian King's respect for Apollo. From some twenty-
five miles northeast of Miletus comes the inscribed
letter of Darius to Gadates, chiding the Persian

official for taxing the sacred gardeners of Apollo and
making them do secular work, in disregard of the fact
that the god had "spoken all the truth to the Persians".
This document has been doubted by some scholars as a
later forgery, but the majority accept its authenticity. What local Apollo had sacred gardeners as his
servants is not known, but the reference to the oracles
of the god appears to be general, and might include
Didyma. Another example of Darius' piety towards
Apollo occurs after the Ionian revolt during the expedition to Marathon. Herodotus records that when the
Persian fleet approached, the Delians fled to Tenos.
But Datis, the commander, sent for them to return,
assuring them that Darius had instructed him not to
harm the island of Delos or its inhabitants, where the
two deities, Apollo and Artemis, had been born. There
can be do doubt on the authenticity of this account.
Of course it can be explained away on the ground that
Darius had no real religious feelings for Delos, but
was simply using the occasion for propaganda. However,
even if this cynical interpretation were completely
true, exactly the same motives could by found for a
gesture of patronage towards the Didymaean Apollo. In
the earlier part of his reign, when Miletus was a loyal subject of the Persian king, it may well have seemed
prudent to recognise the importance of its great sanctuary by conferring on it the rights of asylum which
were already enjoyed by the Artemisium at Ephesus. If
so, it is possible that in return the Branchidae may
have shown their gratitude by loyal responses from the
oracle. Later when the Ionian revolt broke out, led
by Miletus, it is not likely that the priesthood put up any
serious protest, but they may have been less enthusiastic
in favour of the rebellion than most of the Milesians,
and this fact may have been remembered against them.(23)
    These considerations may well have made the
priests of Branchidae less favourably disposed to a
policy of war with Persia. Though the actual story of
the response to the Carian enquiry about alliance is
unlikely to be historically sound, it may well represent correctly enough the attitude of the priests of
Apollo. In this it may be a mere coincidence, but the
priesthood of Delphi appear to have adopted a very
similar policy. At the time of Cyrus' conquest of
Ionia, for instance, the Cnidians had attempted to
convert their peninsula into an island by cutting a
canal across the isthmus. When the workers on the
project suffered a phenomenal number of casualties,
Delphi was consulted and prohibited the canal and even
any attempt to fortify the place. One may compare
this prohibition with the contemporary response of the

Branchidae on the subject of Pactyes. The Delphic
attitude to the Ionian revolt itself appears in the
remarkable oracle given to the Argives when they enquired before the battle of Sepeia. After replying in
particularly ambiguous terms to the questions about
Argos' prospects in the war, the Pythia gratuitously
added a forecast of the fall of Miletus. (The date of
the prophecy must have been after the defeat of the
Ionians in the battle of Lade, when the fate of the
city was sealed.) "And then indeed, Miletus, deviser
of wicked deeds, you will become a feast and bright
gifts to many, and your wives will wash the feet of
many long-haired men, and others at Didyma will care
for our temple." The sack of the city and the enslave-
ment of the female population are prophesied with
only the conventional minimum of poetic periphrases
But the most significant feature is the downright and
explicit condemnation of the Milesians for their wicked acts. The only obvious meaning is a condemnation
of the revolt against Persia. Delphi also foresaw
that the temple at Didyma would pass into other hands,
but it is not possible to tell from the wording whether the priests regarded this as the convenient elimin-
ation of a rival oracle centre or as a disaster to
Greek culture. (24)
     According to Herodotus this prophecy was exactly
fulfilled. Miletus was taken: the majority of the
male population were killed, and the women and children enslaved. The survivors, in accordance with the
usual Persian practice, were transplanted from Ionia
to Mesopotamia where they were settled near the mouth
of the Tigris. The city and its farmland were occupied by the Persians and the uplands were given to the
Carians. Thus the Queen of Ionian cities went down
in destruction.
     Its sanctuary at Didyma was joined with it in the
same fate. If Darius had earlier shown patronage towards Apollo, the Ionian revolt blotted out such relations and no distinction in treatment was made
between Miletus and the Branchidae. According to
Herodotus "The sacred place, both the temple and the
oracle, were pillaged and then set on fire". For more
than a century and a half the prophetic source was
silenced, even though in the intervening years Miletus
the city rose again from its ruins. (25)
     That spoils of the temple were seized by the Per-
sians is very probably demonstrated by a find made at
Susa by the French excavators and now exhibited in the
Louvre. It is a colossal model in bronze of a knuckle-
bone, the kind of object used by Greeks for games of
chance. It bears an inscription, which will be dis-

cussed more fully later, recording that it was dedicated to Apollo by two Greeks as a tithe from their
spoils. As such it had evidently stood in the precinct at Didyma and when it was plundered, had been
carried off to the Persian capital. (26)

Chapter Two

THE ARCHAIC PERIOD FROM THE ARCHAEOLOGICAL REMAINS

If we turn from the literary sources to the archaeological evidence for the archaic period at Didyma,
again one has to note a great shortage of material.
Here the primary cause is that the site was ravaged
by the Persians in 494 B.C., and when after nearly two
centuries rebuilding began, it was carried out on a
colossal scale which largely demolished the earlier
remains. In fact it is remarkable in view of the size
and situation of the Hellenistic temple that the German excavators have been able to detect so much of the
earlier buildings.
    If the cult at Didyma began in pre-hellenic
times, as Pausanias believed, no traces have been
found of buildings of that period. Isolated sherds of
the proto-geometric period have been collected east of
the temple, and more plentiful specimens from the
eighth century onwards occur generally. The earliest
structure excavated by the Germans is a wall of sun-
dried brick some three feet thick which enclosed on
three sides an oblong area 10.20m. (40 feet) by 9.30m.
(36½ feet) lying E. and W. The wall on the fourth
side had disappeared. So the structure may have extended further in length to the east. Evidently a
space of this area could not have been roofed (for the
excavators dated the work to the late 8th or early 7th
century). So the wall was simply a "<u>sekos</u>" enclosing
a sacred place. Judging by its thickness the wall
may have been quite high so as to shut out all view
of the interior. No traces of buildings inside the
enclosure were found, and there may well have been
none. One can conjecture that it contained the sacred spring and one or more sacred bay trees. Also
there may have been one or more altars, but whether
at this early period there was any statue of Apollo
may be doubted. (1)
    If Miletus was already founding colonies such as

Cyzicus in the eighth century, this building will be
contemporary with that period of expansion. If the
Milesian colonies date from 675 B.C., it may precede
them. But at any rate it is likely that by this time
Miletus had won control of the sanctuary. In fact this
enclosure wall may represent the Milesians' decision
to develop the place as their oracular centre.

That the seventh century was a period of growth
and prosperity for the Branchidae can be conjectured
from the next building put up shortly before 600 B.C.
It was a portico with mud-brick walls and an open
front supported on wooden pillars, and it stood to
the south of the sacred enclosure facing towards it.(2
The purpose of the building will have been twofold:-
to shelter the increasing number of visitors to the
shrine, whether enquirers at the oracle or others,
and to protect the growing number of offerings which
were accumulating through their pious gratitude. As
the German excavators point out, the portico must have
been about contemporary with the battle of Megiddo and
the Pharaoh Necho's gift to Apollo. It need not be
supposed that the building was specially erected to
contain the Egyptian dedication, but it is an interesting example of the important offerings which the
Branchidae were now receiving and housing properly.
It is possible that by this time a small roofed shrine
(a naiskos) had been built inside the geometric precinct wall, but generally the site did not take on
its developed appearance till after the middle of the
6th century B.C. By that time already the nearest
rivals to the Branchidae had won a conspicuous lead.
About 570 B.C. on Samos the architects Rhoecus and
Theodorus had begun the first large Greek temple of
marble in honour of Hera. Some ten or fifteen years
later an even larger temple was begun at Ephesus to
the glory of the local Artemis. Croesus, king of
Lydia, assisted with funds which helped to provide a
remarkable feature - huge Ionic columns with human
figures carved in relief on the lower part of the
shafts. Soon after the middle of the sixth century
Miletus followed Samos and Ephesus in building a great
new marble temple on the colossal scale which the
current fashion demanded. Exteriorly it resembled its
two rivals, as an Ionic peristyle building with sculp-
tured bases on the facade. But the structure was
essentially not a roofed building, but a walled courtyard, containing still a sacred spring, a grove of
laurels and a naiskos, within its perimeter. Croesus
was credited by Herodotus with having given vast dedications to Apollo. So his funds at Didyma as at
Ephesus may have helped with the erection of the

24

building, though the bulk of the work must have been done after his fall. The capitals have been dated by style about 535 B.C. and the statuary in relief on the columns 530 B.C. or a little later. Our literary sources suggest that Miletus continued to thrive after the Persian conquest of Asia Minor, and the work at Didyma appears to have gone ahead unhindered.(3)

When the main building was completed, the final stage was to replace any previous naiskos by a new inner shrine with a bronze cult-statue of an up-to-date type. (4) It was in form a small Greek temple with columns on its facade, standing in the farther, western, half of the sacred courtyard. In front of it lay the sacred spring, the bay trees and probably one or more altars. But the main altar of sacrifice, as was usual in Greek cults, lay outside the temple in exact alignment with the central facade of the buildings. Pausanias, the guide-book writer, who had a considerable knowledge of Asia Minor, mentions it in connection with the altar of Zeus at Olympia. According to him the altar at Didyma was one of a small class which were built out of the ashes of the sacrifices. Also both at Olympia and at Didyma the foundation of the altar was attributed to Herakles. The site was found by the German excavators: a circular limestone base nearly 8 m. (26½ feet) across with two entrances; one on either side. The middle was a hollow in which were found burnt animal bones, sherds of pottery and votive-gifts of lead dating from the 7th and 6th centuries. One is to imagine the centre of the altar heaped up into a pyramidal mound of ashes and fragments from the sacrifices mixed with blood. Pausanias regarded it as not very imposing in size compared with the famous altar at Olympia. (5)

The altar, as we have seen, faced the eastern facade of the archaic temple. If we are to picture a priest or a worshipper proceeding from the altar to the sanctuary he would first mount a flight of stone steps of the usual kind surrounding Greek temples before he reached the level of the column-bases and entered through a double colonnade and a deep porch. This eastern end of this archaic temple has completely vanished in the destruction and restoration which occurred on the site, but its general lines can be reconstructed with probability from the surviving foundations of the western half. So we may assume that one entered the temple itself by a central door and found oneself at the head of a short flight of steps bringing one down to the level of the inner court. The floor of this court was not raised when the archaic temple was erected around and above it.

The reason for this curious treatment of the site doubtless lay in the need to have access to the sacred spring. If the general surface of the court had been filled in to be on a level with the stylobate of the temple, the spring would have to have been left in a deep pit - a very unsatisfactory arrangement. Where exactly the sacred spring lay in the court cannot now be established with any degree of certainty. The history of Didyma suggests that the spring, though providing the original occasion for the sanctuary, was not itself very constant. More than once it vanished and re-emerged. The erection of large buildings round it may have served unintentionally to interfere with the flow of water. In any case it is understandable that the archaic architects preferred to leave the spring at its original position and level, even when enclosed in a large temple.

After the temple itself the inner shrine - the naiskos - was rebuilt. This not only brought it into harmony with its new majestic surroundings, but also made it a suitable place to house a new cult statue of the kind which had only been possible to make in the previous thirty or forty years. The technique of casting life-size statues in hollow bronze had been developed in Samos in this period, and had been taken up on the Greek mainland. The Branchidae then commissioned a famous sculptor, Canachus of Sicyon, to produce the cult statue for the shrine. Pausanias, who evidently knew both places, recorded that at Thebes in the temple of the Ismenian Apollo the cult statue was exactly similar in size and appearance to that at Didyma and that in fact they were both made by Canachus. The only difference was that the statue in Thebes was of cedar-wood, the one in Didyma of bronze. Neither Pausanias nor any other source records which was made first. So it might be tempting to suppose that Canachus first erected the type for Thebes in what must have been a cheaper material and then, perhaps because the fame of the work had spread to Ionia, was invited to come to Didyma for the more distant and expensive commission. (6)

The general appearance of the statue can be conjectured by combining the description given by Pliny the Elder with representations on coins and reliefs. No copy in the round exists. Evidently it was one of the latest examples of the original Kouros type: a nude male figure symmetrically posed facing forwards with the left leg advanced. The left arm holding the traditional bow was somewhat lowered, the right arm was stretched forward at a right angle to the body and supported on the palm the figure of a stag. This

last addition was the most unusual feature, but Pliny
spends more words is describing a curious detail of
its construction. Apparently the stag was separately
cast and so lightly poised that it was possible to
pass a thread under its feet by rocking the figure to
and fro on the hand of the god. It sounds like the
kind of tiresome trick invented by a temple guide to
entertain tourists, and one may wonder uneasily whether
by the Roman period the cult-statue was subject to
such undignified displays. (7)

If instead the stag is considered as an attribute
of Apollo, it raises a curious problem. His sister,
Artemis, from the seventh century B.C. was regularly
shown holding a deer by its antlers - perhaps a speci-
alised development from the primitive scheme of the
goddess, mistress of animals, grasping two beasts
heraldically disposed on either side of her. But
Apollo is very rarely shown grasping a stag. One
statue only of this type is recorded as dedicated at
Delphi at an uncertain date. But even the type
grasping a deer by the antlers is essentially different from one with an animal standing on the palm of
the hand. Art historians are led to think of some
Oriental source. E. Bielefeld called attention to a
Hittite seal, as an earlier analogy, but this has now
been shown by R. Ghirshman to be unsatisfactory. He
has called attention instead to a limestone relief of
Urartian workmanship, datable to the eighth century
B.C. It shows a male robed figure holding in the
right hand raised a pine-cone and on the flat palm of
the left hand a young animal - Ghirshman says a fawn.
The derivation of Urartian art from Hittite and
Hurrian prototypes is generally recognised and the god
himself in the relief was probably intended to represent the Hittite Teshub. (8)

It would not be surprising if the cult of Apollo
practised by the Branchidae and dating back before the
Hellenic colonization had retained traces derived from
previous Asian cultures. The link might have been
partly supplied by whatever form of cult-figure had
preceded the Apollo of Canachus. It might have dated
back to the early seventh century at least, and might
have shown the same motif of a stag standing on the
palm, which may then have been included in the speci-
fication which the Branchidae gave to the foreign
artist, Canachus. The only difficulty against this
theory is that if the statue of the Ismenian Apollo
was made before that of Didyma presumably it would
not have included this Asian motive. Here all one
can say is that two alternatives are open:- the
Ismenian statue may actually have been later and may

have reproduced the Didymaean Apollo in every detail,
or when Pausanias refers to their great resemblance to
each other he may only have been referring, as his
words suggest, to the general appearance and not to
the particular attributes.

The German excavators conjectured from the scale
of the naiskos that the Apollo of Canachus was not
much over human size. The representation of it on
the relief from the Theatre of Miletus shows the hair
across the forehead in heavy ringlets, and this taken
in conjunction with the rest of the evidence points to
a date of construction well into the last quarter of
the sixth century B.C. In fact the statue may not
have been installed for as long as twenty years when
the temple was sacked and the Apollo removed to
Ecbatana, the old Median capital. This transportation
into its conqueror's land, as Erika Simon points out,
is less to be thought of as a sign of artistic appre-
ciation of the work than the removal of the enemy's
gods in the manner of the Assyrian conquerors. (9)

So far the archaeological evidence, though according with the literary traditions and supplementing
them, does not cast much light directly on the functioning of the oracle. But fortunately three inscriptions have been found, which though very fragmentary
give positive proof that Apollo was available to be
consulted by oracular methods in the sixth century B.C.
All three inscriptions are written in the archaic
form, boustrophedon, i.e. in lines reading alternately
from left to right and from right to left. This is a
sufficient guarantee of their antiquity. The first,
a stone from Didyma, is now lost, but copies and a
squeeze preserve its contents, which have in themselves a primitive character. (10) Someone, presumably the community of Miletus or certain individuals,
had enquired for authority to engage in plundering,
whether some objects might be taken for booty or some
people made the victims of privateering. The details
of the question are lost, but its general meaning is
sufficiently certain. Apollo's answer is preserved
intact:- "The god said; 'it is right to do as your
fathers did'." The four words of Greek are a slender
foundation for any discussion, but several points can
be noted. The answer is in prose, not in verse, as
so many other oracles, including later ones from
Didyma, are. The god does not, at least in this
instance, use the first person as normally in Delphic
verse responses. The text is so brief and direct that
it gives no indication how the answer was evoked. On
the one hand it shows no sign in its form of the typical alternative question answered by a "yes" or "no",

which could be produced by drawing a lot. But it
would not be impossible that the whole answer itself
could have been written on some form of object, which
would have been drawn out to give the god's reply.
The instruction to follow ancestral custom is typical
of oracular advice, and therefore it would be appropriate for it to have been one of a series of previously
prepared answers available to be assigned by chance
on the god's inspiration in response to the enquiry.

The other two inscriptions were found in Miletus,
but there is little doubt that the oracular responses
which they record were given at Didyma. One is concerned
with the regulations governing the worship of Herakles.
The words of enquiry and the response are both only
preserved in fragmentary form, but the general lines
seem to be that Apollo was asked whether women were
to be admitted to Herakles' temple and also with regard to the use of vegetables in the rites. The sense
of the reply is lost, but once more it is introduced
with the phrase "the god said". Also the response was
certainly not written in hexameters, and probably not
in verse but prose. It appears to have been too long
to have been produced by a method of drawing lots. (11)

The third response recorded in an inscription is
unfortunately the most fragmentary. It may, judging
by the script, be the earliest of the three. The
remains contain the words: "I utter - I said on the
previous night. To him who obeys, it will be better
and more good; to him who obeys not, the opposite."
This much of the text seems reasonably certain. As
Rehm remarks, only a god could encourage and threaten
in such terms as these, and the standard oracular
formula "better and more good" seems to have been
used. If so, the natural interpretation of the document is that Apollo is speaking in the first person
and in prose. He seem also to refer to some message
which he gave the previous night. Again the reasonable conjecture is that someone, the prophet or another, had enquired about the genuineness of a command
uttered by the god in a dream. The oracle when consulted had confirmed the command with a threat against
disobedience. (Curiously enough, centuries later evidence is again found of the oracle being asked to
confirm a dream.) In this instance it is quite impossible to go further and determine what was the subject of the command. But some indications of the
oracular procedure can be inferred. The reply was in
prose, as also in one of our previous examples and
probably in both. So we can say that there is no inscriptional evidence that the oracle of the Branchidae
in the archaic period ever spoke in verse. But also

for the first time among our literary or epigraphic
examples Apollo speaks in the first person. So it
would be unreasonable to conjecture that the response
was obtained by drawing lots or by some other imper-
sonal method. The form points to ecstatic prophecy,
even though the inspiration confined itself to prosaic
expression. (12)

The inscriptional evidence proves what our literary sources allege, that there was an oracle of Apollo
functioning at Didyma in the archaic period. One may
ask whether the material remains in any way suggest an
adaptation to suit the working of the oracle. Three
features might be interpreted in this sense. First
of all, from the earliest buildings found on the site,
one feature was a circuit wall shutting off the sacred
area and probably (judging by its thickness) high enough to exclude proceedings from the gaze of spectat-
ors outside. The functioning of an oracle, particularly if it involved ecstatic prophecy, usually took
place in an adyton, a place barred to approach, and
in later periods was always in the innermost sanctuary. A lofty circuit wall was the nearest equivalent which primitive periods could supply. The tradition of the high-walled enclosure continued to dom-
inate the design at Didyma down to its latest building, and the pattern of buttresses originally required
to strengthen a construction of mud-brick may explain
the repetition of the design in the high stone walls
of the archaic and Hellenistic temples. Whether it
could therefore ultimately go back to eastern origins
and link with the typical Mesopotamian sanctuary consisting of rectangular courts enclosed in buttressed
walls of mud-brick is a difficult question. (13)

Another feature in the design is also, as we have
seen, probably connected with the practice of divination. The maintaining of the same level approximately for the base of the inner sanctuary walls was
determined by the need to have access to the sacred
spring, and this was required because of its prophetic
properties as a source of inspiration. If the oracle
had not been essential to the worship of Apollo the
building within as well as without might have developed on the lines of the typical archaic temple.

Finally a remarkable dedication already mentioned
which has survived from the archaic temple of Branchidae may be discussed and a suggestion made about its
possible significance. Early in this century the
French archaeological expedition to Iran found on the
acropolis at Susa a peculiar object of bronze. This
took the form of a colossal knuckle-bone, more than a
foot in breadth and eight inches in height and weigh-

ing just short of 200 lb. avoirdupois. It bears an
inscription "These offerings Aristolochus and Thrason
dedicated to Apollo as a tithe from the booty.
Pasikles the son of Kydimandros cast it". The reference to offerings in the plural is probably to be
explained by the hypothesis that the original dedication consisted of two bones, one of which is lost.
This conjecture of Haussoullier is strongly reinforced
by the fact that the surviving bone has a handle on
one side which can best be explained as providing the
link for a chain which originally joined the two dedications together. Probably only one of the two was
inscribed.

The Ionic script, the dialect and the proper
names all prove that this object was originally dedicated at a shrine of Apollo in Ionia and removed as
spoils of war to the Persian capital. Also the form
of lettering shows that the original dedication was
made in the earlier half of the sixth century B.C.
Though it is not absolutely proved, the obvious supposition, which has been universally accepted, is that
the offering was made by two Milesians to the Apollo
of Didyma, and that it was looted by the army of Darius
in 494 B.C. and never returned to its proper home. It
now rests in the Louvre and is a remarkable illustration of the history of the oracle of Branchidae. (14)

Why did the offering take the form of a knuckle-
bone or a pair of knucklebones? The choice of the
dedication seems to have no connection with the source
of profit. It is extremely rare, if not unique, as a
votive offering. The traditional association of
knucklebones throughout antiquity was with games of
chance, in which they took the place of dice, and
therefore often with children's toys. It might possibly have alluded, though the idea is rather far-
fetched, to the element of chance in securing a rich
prize. But another use of the knucklebones as dice
may have been involved. In the procedure of various
oracles the will of the gods was determined by drawing
lots, and knucklebones could obviously be used in this
procedure. They could be inscribed with "yes" or "no"
or their equivalents, and the throw could determine
the answer to an alternative question.

There is no evidence elsewhere to suggest that
the drawing of lots or throwing of dice was practised
as a method of divination by the Branchidae. But in
view of the extreme paucity of reference to the subject it would be dangerous to argue from silence that
it was not used there. Certainly lot-oracles were a
common enough institution in Asia Minor in later times
judging by the inscriptions giving tables of answers.

So without feeling great assurance in the suggestion one may propose that the two Milesians chose to dedicate knucklebones to Apollo because he had given them some favourable response by lot, which they had seen fulfilled in a prosperous venture and had acknowledged with a tithe of their profits in this remarkable form

It would be interesting and a notable coincidence if the dedication of Aristolochus and Thrason could be connected with the earliest of the oracular responses which we have discussed. Both are concerned with booty, if the inscription on the knucklebone is to be taken in that sense, and as the names of the enquirer about the right to privateering are lost, it would be possible to identify them with Aristolochus and Thrason, and suppose that we have both the oracular consultation and the fulfilment recorded. But actually the form of the lettering would suggest that the dedication was at least a generation earlier than the enquiry. The most that can be said is that Apollo's response indicated that he regarded piracy as a practice sanctioned by ancestral tradition, and the presence of the knucklebone dedication in the precinct may have been a good demonstration of the truth of this answer.

If then we try on the basis of the literary and archaeological evidence to formulate a statement of the methods of divination used at Didyma in the archaic period two possibilities are indicated. The form of the responses recorded in inscriptions suggests that the god spoke, and this would fit with the legendary examples in which Apollo gives discursive replies. One pictures them as being produced by some form of trance and possession like that attributed to the Pythia. The knucklebone dedication also suggests, but more hypothetically, that there may have been an alternative method of divination by lot. Delphi in the 4th century B.C. and probably earlier supplies evidence for the co-existence of these two methods. In fact it would have been possible to produce a reply to the Cymaean enquiry about the surrendering of Pactyes by drawing lots to decide an alternative question on the subject. But the actual form of Herodotus' narrative is not particularly suited to this interpretation. So the possibility of a lot-oracle operated by the Branchidae in addition to a system of ecstatic prophecy must be left as "not proven".

Chapter Three

FROM THE FALL OF MILETUS TO THE REVIVAL OF THE ORACLE
(334 B.C.)

The fall of Miletus had shocked the Greek world. In
Athens the tragic poet, Phrynichus, in the following
spring (493 B.C.) recorded the event in what was the
first play known to deal with a contemporary subject.
The rash dramatist was fined by the Athenians for
"reminding them of their own kinsmen's troubles", and
the tragedy was banned. For fifteen years the Persians remained in control of the place. They themselves had taken possession of the city and the plain:
the surrounding hills were given over to the Carians
of Pedasus. Didyma, wasted with fire, lay in
ruins. But the Greek victories in the Persian war,
culminating in the battle of Mycale, just up the coast
from Miletus, reversed the situation. Ionia was freed
from the Persian rule, and the Milesians could resume
their independence. (1)
    Though Herodotus describes Miletus as desolate
after its fall and records the removal of the inhabitants to Mesopotamia, it is evident that some escaped death or deportation. In fact Herodotus himself in
describing the battle of Mycale tells how the Persians
rashly chose the Milesian contingent in their forces
to guard the passes to the rear because of their local
knowledge, and when the battle went against them suffered a murderous vengeance at the Milesians' hands. (2)
So though in 479 B.C. the citizens who assembled to
restore Miletus were a small residue of its original
inhabitants, continuity was not lost. So far as
Didyma was concerned, this showed itself almost at once
in a pathetic piece of ceremonial. The Molpoi, the
religious guild of singers attached to the temple of
Apollo Delphinios at Miletus, whose president was the
official who gave his name to the city's year, revived
the annual procession to Didyma, which had evidently
been the main festival connecting the city and its
oracular sanctuary.

From the Fall of Miletus to the Revival of the Oracle
(334 B.C.)

The regulations for the procession are preserved in a
inscription re-copied about 100 B.C., but recording
that the contents were first inscribed in 450/49 B.C.
and from an earlier date in the document itself it is
clear that the ceremonial was at least partly revived
in 478. Some of the topographical details of the
regulations elude one, but the general effect is clear
that under the control of the Molpoi the city of Miletus annually renewed its homage to Apollo of Didyma
from the earliest opportunity after the victory of
Mycale. (3)

Why this duty fell on the sacred guild of Apollo
Delphinios has an obvious explanation. By Darius'
order not merely had the temple of Didyma been destroyed, but also its priesthood had been removed to
Central Asia. There was no family of Branchidae any
longer on the spot to organise a revival of the services. Another Apolline guild in Miletus with important connections with the city's magistracy was the
only body available to undertake the task. What remains uncertain is how much further they went beyond the
revival of the annual festival. Those who comment on
the regulations reasonably suggest that they imply as
a minimum a certain clearing of the debris on the sit
of the temple, so that the altar and perhaps other
parts of the sacred buildings were accessible to the
procession. Dangerous structures must have been made
safe. But one point is clear: the oracle was not revived. (4)

The failure of the Milesians to do this need not
surprise one. The removal of the Branchidae to Central Asia had left a complete gap in the tradition of
oracular prophecy. Also the physical restoration of
the city of Miletus itself must have been a demanding
task. In addition, the newly won independence was
not peaceful or free from internal dissensions.
Twice in the fifties and forties of the century for
several years Miletus revolted from its membership of
the Athenian league, and there is evidence for citizens fleeing to the island of Leros and to Teichiuss
to set up independent communities. Again by decree
certain citizens and their descendants are banished
for ever. In 440 Miletus was involved in a dispute
with Samos and called in Athens to support her. The
early years of the Peloponnesian war were comparatively quiet, but after the Sicilian expedition's disas-
trous end the Milesians set about organising a revolt
from Athens, and until near the close of the war supplied Sparta with its chief base in Asia. The
Spartans in turn handed Miletus over to their new ally
Persia, as part of the terms of alliance; an action

bitterly resented by the citizens. But this was only
the beginning of a political seesaw, in which Miletus
was alternately freed from Persian overlordship and
once more subjected to it. At one time it was seized
by Maussolus, the Carian dynast. These external
interferences were doubtless also reflected in internal political struggles. For instance, in 401 B.C.
when Miletus alone of the Ionian cities preferred to
support Tissaphernes rather than Cyrus the younger,
we find that a group of Milesians expelled from the
city joined Cyrus and expected him to restore them.(5)
     Therefore one need not find it improbable that
in the century and a half which followed the sack of
Miletus no effort had been made to rebuild the temple
at Didyma on its original scale or to revive the oracle once operated by the Branchidae. In fact we have
one piece of evidence to show that by the mid-fourth
century Miletus looked to Delphi as the great Apolline
sanctuary and international centre. A limestone base
for two life-size bronze statues has been found there
with an inscription recording that the figures were
Idrieus and Ada, the brother and sister of Maussolus,
dedicated to the Pythian Apollo by the Milesians. The
base also bore the artist's signature of Satyrus of
Paros, who was one of the sculptors concerned with the
building of the Maussoleum. The dedication can be
plausibly dated to 345 B.C. just before Idrieus' death.
It is uncertain whether we should suppose that the
Milesians were at the time under the overlordship of
the Carian dynast or were merely demonstrating prominently their good relations. But the choice of Delphi
as a place of dedication to Apollo is significant.
After 300 B.C. the statue group would certainly have
stood at Didyma. Also the friendly relations with
Delphi may have had an effect on the Milesians when
they came to revive their own oracle. (6)
     The fourth century, then, had been for its first
sixty-five years a disturbed period and one of recur-
rent foreign dominance for Miletus. Hence though the
city probably grew economically it was not the powerful and successful Queen of Ionia which it had been
in the sixth century. Instead Ephesus with its great
temple of Artemis just outside its walls tended to
become the new centre of commerce for the western
coast of Asia Minor.
     When Alexander crossed into Asia in 334 B.C. the
Persians garrisoned Miletus, still a much more strategically powerful place than Ephesus, and evidently
meant it to be their chief base on the western coast.
But by his lightning victory at the river Granicus
Alexander destroyed the main Persian armies of Asia

From the Fall of Miletus to the Revival of the Oracle
(334 B.C.)

Minor and so was able to approach Miletus from the
landward side with his troops while his fleet by a
quick movement cut in by sea before the much larger
Persian fleet arrived. The mercenary garrison in
Miletus was prepared to resist, the Milesian magistrates tried to negotiate for neutrality, but Alexander, wasting no time in discussion, took the place
by storm. There probably was a party favouring Alexander in the city in opposition to a magistracy whose
feelings for the Greek cause seem to have been very
doubtful. The general picture which we get at this
period is that the Ionian and Aeolian cities were
ruled by pro-Persian oligarchies, or tyrants, who held
down popular movements which would willingly have
supported the cause of independence. In accordance
with this situation Milesian politics showed a volte-
face in favour of Alexander. He was nominally elected
chief magistrate (Stephanephoros), for the year. Also,
at least according to the rather written-up version
which has been preserved for us from a contemporary
source, the oracle of Didyma was revived again to play
a part in supporting Alexander's cause.(7)
    Our source is no less a person than Callisthenes,
the kinsman of Aristotle, who accompanied the expedition as a chronicler and a kind of Public Relations
Officer. He had already won a reputation as the auth-
or of a history of Greece in ten books. As Alexander's conquering advance developed, Callisthenes wrote
and sent back to Greece accounts of "the Deeds of
Alexander" in a series of instalments. These were, as
one might expect, eulogistic in tone and tended to
stress the theme that Alexander was guided and helped
in his successes by supernatural powers. So it is in
keeping with this treatment that Callisthenes recorded
the revival of the oracle at Didyma and its production
of prophecies in Alexander's favour. We must notice,
however, that he told the story in a very strange
way:- "Apollo had abandoned the oracle at Branchidae
from the time when the sanctuary had been looted by
the Branchidae, who had joined the Persian side in the
time of Xerxes, and the spring had failed. But at
that time (evidently after Alexander's restoration of
Miletus' independence) the spring burst up, and the
ambassadors of the Milesians brought to Memphis many
oracular prophecies concerning the birth of Alexander
from Zeus, the victory that was to be won at Arbela,
the death of Darius and the revolts in Sparta."
Callisthenes dated the revival of the oracle of Didyma
at some point between the recovery of the city of
Miletus and Alexander's stay in Memphis in the spring
of 331 B.C. We need not take too seriously the

alleged prophecies. It would not be surprising if
those who produced them for transmission to Alexander
were already prepared to acclaim him as the son of a
god: a notion which had just received a full meaning
from his visit to the oracle of Ammon. The victory
over the Persian King and that King's death were probably forecast in vaguely grandiloquent prophecies which
need not have borne any precise reference to the
events. Similarly it would even have been plausible
enough for the Milesians' responses to have contained
some veiled warning of troubles in Greece in Alexander's absence, though one may conjecture that they
indicated tactfully that the king's enemies would be
defeated. All we need suppose is that Callisthenes is
telling the truth when he records a revival of the
oracle at this time and the arrival in Egypt of prophecies which he could later interpret as fulfilled by
Alexander's successes. Evidently Callisthenes was
writing after these alleged fulfilments: otherwise,
not earlier than the death of Darius which occurred
in the summer of 330. But also Callisthenes did not
write later than the spring of 327 when he was arres-
ted by Alexander, accused of complicity in the Pages'
conspiracy, and died in captivity. (8)

Evidently Callisthenes wrote when he was still at
liberty and acting as the favoured panegyrist of Alexander. But in this connection his story about Didyma
has an extraordinary slant. It is clearly bitterly
hostile to the Branchidae, the original prophets of
Apollo. Instead of representing them as the unwilling
victims of the forces of Darius in 494 B.C., they are
collaborators with Xerxes fifteen years later in loot-
ing the temple. This picture is in flat contradiction
of Herodotus' account, and modern scholars have rightly
agreed in rejecting it. It is known to us first from
Callisthenes and the occurrences of this version in
later authors can all safely be traced to him as their
source. (9)

We may well ask why a historian of repute should
have ventured to put out a story which was such a
travesty of the facts. The reason is clear enough if
the situation at the time when it was produced is examined. As we saw, it follows from Callisthenes' references to the fulfilment of prophecies that he was
writing in 330 or later and not after 327 B.C. This
is the very time when Alexander in his march into
Central Asia reached in Bactria the place to which the
Branchidae had been removed by Darius. Also at this
time according to some of our ancient authorities
there took place an episode which, if historic, should
be regarded as among the blackest in the record of

Alexander's deeds. The version of the fall of Didyma
given by Callisthenes is only known from three passages in Strabo where he paraphrases what must have
been a fuller narrative. Callisthenes evidently attributed the destruction of the temple and the oracle
centre not to Darius' army, but to Xerxes, and made the
occasion not the Ionian revolt (when presumably we are
to suppose that the Branchidae collaborated with the
Persians and escaped destruction), but when after
Salamis the Persian king in fury determined to avenge
himself on the Ionians for failure to fight loyally in
his cause. The story ran that he burnt all the Ionian
temples, except that of Artemis of Ephesus, and that
the Branchidae plundered their own temple's treasures
and handed them over to the Persians. As after this
sacrilege and treason they could not remain in Ionia,
they had joined Xerxes in his journey back to Persia
and had been settled by him in Bactria well away from
any other Greeks. One must suppose that Callisthenes'
motive in recording this fantasy was to explain why
Alexander when he encountered the descendants of the
Branchidae in their Bactrian home proceeded to massacre the whole population, man, woman and child, and
even to destroy the buildings of their town. The justification which Callisthenes produced was that Alexander felt horror and revulsion at the sacrilege and
treason of the Branchidae, and in view of the source
of this narrative and the tone of other passages we
cannot doubt that it was told as a justifiable act of
vengeance. Later authors evidently did not always
regard it in this light. The two great contemporary
sources whom Arrian followed, Aristobulus and Ptolemy,
seem both to have omitted the event entirely, and
therefore, it has no place in Arrian's history.
Aristobulus' reasons are obscure. Ptolemy was deliberately producing an account of Alexander which would
cut out the mythological element, but also would not
reflect adversely on the king who was responsible for
founding Alexandria and whose tomb there gave the
Ptolemies such ground to' pose as his true successors.
If the act of omitting an event of this magnitude seems
extraordinary, one may note again that Plutarch left
it out entirely from his life of Alexander, but by a
reference elsewhere in his works indicated that he
both knew the story and accepted its historicity, when
he wished to illustrate the belated occurrence of divine vengeance.
     Of the writers extant who recorded it, the table
of contents of the seventeenth book of Diodorus Siculus
lists the event, but by an unfortunate accident that
part of the work is lost through a lacuna in all sur-

viving manuscripts. Curtius Rufus tells the story in
detail. His immediate source is obviously not Callisthenes, but, as elsewhere, some later writer who enjoyed producing a sensational picture of Alexander as
a ruthless tyrant. He adds a curious detail which
does not appear in Strabo's brief paraphrase of Callisthenes. So we do not know whether it went back to
a contemporary narrative. Alexander commanded the
Milesians in his army to be called together. They
had a long-standing hatred of the Branchidae. The
king invited them to decide freely the fate of these
people, whether they attached more importance to their
Greek origin or to their subsequent outrage. When the
Milesians disagreed with eath other, the king reserved
the decision to himself and finally resolved on their
destruction. Curtius' comment is that it might have
been just retribution on the original traitors, but
not on descendants who had never even seen Miletus.

Modern scholars, such as Tarn, have mostly been
unwilling to accept the truth of the massacre of the
Branchidae. (10) They are not interested in it as a
moral tale and cannot see it in Callisthenes' light
as redounding to Alexander's credit. Hence Tarn was
prepared to believe that the whole story was an invention of Callisthenes. But this is a very unjustifiable judgement. The fragments of Callisthenes' history which are preserved show clearly that in other
instances he was prepared to write up an episode introducing an element of fantasy, but not that he
invented happenings which had never occurred at all.
For example when Alexander managed at Pamphylia to
lead his troops along the shore, the sea was described
by Callisthenes as receding in homage to the king.
The picture is imaginary, but it does not discount the
fact that Alexander did follow successfully this
rather venturesome route in conditions which proved
favourable. Similarly, it is more reasonable to suppose that Alexander actually ordered the execution of
the Branchidae and that Callisthenes then wrote it up
as an act of Panhellenic retribution.

If one accepts the deed as historic, the question
is what was Alexander's motive. To some extent it may
have been what Callisthenes suggests - horror at the
sacrilege and treason of the Branchidae. But perhaps
we may rephrase this slightly differently by saying
that Alexander or his advisers saw in the Branchidae
a convenient opportunity to stress the object of
Alexander's campaign as retaliation for the Persian
wars on Greece. This aspect had already been emphasised by the deliberate burning of Persepolis two
years before, but since then Alexander's campaigns had

taken on rather the character of the successor of the
last Darius avenging himself on his enemies. There
may well have been those in Alexander's councils who
thought that a new demonstration was overdue, that the
king had not forgotten his obligations to the Hellenic and Macedonian cause of vengeance.

But apart from the motive of demonstrating a
Panhellenic crusade, there may also have been other
influences at work. It is curious that Curtius Rufus
brings in a consultation of the Milesians in Alexander's army. As he tells the story they are not the
decisive factor, because after mentioning their bitter
hatred of the Branchidae he rather strangely makes
their vote uncertain and leaves the final decision to
Alexander personally. This may be the modification
of the story introduced by Curtius' source, who wished
to end by condemning Alexander for his tyrannical
cruelty. May one conjecture that an earlier version
represented the Milesians as consulted and voting un-
hesitatingly for execution?

It may seem strange that the army could be represented as containing any appreciable contingent from
that one city, and perhaps our source here engages in
picturesque exaggeration, but curiously enough it is
quite possible that one member of the expedition later
to become famous was Demodamas of Miletus, whom we
encounter later as a loyal upholder of Apollo of Didyma. (11) At any rate, after the expulsion of the
Persian garrison from Miletus by Alexander, a party
in the city evidently gave Alexander their strong
support, and this was recognised by Callisthenes in
his pointed account of the prophecies issued by the
revived oracle at Didyma. Hence it would not be surprising that Alexander had some Milesian followers in
the expedition. But here another factor is worth con-
sidering. The pro-Alexander party in Miletus had tak-
en a new initiative. They had revived the oracle,
silent for more than a century and a half, and used it
to back strongly the Hellenic cause. One can imagine
their consternation if they had been told that Alexander had at last rescued from the wilds of Bactria
the original family of the Branchidae who would shortly be returning to take up their ancestral rights in
Apollo's sanctuary. Curtius' description of the contemporary Branchidae may be due to the imagination of
himself or his source. "Their ancestral habits had
not yet died out, but they were now bilingual and were
gradually deteriorating from their native speech."
But it might not be so much the incongruous nature of
the restored Branchidae which would offend the Milesians. The real problem is that evidently for four or

five years a new vested interest in the oracle of
Didyma had been created. If the Branchidae were restored, the control of the sanctuary of Didyma would
presumably be challenged and perhaps alienated from
its new holders. It is an imaginative reconstruction
of the situation, but one may venture the hypothesis
that a group of Milesians in the army decided to fore-
stall any such eventuality by quick and dastardly
action. They brought to the ear of Alexander and his
staff a new version of what had really happened at
Didyma:- that which Callisthenes was to publicise.
They accused the Branchidae of being descendants of
traitors to the Hellenic cause. Perhaps they were
literally believed: perhaps it was cynically recognised that the massacre of these descendants of alleged traitors would make a good demonstration of Alexander's avenging justice. Also it was a guarantee
that the oracle of Didyma, whose propaganda value was
already recognised, did not fall into the hands of
dubious semi-orientals. The deed was done: and Callisthenes wrote it up to the credit of Alexander and
the glory of the newly revived oracle of Apollo of
Didyma.

Owing to the very limited evidence of Strabo's
summary of Callisthenes on the subject it is difficult
to picture what this revival involved. The one point
emphasised is the re-emergence of the sacred spring,
which according to this statement had died out on the
fall of Didyma. This tallies with the fact that later
accounts of the oracle's working, mostly dating from
late Imperial times, refer to the spring as the source
of prophecy. Strabo's words would seem to imply a
spontaneous gushing forth, evidently interpreted by
Callisthenes in his usual way as a divine manifestation in favour of Alexander. We can presume that
human agency may well have played a greater part in
the result than Callisthenes suggested. Whether the
organisation and methods evidenced centuries later
were already instituted in 334 would be hard to prove,
but it is actually quite probable. For though the
spring, as no doubt in primitive times, was the local
source of inspiration, the arrangements for eliciting
prophecies were evidently remodelled on the oracle at
Delphi. The Branchidae as we have suggested were
hereditary prophets, and no doubt both received the
inspiration from Apollo and uttered it to the enquirer. But in 334 the restoration was the work of the
Milesian democracy, and it would not be appropriate
for them to hand over the functions to a family of
prophets. Instead the office of Prophetes was made
annual, appointed by lot (probably out of a short

list). Its standing became considerable, ranking in
seniority even above the position of Stephanephoros,
which was the eponymous magistracy of Miletus. As it
also acquired over the years expensive obligations,
such as feasting the townsfolk at his cost on stated
festivals, in practice the prophetship tended, especially in Roman times, to fall into the hands of a
group of leading families. But it remained in form
at least an annual democratically elected office.

Clearly such a short-term official could not be
expected to act as the vehicle of the god's inspiration. For this purpose as at Delphi a woman was chos-
en the prophetis. She appears in the few literary
references to the functioning of the oracle. But,
like the Pythia at Delphi, among all the mass of inscriptions she is scarcely recorded. A pair of fragmentary texts named the prophetis officially, and a
sarcastic graffito referred to another.(12) But while
the names of some fifty male prophetai are known, the
woman at the centre of the operation is almost disregarded. Presumably, like the Pythia, once appointed
she held the post for life or at least indefinitely
long. How she was chosen we are not told. In
late periods, judging from our two inscriptional instances, she tended to come from prominent families.

In one other respect Delphi was imitated at Didyma. While the three responses of the Branchidae
preserved on stone appear to be in prose, all the inscribed oracles of the Hellenistic and Roman periods
where they offer a verbatim text are composed in hexameter verse. This had been the classical form for
the Pythia's replies, though by the late fourth century it was probably already being abandoned in favour
of prose and by the Roman period Plutarch could write
a treatise on the problem why the Pythia had ceased
to prophesy in verse. But once the hexameter was
adopted at Didyma it was retained with a conservative
tenacity long after it had been abandoned at Delphi.

We may suppose, then, that by some method, the
Milesians claimed in the years following 331 B.C. that
they had access once more to the sacred spring at
Didyma and produced the prophecies which Callisthenes
was able to cite. But the archaeological and epigraphic evidence suggests that they did not immediately
commence the erection of the stupendous temple which
rose on the site of the original shrine of the Branchidae. This is not surprising as it was on such a
grandiose scale that it is hard to imagine that any
Greek city could have undertaken it unaided. Perhaps
the Milesians may have hoped that Alexander could be
interested by the diplomatic use of oracular responses

and would supply the funds needed. But he was too
preoccupied up to the time of his early death to undertake such projects. Thirty years were to pass
until at last they were to find their royal benefactor
in the person of Seleucus Nicator.

Chapter Four

THE HELLENISTIC PERIOD

Seleucus I, Nicator was to be the first of his dynast
to begin the great series of royal benefactors of
Didyma. Appropriately enough our literary authoritie
preserve a number of oracles which they describe as
responses given to him. Two of them are of a traditional type of legend - Apollo with proper oracular
ambiguity foretells the king's end, but the meaning i
not originally understood. According to one story,
while Seleucus was only a young soldier following
Alexander in the war against the Persians, he consult
the oracle of Didyma whether he should return to Macedon. The response of Apollo in a single hexameter
verse was:-

> "Haste not to Europe: Asia is far better for
> you."

So Seleucus acting on the oracle's advice arranged
to stay in Asia and embarked on the career leading to
his kingship. Actually he did not set foot on Europ-
ean soil again until about half a century later in
281 B.C., and his return to Europe was immediately
followed by his assassination. Appian saw in this
conjunction of events the ultimate fulfilment of
Apollo's early prophecy. Modern scholars mostly prefe
to regard it as an ingenious instance of <u>vaticinium</u>
<u>post eventum</u>. The advice to remain in Asia might hav
been given by the oracle of Didyma as a genuine piece
of advice without any distant foresight, and then hav
been revived when Seleucus' assassination gave it a
new significance. But on the whole the story is more
likely to be a legend. (1)
It is associated in Appian with a second prophecy about Seleucus' death which perhaps he also meant
to attribute to Didyma, though the source of the oracle is not clearly stated. It is a much more conven

tional fiction based on the traditional motive of an
ambiguous place-name. The prophecy ran:-

> "By avoiding Argos you will arrive at your fated end.
> But if you approach Argos, then you may perish
> untimely."

Seleucus accordingly avoided all the many places in
the Greek world called Argos, but when in 281 B.C. he
landed in Europe at Lysimacheia, he noticed a large and
conspicuous altar. On enquiring about it, he was told
that the natives called it Argos, and immediately
afterwards was assassinated by Ptolemy Ceraunus. This
motif based on the homonymity of place-names is so
conventional in myths about prophecies of death that
is can be discounted completely.

The deaths of kings are events which attract the
formation of legends. More plausible, as probably
based to some extent on fact, is another response of
Apollo Didymeus for which we have the reported evidence of Seleucus himself. In 312 B.C. after taking
refuge with Ptolemy in Egypt he decided to make a daring attempt to recover Babylon, his former satrapy,
from the control of his enemy, Antigonus. He started
on this venturesome expedition with only a thousand
men, and needed to use all his powers of persuasion to
raise their drooping morale. Besides appealing to
their pride and his own record of achievement, he told
them 'to be confident in the pronouncements of the
gods and believe that the conclusion of the expedition
would be worthy of the attempt. For when he had consulted Apollo at Didyma, the god had addressed him as
king, and Alexander had stood by him in a dream by
night and had clearly revealed to him his future sovereignty, which it was fated that he should receive
in the course of time'.(2)

It was premature for Seleucus to represent the
oracle as addressing him with the title of king. It
was not till six years later in 306 B.C. that Antigonus was the first of the Diadochi to assume the
diadem and the royal title, followed in the next year
by Ptolemy, Seleucus and Lysimachus. But for some
time before the title had been used unofficially in
flattery of the Macedonian marshals, for instance by
the Athenians in welcoming Demetrius in 307 B.C. So
there would be nothing extraordinary if an oracle
before 312 B.C. had used the title hyperbolically in
addressing Seleucus. It is easy to imagine a suitable
occasion. In 315-12 B.C. Seleucus in Ptolemy's service had commanded a fleet off the Ionian coast and in
313 had actually been called to assist the satrap of

Caria. So he might well have had occasion to visit
Miletus and Didyma. As the history of Alexander had
shown, the Milesians were prepared to apply the prophecies of Apollo of Didyma very positively for political ends. Hence an enquiry from Seleucus about his
future might well have been made the occasion for a
demonstration of loyal support by addressing him in
some high flown compliments. But of course Seleucus
also may have greatly exaggerated, if he did not invent, the support of the oracle, so as to encourage
his troops. The interesting and significant point
which need not be doubted is that already in 312 B.C.
we find Seleucus recognising Apollo of Didyma as his
special patron.

The god appears again in this character in an
oracle recorded by a very late source. Libanius of
Antioch, the orator, in 356 A.D., when referring in
enthusiastic terms to Daphne, the famous sanctuary of
Apollo outside his native city, describes it as being
"all in all to Seleucus - Moreover an oracular response led him on, which in times of difficulty he had
received from Miletus, and had recovered his courage.
For it promised him future good fortune and enjoined
him that, when he had taken over the sovereignty of
Syria, he was to make Daphne a sacred place." Libanius' context for the oracle is vaguely indicated, but
it looks as if he meant to refer to the same circumstances as the response addressing Seleucus prematurely
as king. But the content of the prophecy does not fit
It would be very unlikely that the oracle would have
been so precise as to mention the sovereignty of
Syria; still less that it would have prescribed a
foundation of a sanctuary at Daphne. At most the
original response might have added to its forecast of
Seleucus' good fortune some proviso that he should
recognise Apollo's good will by some benefaction. On
the other hand it would be very likely that when
Seleucus founded Antioch on the Orontes in place of
Antigoneia in 300 B.C. he established and consecrated
the sanctuary and grove of Apollo in its suburbs at
the same time and obtained some oracular authority for
the new foundation. If so, Didyma would have been the
obvious place at which to seek it. It looks as if two
possible consultations have become confused in our
sources as represented by Libanius. (3)

The legends of Seleucus and Didyma are of rather
dubious historicity taken individually, but the general picture which they suggest is correct. Of none
of the other Diadochi were any stories told connecting
them with that oracle-centre, and this is exactly what
the inscriptions from the site confirm. Evidently

Seleucus Nicator and the later members of his dynasty
throughout the third century B.C. maintained a very
special relation with Miletus and its Apollo. This is
also illustrated by Seleucus' coinage, which from
300 B.C. regularly was stamped with the laureate head
of Apollo or the prophetic tripod. (4)

The inscriptional evidence from Didyma starts in
the year 300/299 B.C. A year before in the battle of
Ipsus the great empire of Antigonus and Demetrius had
been crushed, and Seleucus' position as lord of the
Eastern half of Alexander's conquests established.
But the coastal cities of Ionia still remained in control of Demetrius. However, this did not prevent them
from being open to penetration by Seleucus' diplomacy.
Also owing to his falling out with Lysimachus he soon
found it to his interest to come to friendly terms
with Demetrius and even to strengthen this rapprochement by a marriage alliance. (5) In these circumstances it is not surprising if Seleucus saw Miletus as a
useful base for influence in Ionia and the projected
temple at Didyma as a convenient means to win the
city's support.

From the texts of two decrees of the Milesian
assembly, one in honour of Antiochus the heir apparent
datable to the later months of 300/299 and the other
in honour of Queen Apame dated to 299/98, it is clear that
the king had invited an embassy from Miletus to visit
him and discuss the building of the temple at Didyma.
In view of Seleucus' earlier relations with the oracle
and his adoption of Apollo as his patron this invitat-
ion would be completely plausible. The king offered
the ambassadors financial support for their temple,
and the queen her good will, for which she was honoured in the second decree by the erection of her
statue. Antiochus "in rivalry with his father's
policy about the sanctuary", as the wording goes, had
undertaken to construct in Miletus a large colonnade
a furlong in length. This covered building would
provide protection for shops and market stalls, and
the proceeds derived from letting the sites were to be
assigned to finance constructions in the sanctuary at
Didyma, which were to be regarded as Antiochus' dedications. In response to this benefaction the first
decree provided for the appointment of an architect
for the colonnade and a commission to manage its proceeds, while Antiochus was to be honoured with all
the usual civic privileges and a bronze equestrian
statue. (6)

Evidently from these decrees the king had himself
taken a certain initiative in the matter, in which he
was supported by his wife and his son. But it is sig-

nificant that in both decrees there occurs the name of
a Milesian who was in a special position to interest the
king in the subject. The proposer of the first decree
was Demodamas, the son of Aristides, who, had probably led
the embassy to Seleucus, and the second decree is described as based on a report which he had submitted to the
city Council. Also at the end of the same decree
Demodamas' name comes first in the list of the three com-
missioners. He can safely be identified as a citizen
of Miletus who had already won prominence as a member of
Seleucus' court.

Pliny, the Elder, when describing the farthest
bounds of the ancient world, mentions the Jaxartes and
Alexandria Eschate, Alexander's most northerly foundation. The spot was marked by altars which Pliny says
were set up by Hercules and Dionysus and by Cyrus, Semiram-
is and Alexander, all of whom treated it as their limit in
that direction of the world. "But Demodamas, the general
of King Seleucus and King Antiochus, crossed the
river - and set up altars to Apollo of Didyma." (7)
This daring expedition of Demodamas far north into Central
Asia is usually supposed by modern scholars to have
taken place before Seleucus' expedition to India in
306 B.C. At any rate it is plausible to suppose that by
299 B.C. Demodamas had high standing at Seleucus' court
as an experienced and trusted marshal. Such a man
would have the ear of the king and could raise with
him the subject of the temple at Didyma with local
knowledge of the problem, while, as we have suggested,
it might appeal to the king as a suitable direction in
which to show himself a pious benefactor.

It is not possible to prove from our extant
sources what the position was at Didyma in 299 B.C. More
than thirty years previously the sacred spring had
been uncovered and prophecies produced. In 299 the
building of the temple is mentioned as if it were a
work already in operation, but what had been done in
the interval remains quite uncertain. Building accounts have been discovered in plenty for the period
from the middle of the third century B.C., but none
for the period before 300. The only inscriptions
which might indicate some progress are very fragmentary catalogues of sacred treasures, which if correctly dated about 310 B.C., would show that by that
time Apollo had acquired a number of dedications,
including some of gold and silver, which would presumably have been housed in some building for their safe
keeping. (8) One would naturally suppose that,
apart from any clearing of the site and removal of the
ruins of the previous temple, the next step would be
to erect a central shrine, like the naiskos in the

archaic temple, which could hold dedications and house
a cult-statue. Actually the remains of the new
naiskos are such that archaeologists can believe it
was built either in the last quarter of the 4th century or just after 300 B.C. (9) At any rate we may
suppose that progress had at best been very slow and
cramped for lack of funds, so that a case could well
be made to King Seleucus that assistance was badly
needed. What would be interesting to know is whether
from the beginning the Milesians had had in their
plans the grandiose scheme of the actual temple as
later built, or whether designs on this vast scale
were only drawn when it appeared that help on a com-
mensurate level could be expected from King Seleucus.
One rather dubious reference might be taken to suggest
that the plans may have been there from a very early
date. Vitruvius, when listing famous architects and
their works, names as those responsible for the restored temple of Artemis at Ephesus Demetrius and
Paeonius and goes on to say "At Miletus the same
Paeonius (of Ephesus) and Daphnis of Miletus built a
temple for Apollo in the Ionic style." He must be
referring somewhat loosely to the temple at Didyma.
But the interesting question is whether the same architect could be responsible for both buildings. The
temple of Ephesus was burnt down in 356 B.C. and its
restoration was begun soon after. The work was largely accomplished, but still incomplete, when Alexander
freed the city from the Persians in 334. So if Vitruvius' statement can be taken as evidence that at
Ephesus Paeonius was the junior architect or successor
to Demetrius, the original designer, it would be possible that he was active in the thirties of the century, and could have drawn up the plans for the restored temple of Didyma at any time after the oracle
had been revived. (10)

The implication from the inscriptions already
mentioned is that Seleucus in 300 B.C. had taken some
large step to help the construction. Probably he gave
a considerable capital sum, and in his honour his
statue was set up on a huge base in the Delphinium at
Miletus. (11) His son and heir apparent, as we saw,
adopted a different and complementary method. By
providing a very large building at Miletus which could
produce a regular income he created a permanent endow-
ment for the sanctuary at Didyma. It has been noted
that the wording of the decree setting up the trust
is somewhat general. The money is for the "equipping
of the Sanctuary". The officials responsible probably
looked ahead, and supposed that sooner or later the
temple would be finished and then the annual income

from Antiochus could legally be applied to any other
works at Didyma. But they had scarcely foreseen how
long and expensive the construction of the temple itself would be and that in fact it would never be completed.

Besides giving financial help Seleucus made one
great gesture of piety and sentiment. He found in the
old Median capital of Ecbatana the original bronze
cult-statue of Apollo Philesius made by Canachus. It
had evidently been removed by the Persian forces in
494 B.C. not, as one may suppose, on aesthetic grounds,
but to transfer Apollo to a new home in the land of
his conquerors. Seleucus proceeded to send the statue
back to the Milesians. He had a precedent for his
action, since Alexander had restored to Athens the
original statues of Harmodius and Aristogeiton
by Antenor, which had been removed by Xerxes. The
Apollo was installed by the Milesians in the restored
naiskos and remained to be admired by future generations down to the end of paganism. (12)

The gratitude of the officials of Didyma to
Seleucus may have been shown in the creation of a
suitably honorific legend. In the latter years of
Seleucus' reign he was already hailed as the son of
Apollo, as is illustrated by some lines of verse inscribed at the end of a poem to Asclepius found at
Erythrae. "Praise with hymns at the libations of
Apollo of the dark hair his son Seleucus, whom the god
of the golden lyre himself begat; praise him and for-
get not." The appropriate legend is found in Justin.
Seleucus' mother, Laodice, had a dream that Apollo had
made love to her, and as a reward had given her a ring
engraved with an anchor, and had instructed her to give
it to the son whom she bore. Next morning when she
woke a ring with this emblem was found in her bed.
Also her son when born had a mark in the shape of an
anchor on his thigh and this characteristic symbol was
said to be hereditary. Justin links the legend of the
dream with the dedication of Daphne to Apollo by stating that the twin foundations of the city of Antioch
and its sanctuary were made by Seleucus in memorial
to his mortal father and his divine progenitor. But
this connection does not exclude a link with Didyma,
since, as we have seen, that oracle-centre was credited with having commanded the foundation of Daphne.
The association of the anchor with Seleucus appears
first in his coinage struck at Susa c. 305 B.C., and
is repeated variously on his coins throughout his
reign. This does not prove that the legend of Seleucus' divine birth is as early in origin. For other
authorities know of different stories about Seleucus

and a ring with an anchor foretelling his sovereignty, which do not involve Apollo. It appears as if Seleucus adopted the anchor as his badge for reasons which we cannot tell, and then a legend explaining his connection with it developed and ultimately involved the story of his birth from Apollo. Bevan may have been right in his original conjecture that this version was the invention of Apollo's priests at Didyma. (13)

With the cult-statue safely returned and funds for a rebuilding assured the Milesians could go ahead with their work of reconstruction. The new temple was not merely laid out as a larger version of its predecessor, but it also contained some highly remarkable new features. (14) In size it was 118.34 m. in length and 60.13 m. in breadth at the first step, making it just a few metres larger in both dimensions than its great rival, the temple of Artemis at Ephesus. The colonnade round all four sides was of two rows of columns 19.70 m. high to the capital - a height which was only slightly exceeded centuries later in the temple of Zeus at Baalbek. The prodomos also contained three rows of four columns each. So far the design of the temple was in accordance with the other large Ionic temples of Asia Minor. But at this point the plan of the temple was modified in the strangest manner. For the prodomos did not lead by a great central doorway to the cella, but where the doorway should have come, the worshipper entering the building found himself faced with a blank wall 1.495 m. high with above it a colossal window 5.63 m. wide. Consequently the worshipper in the prodomos could not look into the temple. Instead, just above his eye-level beyond the embrasure of the window stretched the floor of a large room 14.04 m. by 8.73 m. with its roof supported on two columns. Through the doors of this room, opposite the window, the spectator on ground level outside could just see the upper part of the naiskos in the inner court. There was no direct approach to this room from outside the temple, but it was connected with the inner court by a monumental stairway of twenty two steps, 15.25 m. wide, which led down by the triple doorways of the room to the ground level in the heart of the temple. This inner courtyard, as in the archaic period, contained the sacred spring, the naiskos with the cult-statue, various altars, and probably a grove of bay trees. It was open to the sky, but cut off from the outside world by towering walls, which are 22 m. to 25 m. high and were probably designed to reach a height of nearly 28 m. above the floor of the adyton. This was never completed, but even as it stands at the present day

the effect is overwhelmingly impressive. A plain unbroken wall of this height would have been unbearably
dull. So the surface is diversified by eleven pilas-
ters on each side and five on the end wall corresponding to the centre of the interspaces of the columns
in the exterior colonnade and springing from a basement running round the adyton at a height of 4.92 m.

    This inner court could only be reached from the
outside world by two long sloping passages built in
the thickness of the wall and leading from the prodomos
near the angle of the wall on its north and south
sides. The passages were only wide enough and high
enough for a normal man to traverse and could not admit two abreast. At the adyton each opened into a
sort of small pavilion giving access to the court.
While the grand staircase leading up to the room with
two columns was designed for processions, these passages were evidently meant to control access, which
could only be obtained in single file. The difficulty
produced by the steep slope was fully recognised by
the architects. The marble floor of the passage is
heavily scored in a regular pattern to prevent slipp-
ing. (14)

    The building contains one other remarkable feat-
ure. From the room with the two columns overlooking
the prodomos two staircases mounted one at either end
in the thickness of the wall. As they now stand, they
end abruptly at the third flight, so that their exact
function can only be conjectured. They could have
given access to a room above the ceiling of the room
with the two columns or to the pediment floor. One
may reasonably suppose that they had some regular and
important use and were not merely service staircases
needed for the construction of the upper levels, (15)
for the roof of the staircases was decorated with a
beautiful design in relief and painted, showing a
running pattern of Greek keys. But possibly the top
of the staircase was unroofed as there are careful
arrangements at the bottom step to drain off any water
which came down the staircase.

    Detailed conjectures about the purposes of these
special features of the temple are more appropriately
postponed to a discussion of the whole procedure of
the oracle. (16) Enough has been written to show that
the temple of Didyma as rebuilt in the Hellenistic
and Roman periods was a highly remarkable and elaborate structure. Consequently as has been pointed out
by earlier scholars, its history is more like that of
a medieval Gothic cathedral, which also it more resembled in scale. The Parthenon, though smaller, with
all its elaborate sculpture was completed in some sixteen

years. The temple of Asclepius at Epidaurus in the fourth century B.C. took only four years, eight months and ten days to erect. At Didyma, if we leave on one side the uncertain amount done before 299 B.C. and take the start from that date, fragments of accounts show the work still in progress more than two centuries later, and literary references and stylistic considerations suggest that it was continued for another couple of centuries at least under the Roman emperors. Pausanias writing under Marcus Aurelius described it as unfinished, and it is probable that after Caracalla work ground to a halt and was never resumed. By that time the general appearance must have suggested that the temple was near completion.

Evidently the work on the building was not allowed to interrupt seriously the functioning of the oracle. For intermittent evidence for its activity occurs throughout all these centuries. Presumably once the spring and the <u>naiskos</u> were suitably fitted up, and the <u>adyton</u> surrounded by the lower courses of its circuit wall, the operations of the prophets could be carried out, even if they lacked the full dignity of their proper setting. Van Essen has calculated that as the ground-floor of the <u>adyton</u> was 5 m. below that of the peristyle a wall some 1.5 m. to 2 m. in height would already prevent one from seeing the interior. (17) This height must have been achieved quite soon. But the political history of Miletus in the third and second centuries was seriously interrupted by constant changes of overlordship. Though throughout the period the city may nominally have remained free and independent, in practice the Hellenistic monarchs probably exercised a great deal of interference, and the chequered pattern of changes of supremacy must have disturbed the administrative and economical progress of Miletus and therefore its sanctuary.

It is impossible owing to the defects of our historical evidence to give a precise account of the complicated changes of sovereignty which affected Miletus. There is no literary account of the period, and deductions have to be based on casual allusions in ancient authors and contemporary inscriptions, which are rarely precisely dated. But an approximate sketch will suggest under what conditions the temple of Didyma grew and the oracle functioned.

In 299 B.C. Demetrius Poliorcetes had been the king in control of the Ionian coast, but the rapprochement between him and Seleucus had given the latter an opportunity to intervene in Miletus. They soon fell out again and by 290/89 B.C. Lysimachus had taken

advantage of Demetrius' preoccupations in Greece to
seize Ionia. He treated some of the cities, such as
Colophon, with ruthless authority, but Miletus does
not seem to have suffered particularly at his hands.
However, as Lysimachus was no friend of Seleucus,
Syrian influence must have waned. In 287 B.C. there
occurred the brief spectacular episode when Demetrius
in his last desperate effort to assert himself landed
at Miletus with an expeditionary force designed to
retrieve his Asian territory from Lysimachus, but also
with more high-flown plans of conquest directed
against Seleucus himself. His intentions in this direction seem to have been foreseen by Seleucus, who
made a colossal effort of diplomacy to win over Miletus in advance. In the previous winter 288/7 he sent
an ambassador to the city bringing a huge consignment
of offerings, which he asked the Milesians in a letter
to dedicate at Didyma for the health and prosperity
of the Seleucid kings and the safety of the city. The
magnificent benefaction was recorded at Didyma by in-
scribing the king's letter itself, which contained a
list of the royal gifts. These ranged from "a big
lamp of bronze" to various gold and silver cups and an
antique Persian wine-cooler. The ambassador also
provided massive quantities of incense, to which the
Syrian kingdom had access, and offered as victims a
thousand sheep and twelve oxen. (18)

It is more than a mere coincidence that Seleucus
sent this huge and unprecedented gift only a few
months before Demetrius' attempt on Miletus. The generosity of the presentation was immense and might well
have evoked some warm response from the oracle. But
if so, it is not recorded. If by linking the prosperity of the Seleucids and the safety of the city in
one invocation, the king had hoped to purchase the
loyalty of Miletus, politically it was a failure. Next
summer Demetrius sailed in with his fleet, and was
enthusiastically welcomed by the Milesians. But,
after initial successes in conquering Ionia and Lydia,
he left for the East where he fell into the hands of
Seleucus and never regained his freedom. Lysimachus
resumed his control of the Asia Minor coast. He punished Miletus for its disloyalty to him by requiring
some heavy indemnity. For five years later (283/2
B.C.) the citizens are actually found negotiating with
Cnidus for a state-loan to meet the second instalment
due to the king. (19)

In 281 B.C. Seleucus at length marched west to
settle with Lysimachus. They met in the battle of
Korupedion, where Lysimachus was killed, and the victorious Seleucus marched on to take over his kingdom,

but instead fell a victim of assassination. So just
when it seemed that Seleucus would finally establish
his sovereignty over Asia Minor, his empire collapsed
into confusion, and Ptolemy II, who had great am-
bitions to control the Aegean by his naval power, chose Miletus as a suitable base of operations. Once
more the Hellenistic monarch began by making a generous
gift: this time ceding royal lands, presumably property of Seleucus which he had occupied. (20) But
Ptolemy's navy proved little protection to Miletus
against a new threat by land which was ravaging Asia
Minor. In 278 B.C. three tribes of migrating Celts
crossed into Asia, and settled in the mountainous
stronghold of Galatia. Like their kinsmen who had
invaded Italy a century before, they were not so much
interested in the conquest of territory as in the
amassing of plunder, especially gold. The cities of
Ionia fell easy victims to these savage raiders.
Miletus was one of the places to suffer, and the result so far as Didyma was concerned is illustrated by
a pathetic entry in the temple records for 277/6:
"The following survived from the war in the possession
of Apollo - one embossed cup and one ox-horn set in
silver." All the great offerings of Seleucus I and
the other treasures amassed over the years had vanished in one Gallic raid. (21)
     To protect themselves from the recurrence of such
perils the Milesians adopted the dangerous expedient
of accepting a garrison from a Hellenistic king. This
at least is the probable explanation why shortly
afterwards the democracy was overthrown by a tyrant,
Timarchus the Aetolian, who appears to have been originally a mercenary commander under Ptolemy II, but
later rebelled and attempted to create an independent
autocracy and even waged war on Miletus' neighbours in
a bid to extend his power. The democracy remained
suppressed under this militaristic dictatorship till
259/8 B.C. when at last with the help of Antiochus II,
who had lately come to the throne of Syria, Miletus
regained its political freedom. (22)
     The interlude of Ptolemaic influence in Miletus
had lasted some sixteen years and left little trace
there, but it may have had one reflection in Greek
literature. Callimachus, the great contemporary poet
of Alexandria, wrote one poem entitled Branchus, addressed to Apollo and Zeus as the gods of Didyma, and
elsewhere in his Iambics referred to the legends of
the Branchidae. It was typical of Alexandrian poetry
to collect and reproduce local traditions which up
till then had failed to find a place in Greek poetry.
But the Ptolemaic interest in Miletus probably added

special point to Callimachus' contemporary references. (23)

The oracle of Didyma also appeared about this period in the poetry of Callimachus' contemporary and rival Apollonius of Rhodes. In his lost poem on the foundation of Caunus he told how when Io was carried off by pirates - the rationalised version of the myth - her father Inachus sent Lyrkos the son of Phoroneus, among others, in search of her. He failed in his mission and in despair at returning unsuccessful he settled in Caunus in southern Caria and marrie a native woman, Heilebie, the daughter of Aibialos. They had no children. So Lyrkos went to consult Apollo of Didyma and received the reply that he would have children by the woman with whom he first had intercourse on leaving his ship. On the voyage back he put in at Bybastos where Staphylus ("Grape-bunch"), son of Dionysus, hearing of the oracle made Lyrkos drunk and chose Hemithea, one of his two daughters to sleep with him. Lyrkos was dismayed in the morning to find what had happened, but gave Hemithea a belt, which in the usual manner of such Greek legends, led ultimately to the recognition of Basilus ("Sovereign" the child of this union, who became king of Caunus.

The story is a very typical Hellenistic romance, which was also told by Nicaenetus, an elegiac poet o Samos. Except for the names it contains the minimum of genuine local tradition, for it is obviously modelled on the Attic legend of the begetting of Theseus There the childless Aegeus consults Delphi and on his journey home is seduced similarly by Pittheus of Troizen. It was probably Nicaenetus or Apollonius wh invented this version of the story for Caunus and chose to make Didyma, not Delphi, the scene of the consultation as the nearer oracle centre of rising repute in the third century B.C. The supposition tha the story is only a Hellenistic fiction is confirmed by the fact that Diodorus Siculus records a quite different legend about Hemithea ("Half-Goddess") the daughter of Staphylus. This involves no reference to the oracle of Didyma though it does incidentally trac the origin of the Aniadai, the oracular family of Delos. Instead it serves to explain the origin of th local cult of Hemithea, at Kastabos, on the promontor of Cnidus, and to provide the reasons for the local taboo on wine and pigs in its ritual. This is obviously the correct and original legend. As Diodorus states "there are many different accounts related to her (Hemithea), and we shall tell the most prevalent and that accepted by the local inhabitants". So the story of Hemithea and Lyrkos can be taken only as

showing how in the mid third century B.C. Didyma was
winning a new place in Hellenistic literature, sometimes in stories modelled on the traditional legends
about Delphi. (24)

With the fall of the tyrant, Timarchus, the
Seleucid influence in Miletus was revived. Antiochus
II was recognised as a benefactor of the city in help-
ing to overthrow the tyrant and restore the democracy,
and these good services were acknowledged in a manner
which was in the Greek tradition. Appian records that
the Milesians were the first to confer on him the
epithet Theos ("God") which became his traditional
title distinguishing him from his namesakes in the
dynasty. This can be taken to mean that the people of
Miletus in recognition of Antiochus' good services to
the democracy set up a municipal cult of him as a divinity. This institution of a new god in the city
would appropriately require the sanction of Apollo,
and it is evident that something of the sort was provided from Didyma, as is shown by a letter of Seleucus
II in which soon after his accession in 247 B.C. he
summed up the relations of his family and the Milesian oracle-centre. "Our ancestors and our father
(Antiochus II) in particular have shown many great
good services to your city both on account of the oracular responses issued from the shrine among you of
Apollo of Didyma and on account of our kinship to the
god himself and also especially on account of the
gratitude shown by your democracy. We see also our-
selves from the rest of your policy to us at all times
in relation to our affairs, as has been displayed to
us by our father's friends, and from the report which
Glaucippos and Diomandros made to us who have brought
from you the consecrated garland out of the innermost
sanctuary with which your democracy has crowned us,
that you have made to our friends a sincere and firm
demonstration and that you are mindful of the benefits
which you have received. We therefore have accepted
the goodwill of your populace and are eager and regard
it as among our chief objects to bring your city to a
yet more distinguished position and to increase the
generosities already existing.....:" (25)

At this point the letter breaks off, but its main
purpose and significance are clear. The authorities
of Miletus evidently regarded good relations with the
Seleucids as a key-stone of their policy and on the
accession of Seleucus II had sent a special embassy
to congratulate him. Seleucus on his part clearly
regarded the association of Miletus as important. He
recalled the past benefits conferred on the city and
made promises for the future. In all this diplomacy

the oracle at Didyma played an important part. The
men of Miletus did not attempt to send the Seleucid
king great material gifts for his accession. Instead
their ambassadors brought a consecrated crown from the
innermost sanctuary at Didyma. It was a garland cut
from the sacred bay trees growing in the adyton. The
king fully recognised the spiritual significance of
this offering, and in return in his letter particularly stressed the connections of his dynasty with
Apollo. He mentioned their claim to be descended from
the god through Seleucus Nicator - a claim endorsed
by Didyma - and he also recalled more recent oracles,
which as he was referring particularly to his father's
services to Miletus probably included one recognising
him not merely as descended from a god, but as being
himself divine. It is a pity that the letter breaks
off just where Seleucus II was announcing his own
beneficent intentions. It would be interesting to know
whether he promised any specific assistance for the
erecting of Apollo's temple. But the rather vague
reference to bringing the city of Miletus into a more
distinguished position suggests that the king intended
to do something for the community, rather than for the
building. Dr. Günther has suggested that this was to
take the form of declaring the territory of Miletus
sacred and inviolate (asylos).

That such a declaration of asylia was made at
some date before the end of the third century B.C. is
proved by an inscription from Cos which records a
decree of the Milesians invoking the recognition of
this privilege in connection with the celebration of
new sacred games - the Didymeia. The document gives
a remarkable eulogy of their local oracle: "The people
of Miletus in accordance with ancestral tradition sub-
sidises public gatherings and contests at Didyma in
honour of Apollo of Didyma, and the city and its territory have been consecrated on account of the fact that
in this place Zeus and Leto were united in love, and
on account of the oracular responses of the god from
which not a few nations and cities and kings who have
obtained the great blessings of the advice from the god
have proclaimed the consecration and asylia on their
own initiative themselves, duly assigning to the city
and to the god their deserved gratitude on these matters. Therefore it is fitting for the people of Miletus, acting in accordance with the oracles that have
been given, to establish the contest of the Didymeia
with a crown as the award and to receive to it the
Greeks in general since the good services have been
conferred by the god on them all in common." (26) Out
of this rather turgid statement, typical of the style

of Hellenistic decrees, we can extract the indications
of four elements which are usually present in these
third century B.C. votes of asylia. The city chosen
for this privilege had to be marked by the presence
of an outstanding cult of some deity; also it had
usually some indication that the place itself had been
chosen by the god. The privilege of asylia was conferred by the decrees of numerous states which agreed
individually to recognise this status, and the basis
was usually an oracular response. The city for its
part normally acknowledged the privilege by celebrat-
ing periodically a festival in honour of the god in
which those recognising its status could participate.(27)
   At Miletus the cult of Apollo of Didyma provided
an obvious example of a religious institution whose
sanctity could consecrate the city's territory. Here
it is reinforced with a legend unknown to extant Greek
literature. The decree clearly indicated that Didyma
claimed to be the place where Zeus and Leto were first
united in love and therefore where Apollo was conceived. Such a claim does not appear elsewhere in our
ancient evidence, and it has been usual since the discovery of the inscription to suppose that the legend
was invented at this point to reinforce Didyma's claim
to sanctity. But recently a small votive statuette
has been found in the stratum of the archaic temple.
It shows a male and female couple who can plausibly
be indentified as Zeus and Leto.(28) Hence Tuchelt
claims that the legend dates back to the archaic period and supposes that there were altars dedicated to
Zeus and Leto in the adyton of the archaic temple
destroyed at the time of the Persian sack. This is
rather an elaborate edifice of hypothesis to erect on
one uninscribed statuette. At most one may admit that
the priests of the late third century may have had
some weak tradition associating Leto with Zeus at
Didyma. Our literary evidence briefly refers to a
cult of Zeus in association with Apollo in the Hellenistic period, and inscriptions from then to Roman times show that Zeus had a sanctuary of his own and was
worshipped under various titles. But in none of this
evidence is he associated with Leto nor does Leto
appear to receive any cult with him until the two
deities are grouped together in statues set up in a
very late revival in the last years of the third century A.D. So the general effect of our evidence is to
suggest that the legend of the union of Zeus and Leto
at Didyma was a Hellenistic invention meant to justify
the sanctity of the place with a view to claiming
asylia. Delos or Patara had already for long asserted
their legendary claim to be Apollo's birthplace. So

this myth that he was conceived at Didyma was the best
that the priesthood could concoct.

As for the recognition of the sanctity and <u>asylia</u>
of Miletus the inscription refers to the spontaneous
proclamations issued by not a few nations, kings and
cities, and connects this with the benefits which
they had received from Apollo's oracles. It is unfortunate that no copy of these pronouncements has
been preserved in inscriptions. Perhaps they were
never inscribed, unlike the vast dossier dealing with
the <u>asylia</u> of Artemis Leucophryene which was published
on stone by Magnesia on the Maeander. Other grants
of <u>asylia</u> were based on a specific consultation of an
oracle and its favourable reply. (The oracle consulted
was usually Delphi, but once Didyma was associated
with it in what was probably the consecration of Teos)
Instead the <u>asylia</u> of Miletus is merely justified by
the general services of Didyma. Similarly in the case
of Magnesia there is no disguise of the fact that the
pronouncements of the different cities were solicited,
but the Milesians assert that their <u>asylia</u> was proclaimed spontaneously - a statement which is difficult
to take at its face value. It is possible that the
truth was, as Dr. Günther suggests, that the declaration was inspired and organised by Seleucus II, and
that he was responsible for stimulating a number of
kings, nations and cities who were in his sphere of
influence to address letters to Miletus offering to
recognise their territory as holy and inviolate. The
differences in this instance from normal procedure may
be correctly explained by the fact that this was the
earliest example of such a proclamation. Seleucus II
was responsible for the next datable instance subsequent to this - the <u>asylia</u> of Smyrna, for which he
consulted the Pythian Apollo, and later examples followed the pattern of that occasion. It is to be supposed that all this religious diplomacy on his part
was not solely inspired by piety. The declaring of
Miletus and Smyrna as inviolate gave the Syrian kings
two valuable ports in Ionia which were protected by a
form of religious neutrality, but could be expected to
support the Seleucids in the spreading of their influence in Asia Minor and the Aegean. (29)

After a discussion of the part of Didyma in the
declaration of Milesian territory inviolate, it is
paradoxical that the next appearance of the oracle in
the city's records is in connection with the military
activity of Miletus. It is, however, all too typical
of the Greek city-state that, while willing enough at
times to engage in diplomacy to limit large scale warfare, the citizens were unwilling to forgo their

traditional border disputes with their neighbours.
The Milesians in their history had shown themselves
ready enough to fight over this kind of quarrel.   In
the latter half of the third century the neighbouring
enemy was Magnesia on the Maeander - a city which ir-
onically like Miletus had its territory declared inviolate.   The object of their contention was the land
of Myus, which had been one of the original twelve
cities of the Ionian League, but by the Hellenistic
period was evidently in decline.   This was probably
due to the silting up of the estuary of the Maeander,
which was resulting from the river's alluvial deposits.   In the end this fatal process was to reach Miletus itself, but at this time it was only seriously
affecting Myus, which lay much further upstream.
With the failure of Myus' channel to the sea it sank
in importance till it was taken over by Miletus, its
southern neighbour, but this involved a clash with
Magnesia, its neighbour on the north.   Our sources do
not show how long this struggle for territory had
lasted, but in 228 B.C. the Milesians considered taking a decisive step.   They had enlisted for the war
with Magnesia a contingent of mercenary soldiers from
Dreros and Milatos in Crete.   It is significant of the
Hellenistic period that warfare of all kinds had become largely a professional activity; citizens had
neither the technical proficiency nor the old-fashioned patriotism of the classical period.   It was easier
and more effective to hire soldiers from those less
developed regions which were the breeding ground of
mercenaries.   On the other hand if the Milesians wanted to have a permanent garrison on the frontier, to
hire mercenaries was not enough.   Their usual con-
tracts were short term, and they might be difficult to
retain in case a better offer of pay turned up.   So
the only safe method was to settle them on the land
which they were hired to defend, and admit them to
membership of the city. (30)   Evidently this was the
policy decided upon by the Milesian magistrates, who
may also have been influenced by a decline in the
city's population, such as would be typical of this
period.   Before the plan was finally approved by the
city, a delegation was sent to Didyma with instructions to enquire "whether it is better and more good
for the people both now and for the future if they
took into the political body the men of Dreros and
Milatos and gave them a share in land and in all the
other things that the Milesians have in common".   The
god's reply in hexameter verse is fragmentarily preserved: " Receive with a welcome as inhabitants the
men who are a help into your city.   For it is both

better and more good..." Evidently Apollo gave his hearty approval, and a similar enquiry a few years later probably also received an affirmative answer.(31)

Some technical features of these documents are worth attention. The city in its enquiries repeats three times the standard formula which we have translated and which was probably the traditional wording when Apollo was consulted by Miletus. The use of the phrase "better and more good" is conventional in oracular enquiries, and ordinarily it introduces an alternative question such as could be answered without ecstatic prophecy by some mechanical means of drawing lots. In fact if only the question and the paraphrased result of the consultation were recorded, a modern scholar would probably have conjectured that this was the method of divination employed. But enough of the answer is preserved verbatim to prove that in each of three instances it consisted in a succession of hexameter verses. They seem to be rather prosaic compositions, but at least it is likely that they are meant to reproduce the words of Apollo speaking through the mouth of his inspired prophetess. So Didyma, at a time when Delphi was abandoning verse in its oracles, still maintained the classical tradition.

The other comment on the subject might be to ask why Miletus consulted Didyma at all. It might have been that there were two bodies of opinion in the city, one in favour of giving citizenship to the mercenaries, the other against it, and that Apollo was called in as arbitrator on a contentious issue. But nothing in our sources suggests this situation. So it may be that tradition dictated that questions of grave importance affecting the city should not be settled without divine approval, and public opinion still supported this procedure. This would imply that even at the end of the third century B.C. the consultation of oracles was treated as a serious religious obligation.

About the same period as the enquiries on citizenship for the Cretan mercenaries, the Milesians consulted Apollo on a religious matter which was a more typical subject for questioning an oracle. The enquiry only is preserved and not the god's answer. It concerned the cult of Artemis Skiris. (32) The goddess was worshipped at Miletus under various titles. In this instance the name was connected with a family, the Skiridai, who evidently continued to be responsible for the management of the cult even after it had been recognised as an institution of the State. One of its practices was a collection (<u>agersis</u>), and the

Skiridai at some date in the later part of the third century B.C. proposed some alteration in those arrangements. Consequently the Milesian democracy decreed to hold a formal consultation of Apollo on the subject. The question was drafted:- "the people of Miletus ask whether it will be acceptable to the goddess and expedient for the people if both now and for the future they perform the collections for Artemis Counsel-giver Skiris as the Skiridai expound the sacred law or as it takes place at present." The answer is not preserved. As the enquiry was framed as an alternative question, the oracle might have been obtained by lots, but we have seen already that Apollo of Didyma tended to discursive replies even in response to such enquiries. Two other points are also worth noting. It was usual for the Pythian Apollo to be asked whether other deities should be worshipped in particular ways. Similarly, the Milesians did not ask Artemis herself what should be done about her collections; they asked Apollo as the general source of guidance. It was assumed that his knowledge covered the wishes of other deities and the best way to worship them. Also by the form of the question it was apparently assumed that Apollo knew the points at issue. Particularly it was not explained to him what it was that the Skiridai proposed. His omniscience in such matters is taken for granted. Again parallels could be found in enquiries at Delphi.

In general these enquiries illustrate the way in which the Milesians referred questions involving significant changes to Apollo for ratification whether they were political or religious. Apollo's advice about citizenship and settlement for the mercenaries was not very successful, if it was meant to guarantee to Miletus the possession of the territory of Myus. In 201 B.C. when Philip V of Macedon invaded Asia Minor, he altered the political map to suit his own strategic wishes. Myus was taken from Miletus and given to Magnesia. This caused Miletus to join Rhodes in calling on Rome for help. After Philip was defeated in 196 B.C., Magnesia and Miletus under pressure from the cities allied to Rome delimited the territory, so that Myus was restored to Miletus. But even under Roman suzerainty the Greek cities still remained free to fight each other, and later the Magnesians won such a decisive victory over the Milesians that they seized the territory of Myus again and expelled the Cretan settlers, forcing them to return to their native land. (33)

The oracle of Didyma does not appear in these events, but about 180 B.C. it gave its blessing to an agreement between Miletus and its other smaller neighbour, Heraclea on Latmus. By this treaty the two communities were to exchange rights of citizenship and to settle outstanding quarrels, such as one involving again the territory of Myus. Before the pact had been concluded, the people of Miletus had referred the issue to Apollo of Didyma, and had received an answer that it would be better to make the treaty. But this time the actual words of the oracle are not quoted.(34)

The involvement of Apollo in this political decision, as in the question of the mercenaries, may have been particularly because the issues in both instances concerned the composition of the citizen body - a serious question affecting the very nature of the community.

It is the last instance of such a political enquiry at Didyma. For though Miletus continued to be free in name, like all Greek cities, particularly those in Asia Minor, it gradually lost all effective independence. So subjects for enquiry such as those recorded in the half century 228-180 B.C. did not arise again. But there may have been other factors also operating. In effect the Roman senate had taken the place of the Seleucids as the dominant power to whom the Milesians must ultimately look in foreign affairs. By the Peace of Apamea (189 B.C.) Antiochus III had been compelled to withdraw beyond the Taurus. Antiochus IV (Epiphanes) tried to exercise influence in the Aegean by his benefactions. He paid for the erection of a new council chamber in Miletus and followed the traditional practice of the dynasty in appointing Milesians, the brothers Timarchus and Heraclides, as his ministers. But in practice he had no real authority in Ionia, and his successors abandoned any attempt at influence there. Their place had been taken for a while by the Attalids, whose territory had been extended after the Peace of Apamea in reward for their military and naval support of Rome. Miletus looked to Eumenes II for help and vowed a sanctuary in his honour in 167 B.C. But even Eumenes found himself treated with suspicion by the Romans - within little over half a century after the Peace the last of the Attalids bequeathed his kingdom to them. (35) The Romans in their relation to oracular centres were very different from a Hellenistic monarch. After the Second Punic War the Senate only consulted officially the Sibylline books and the Haruspices. We never hear of a Greek city using an oracular response to influence the Republican government. So it was to be expected that public consultations of the oracles would decrease and even fall into abeyance - a fact corresponding to the silence that occurs in our epigraphic evidence.

It is interesting, however, to notice that the building of the temple at Didyma only gradually declined. From 219 B.C. to about 170 B.C., over a period of some fifty years, the officials responsible for the erection set up a record year by year reporting in detail the work done together with its cost. Though only extant in fragments, these building accounts have made it possible for Rehm to identify what was executed at different stages and how the various items were costed. (36) Unfortunately the inscriptions only deal with construction and expenditure; they tell us nothing about the source of the money. Presumably the rents of the 78 shops in Antiochus I's colonnade were being expended each year on the building of the temple. Also Miletus itself may have subscribed regularly from the city's funds. Occasional benefactions might have come from wealthy donors, but if so, they have left no trace in our records. So it is reasonable to conjecture that a steady income may also have been derived from the private enquirer at the oracle. This kind of business at this period was not perpetuated by dedicatory inscriptions, such as we shall find occasionally in the time of the Roman empire. But it is plausible to suppose that the oracle at Didyma was still regularly consulted by private individuals, though not by kings and cities. Otherwise it is hard to understand why the costly and difficult work of building should have been pressed ahead with vigour. Also the government of Miletus was probably still generally democratic as the detailed publication of accounts seems to imply. The style of the records suggests the transcript of a diary: - "There were placed in the temple in the gaps left in the door-frame (of the main entrance) eight stones of marble and four stones of limestone of which the measurement was two hundred cubic feet and seven palms. The lintel was brought from the Chresmographeion (the record building) into the vestibule of the temple. When a crane with four legs had been assembled and put in position and one of two legs had been put in position, the lintel was raised and bedded into the doorposts...". (37) Evidently the temple and its precinct must have been a hive of activity for many years. But it appears that after the death of Attalus III and the bequeathing of his kingdom to Rome, the creation of the province of Asia had a prejudicial effect on the position of Miletus. The government of the city under Roman pressure was changed from a democracy to an oligarchy consisting of a governing body of fifty. (Perhaps the populace had

shown too much sympathy for the pretender Aristonicus
but it may be simply the typical effect of Roman
policy.) Whether through political changes or an
accompanying economic decline, the work on the temple
slackened. The form of the accounts published was
changed, and the series appears to have soon ended.
Also significantly they are headed with a reference
to "the decree passed by the magistrates and the
people with regard to the oracle which had been issued
about the erection of the temple". Evidently for the
first time that is recorded Apollo himself had intervened with a response in which one can conjecture that
he had urged the Milesians to hasten the work. How
much effect this had produced we cannot tell, but
evidently it did not last.

The only response recorded verbatim from this
period was inscribed by a private individual who was
concerned with the erection of the temple. It is on
a marble altar dedicated to "Poseidon Asphaleios (the
steady) the Saviour and the Greatest by Andronicus
the son of Potamon, former treasurer and overseer of
the building of the temple of Apollo of Didyma". (38)
He is not otherwise known from the temple records and
from his official title and the style of the script
he must have been active before the last years of the
second century B.C. Above the dedicatory inscription
is engraved a response of Apollo written in hexameter
verse. The enquirers and their enquiry are not recorded, but from the form of the reply addressed in
the second person plural it is probable that the enquirers were the Milesians and not the one individual,
Andronicus. Also from the contents of the response it
is likely that the enquiry concerned an earthquake
shock and that Apollo had been asked how one could
provide some future protection against this danger.
"The god gave an oracle: As the Steady appease Poseidon with sacrifices under this title and ask him to
come in mercy and save the ornament of your city un-
shaken free from danger. For it comes very near to
you. You must guard against it, and pray that thereafter you may advance to old age unacquainted with
troubles." Presumably Miletus or Didyma itself had
experienced a tremor of sufficiently alarming inten-
sity to occasion an official request for a ritual
precaution against serious damage. Apollo suitably
suggested as the protecting deity Poseidon, who since
the days of Homer had been "the Earth-shaker" and
therefore also the appropriate god to preserve from
earthquakes. It appears that Andronicus, who was in
charge of the temple works - a specially vulnerable
target for tremors - had personally undertaken volun-

tarily to erect the altar and offer the accompanying sacrifices for the first ten years. No doubt an individual chosen for his position, especially in the late second century B.C. would be a person of considerable means. But his action was certainly generous. There is no evidence whether the sacrifices to Poseidon Asphaleios continued to be offered later after the original scare had passed.

The first century B.C. in its first half was not a happy period for Miletus. Roman supremacy was felt as oppressive. Consequently the city unwisely supported Mithridates in his first war against Rome and even elected him to the honorary position of chief magistrate in 86 B.C. Miletus will therefore have felt the weight of Sulla's punishment, when Mithridates was forced to withdraw. From this point can be traced an economic decline in the city which continued till the principate of Augustus. (39) As we have seen, this corresponded to a period when the building activity at Didyma appears to have dwindled and perhaps been suspended. But Roman supremacy did not even guarantee protection. Didyma is recorded in the long list of leading sanctuaries of the Aegean which were taken and sacked by the Pirates before 65 B.C. How extensive the loss and damage was we have no means of knowing.

Pompey's victory over the Pirates removed this danger, and for the last time we find the Milesians successfully enlisting the generosity of a Hellenistic monarch. The only surviving dynasty of the original successors to Alexander was the Egyptian, and Ptolemy Auletes by his dissolute and erratic life showed that he only remained in power through Roman sufferance. Shortly before his death an embassy from Miletus succeeded in persuading him to make a generous benefaction - twenty-four and a third talents' weight in ivory for the adornment of the "great doorway", of the temple. (40) This was probably only half of the king's intended benefaction, for his successor, Ptolemy XIII, at an uncertain date before 49 B.C. gave a similar amount of ivory. Evidently this was the quantity estimated to decorate one of the two leaves of the door, and Ptolemy Auletes, who had probably undertaken to provide the materials for the whole work, had contented himself with sending first enough for the one half and left his son to add what was needed for the second. Ever since Ptolemy Philadelphus had explored and developed the routes to Equatorial Africa, Egypt had been the great trading depot of elephant tusks for carving. So the embassy to Ptolemy XII had gone to the obvious source of this material. Also evidently, though the temple was not finished, the main entrance and the adjacent <u>prodomos</u> and the room with two columns must have been <u>fully</u> constructed, as the fitting of ornamental doors could only come appropriately after the awkward process of erection was completed. This must have meant that the general setting for the ceremonial or oracular consultation was at last practically finished.

Chapter Five

THE IMPERIAL ROMAN PERIOD: THE FLOWERING

The wars of Caesar and Pompey and of the Triumvirs
against Brutus and Cassius must have created some interruption in civic life, and still more the Parthian
invasions in Asia Minor. In 40 B.C. Labienus, the
Roman renegade, leading the enemy's army, penetrated
Galatia, Phrygia and Caria. In some places he was
bravely resisted, but in others the local inhabitants
accepted the new conquerers willingly. He destroyed
Mylasa, within some fifty miles of Miletus, but was
then forced to retreat, and Ventidius' victory over
him in the following year ended the immediate danger
from Parthia. The Milesians had been very near to
grave disaster, but they may have benefited from the
risks which they had run. For in 39/8 B.C. an embassy
sent to Rome returned with a grant of "the restoration
of the previous assembly and the laws." This grant of
"freedom and autonomy" as it is elsewhere described in
the official records meant that the Milesians could
reestablish their democratic constitution. (1) This
was a rare circumstance in the cities under Roman control, and presumably the concession was given in recognition of the loyalty of the Milesians in face of a
critical situation produced by the Parthian invasion.
    It may be an indication of the renewed confidence
which this inspired in the prophets of Didyma at this
time that a curious practice started to which we owe
a considerable amount of the inscriptions from the
sanctuary. Since the third century B.C. there had
stood somewhere within the temple precincts a building
which was later demolished. In fact its actual site
now remains undiscovered, but there are so many stones
surviving from the construction and reused elsewhere
that Knackfuss has been able to produce a hypothetical
reconstruction. It was built in the Doric style with
a front consisting of four columns in antis and a pediment. Evidently it was a building connected with the

69

operation of the oracle, and the best conjecture is
that it was the <u>Chresmographeion</u> - the record office
of the responses - mentioned in the building accounts
as we have seen, as some place distinct from the
temple. The German excavators without committing
themselves to this identification call it the Prophets
House. Its exact function can be discussed later in
connection with the question of the oracular procedure
In any event it was evidently a building under the
control of the prophets. For starting about 39 B.C.
it became usual for each of these annual officials to
have his name inscribed on the outside, and also often
to add any reference to events in his year of office
which he chose to record. In a way which seems curious to our taste, but has a parallel at Claros, the
engravers paid no attention to the architectural
elements of the building, but wrote their names and
comments wherever they could find convenient space,
nor merely on the flat walls, but also on the columns
and other ornamental features. This new assertiveness
of the prophets after the building had stood for some
two centuries untouched suggests a new consciousness
of the importance of their office. (2)

The relations of Miletus with Rome continued
thereafter on a correct and dignified footing. But
there is no sign of any special warmth of feeling for
the Principate. Pergamum became the first seat of a
provincial temple of Rome and Augustus in Asia; Ephesus was a regular headquarters for the proconsul; when
Augustus himself stayed for long periods in the East,
he chose Samos for his residence. The only formal
recognition of the Emperor at Miletus was that he was
twice elected to the honorary position of <u>Stephaneph-
oros</u>, for the first time in 17/16 B.C. on the tenth
anniversary of the establishment of the Principate and
a second time in 7/6 B.C. on the twentieth anniversary. The same honour was conferred on Gaius Caesar,
Augustus' grandson, in 1/2 A.D. during his ill-fated
campaign in the East.

In 22 A.D. when the cities of Asia were required
to send embassies to the Senate to justify their
claims to <u>asylia</u> for their sanctuaries, Miletus was
represented by a delegation. Tacitus, who spreads
himself in his account of the various claims, no doubt
drew the details from the Senate minutes, but about
the Milesians he only tells us that they claimed to
derive their right from King Darius - a curious statement which we have already discussed. Evidently their
privilege was approved by the Senate, as we do not
hear of any difficulty arising over it. For practical
purposes it was more strongly based on a recent exten-

sion of the asylia rather than on the antiquarian
claims which interested Tacitus. Julius Caesar had
extended the area of the sanctuary by two miles,
presumably in recognition of some loyal service by
Miletus during the Civil Wars. (3)
    We next hear of Didyma as catching the megaloman-
iac fancy of Caligula. Seutonius lists the project of
completing the building of the temple together with
more fantastic plans attributed to him such as restoring the palace of the tyrant Polycrates on Samos
and "founding a city on the ridge of the Alps". But
it is possible that the emperor had actually taken
some steps towards expediting the erection of the temple. For Caligula certainly had chosen Miletus as a
centre of his worship. Dio Cassius records that he
commanded the league of the cities of Asia to dedicate
a temple there to himself. For as he explained, he
had chosen this city because Artemis had anticipated
him at Ephesus, Augustus at Pergamum, and Tiberius at
Smyrna. But Dio alleges "the true reason was that he
longed to appropriate himself the temple which the
Milesians were building to Apollo, both large and
extremely beautiful". This story is partly true,
partly unconfirmed. Caligula certainly established a
provincial temple in his own honour at Miletus corresponding to the imperial cults at Pergamum and Smyrna.
The foundation of the cult and its building is recorded in an official inscription. At the same time Caligula may have considered it a suitable gesture to the
local inhabitants to help them to complete the Didymeion. Rehm has conjectured that we can find evidence
for renewed activity at the temple in an inscription
(unfortunately undated) honouring a man named Meniscus
who had been on the embassy to Rome in 22 A.D. It is
set up by "the craftsmen from Asia working on the
temple at Didyma". The unusual title of this body
suggests some team of specialists gathered from the
whole province, and therefore would imply something
much more than the local workmen slowly going ahead
with their annual and unending task. If, as is possible, Meniscus was being honoured at the end of a
long career, the team may well have been working in the
late thirties in the reign of Caligula. Our rather
fragmentary evidence then suggests that the Emperor
chose Miletus for the seat of his imperial cult in the
province and gave some generous support towards completing the temple of Apollo. But the supposition that
he meant to usurp Apollo's place at Didyma was probably nothing but the typical scandal which rumour
attached to Caligula's grandiose acts. His speedy fall
and the accession of Claudius will both have abolished

the imperial cult in Miletus and have terminated the
use of the emperor's funds to complete the Didymeion. (4)

For good or ill Didyma did not attract the interest of Nero. His notorious tour of Greece was confined to the mainland. Nor does Vespasian coming from
the East to Rome seem to have any special contact with
it. The first sign of a Roman emperor again taking an
interest in the place is not found till the reign of
Trajan. Meanwhile a group of inscriptions connected
with one remarkable individual shows both the low level
to which civil and religious activity had fallen in
Miletus and the efforts which one man applied probably
with some success to remedy the situation. Tiberius
Claudius Damas is the person, and his career at one
point can be fixed chronologically by the occurrence
of his name on Milesian coins of the reign of Nero.
For the rest we depend on the inscriptional records
which he set up in Didyma and at the Delphinion in
Miletus. These show that he was twice prophet, evidently with an interval of years between. On the first
occasion he records that he undertook the office for
no remuneration in addition to the civic office of
"General" (strategos) and performed all the duties of
those who preceded him. This emphasis on maintaining
traditions is typical of Claudius Damas. For he volunteered to undertake his second prophetship, as he
records, at the age of eighty-one when the office had
remained vacant for the previous years, and he renewed
the ancestral customs. That this claim was not mere
verbiage is shown by the record preserved in the
Delphinion which reveals Damas as reviving and re-
organising the traditional institution of the Molpoi.
Evidently he had a deep interest in the religious
practices of the past and a strong personality to push
through a revival. The summary references in his inscriptions at Didyma point to it as having been another
field of his restoring energy. In view of his advanced age when he held his second prophetship he may
very well have been active at any time between 50 and
90 A.D., and it may be to his credit that when in the
second century A.D. there was a great blossoming of
oracular activity in Asia, Didyma was able to take a
leading role in this renaissance. (5)

The Emperor Trajan himself made an important contribution to starting this new epoch. In 101 A.D. or
in the following year he was responsible for a complete restoration of the sacred way between Miletus and
the temple. The work is described in an inscription
using almost biblical phrases. "The hills were cut
out and the valleys filled up." This was an important

gesture of imperial good will made long before Trajan
had occasion to go east on campaign. Rehm has pointed
out that Trajan showed a certain interest in oracle-
centres, and there may be evidence that his patronage
had been wooed by use of Miletus' oracle. At least
Dio Chrysostom in a contemporary speech mentioning
imperial benefactions to Eastern communities refers
in his usual indirect way to "one of the most notable
cities of Asia which had a claim on the emperor, as
the god had delivered an oracle among them and had
foretold his principate". It looks as though Miletus
had been able to claim that Apollo of Didyma had
foretold Trajan's elevation to the emperorship. It
was a typical kind of legend to create and may have
been assisted in this instance by the fact that Trajan's father had been proconsul of Asia 79/80. If
Apollo had at that time produced any flattering address to the governor a re-interpretation might conveniently prove that it contained a forecast of great
fame for his descendants. (6)

Trajan himself was nominated prophetes, probably
in 101/2, and stephanephoros in 116/117, his last year
of life, but, though Rehm considers the possibility,
there is no evidence that he had visited Miletus on
his way to his Eastern war. The only emperor who came to
Didyma in person in the second century A.D. was
Hadrian in 129 A.D. No description of the visit survives. He evidently was elected stephanephoros, and
in return must have made generous benefactions to the
city. This might be conjectured from Hadrian's general practice. But it is possible also to judge of
it from the reaction of the Milesians themselves. We
find not only statues dedicated by the city, which
could be regarded as a conventional tribute: even the
declaring of the day of his visit as an annual holy
festival is not very remarkable. But Rehm calls
attention to the numbers of small altars - pieces of
over thirty are preserved - dedicated to Hadrian by
private citizens under such titles as Saviour, Founder, and Benefactor. Evidently the Emperor had impressed himself deeply on the inhabitants of Miletus,
and it is likely that this was partly at least by
material gifts. Later in 136/7 at the end of the
Jewish war the city invited him to accept the honorary
rank of "prophet" at Didyma for one year, and the
emperor graciously agreed in a letter whose first
words only are preserved. (7)

These auspicious demonstrations of imperial patronage under Trajan and Hadrian ushered in what can
be reckoned as in some ways the Golden Age of the
oracle of Didyma. In the century and a quarter be-

tween 100 and 225 A.D. we have more recorded responses
of the oracle, whether in literature or in inscription, than for any previous period. Most of them are
not precisely datable, but that they belong between
these years in reasonably certain. Most difficult is
to decide how far this increase in numbers of recorded
enquiries really means a considerable increase in
oracle business compared with other centuries. The
explanation may partly be that in a prosperous age,
such as the 2nd century A.D. in Asia, more money was
available for such an expensive undertaking as cutting
a lengthy inscription on stone. It is also a period
when private individuals liked to record their personal achievements somewhat ostentatiously in this fashion. So the existence of some of our records is to be
accounted for by the social and economic conditions
of the time, as much as by its religious activity.
But the renewed prominence not only of Didyma, but of
other oracles in this period, and even the success of
such a charlatan as Alexander of Abonuteichos are best
explained, as scholars generally agree, by a changed
attitude to religion.

In the couple of centuries between 100 B.C. and
100 A.D. it had been unusual for intellectuals to
think and write of spiritual experience or mystic
contact with the divine. In literature the gods were
mostly treated in conventional terms, and in some ways
the willingness to deify emperors was an indication of
the lack of feeling for the transcendental in contemporary worship. The superhuman was largely measured in
terms of material achievement. But with the turn of
the second century A.D. a change comes over this attitude. It produced what E.R. Dodds has called "an
Age of Anxiety" from the accession of Marcus Aurelius
to the conversion of Constantine. But already before
161 A.D. the altered attitude to the world and its
problems had begun to show. Man in the Augustan Age
had seemed richly confident in the divine purpose nd
his own reason. But a century later neither gave
sufficient support. Tacitus could hint darkly at the
wrath of supernatural powers as having worked behind
the fantastic confusion of Tiberius' reign or the
grisly horrors of the Neronian tyranny, and had to
admit that, though he could not explain astrology
rationally, it was vindicated by sufficient successes.
So one can suppose that to those who felt themselves
living in doubt and distress an oracle which could
speak with the voice of God was a comfort and protection. (8)

With this loss of nerve and failure in self-con-
fidence went a new willingness to accept the vastness

of the physical universe and together with it the
complexity of its spiritual counterpart. The classical world had been prepared at times to admit that
man did not know the gods and that what was told of
them was at best an approximation to truth. Also
philosophers had familiarised intelligent men with the
idea of monotheism. These approaches to the problem
of the government of the universe now tended to combine in superseding the simple legends of paganism.
But also the universe itself had taken on a larger
scale, which had begun to dwarf the anthropometric
dimensions of the Olympian gods. The old conception
of a flat earth with the astronomical phenomena taking
place just above it in the atmosphere had been replaced in the late Hellenistic period by a picture of the
earth as a globe floating free in vast space. The
attempt to establish a heliocentric view of the universe had not won general acceptance. The spherical
earth was still regarded as the centre of the cosmos,
but the size of the earth had been estimated with fair
approximation of correctness, and the sun and the other
heavenly bodies were seen as an elaborate system ex-
tending far into space. This provided a new setting
for a supreme God to govern.

It was agreed that God was probably one and
supreme, but also it had come to be accepted that between Him and man there operated at different levels
many forms of daimones, some of whom had produced the
supernatural phaenomena known to the pious. Plutarch,
the high priest of the Pythian Apollo, was prepared to
discuss the decline of the oracles on the Greek mainland as possibly attributable to the departure or even
the death of the daimones who had operated them. So
rationalism or formal piety was replaced by a new in-
tensity of feeling and variety of belief which gave
abundant scope to the consultations of oracles, whether they supplied comfort to the anxious or information
to the curious.

Before surveying the evidence for actual responses, it is worth mentioning that about this period
Didyma figured in one famous work of fiction. Apuleius inserted into his picaresque novel of the Golden
Ass an exquisite fairy-tale, which at least did not
come from his usual Greek source and may be largely
his own invention. The story of Cupid and Psyche has
no historical setting or local background, but, as in
many Greek legends, the action is started by a response from "the most ancient oracle-centre of the god
of Miletus". It is given verbatim by Apuleius in
eight lines of Latin elegiacs, which he introduced with
the quip:- "But Apollo, though Greek and Ionian, for

the sake of the founder of a Milesian tale, thus
replied with a Latin message." Evidently Apuleius
chose to name Miletus the oracle-centre, as he felt it
was appropriate to his kind of romantic novel.   There
is nothing in the context to suggest that he had any
local knowledge of Didyma, and he puts into the mouth
of Apollo exactly the ambiguities which fit with the
development of his plot.   So the only evidence to be
drawn from the passage is that when Apuleius wrote
(c. 180 A.D.), Didyma as the oracle of Miletus was
well known by repute to him and his Latin readers. (9

In examining the individual responses of the
Didymaean Apollo it is best to try to adhere to a
chronological order as this serves to bring out certain developments in content and style, but in most
instances the dating is only approximate.   The majority are derived from inscriptions, often very fragmentary, none of which contain precise dates and many
of which give no internal indications of their period.
At best the judgement of experienced editors, such as
Rehm, derived from the form of the lettering, can be
taken as a probable guide.   Otherwise some enquiries
which deal with similar subjects, and are not obviously separated in time, are best taken together.

The earliest example on grounds of script is a
very fragmentary enquiry dated about 100 A.D.   The
question concerned some baths and a gymnasium, and was
probably about the erection of an altar in the open
air, since all these words occur separately in the
inscription.   Apollo evidently replied in the first
person and in at least five lines of hexameter
verse. (10)

A much more important and interesting inscription is presumably to be dated in the reign of Hadrian.
It is preserved in situ in the back wall of the
theatre of Miletus beside the entrance to the topmost
flight of steps in the west wing.   The auditorium of
the theatre had been completely rebuilt in the Trajan-
ic-Hadrianic period and this enquiry was made by a
team of workmen engaged on it:-

> "The builders, Epigonus and company (the name
> of the team is partly lost), contractors for
> the part of the theatre, of which the prophet
> of the god, the late lamented Ulpianus, was
> superintendent and the architect Mnemophilus
> was contractor, enquired whether they should
> execute the arching and the vaulting.   And
> should they consider employment given by their
> native city or employment of some other kind."

The god gave his oracle:-

> "For men of skill it is expedient to use sound
> constructions and ingenuities together with the
> suggestions of the best man of good ability,
> while appealing with sacrifices to Pallas Trit-
> ogeneia and mighty Herakles." (11)

The meaning of the text is made obscure by the
use of technical terms and a certain clumsiness of
phrasing in the preamble and more than the usual
amount of vague verbosity in the response itself. But
the general lines of the situation seem to emerge as
follows:- this section of the back of the theatre including the vaulting over some of the passages had
been funded by a benefaction of a deceased prophet of
Didyma, called Ulpian. (The family is known from the
inscription of a Titus Flavius Ulpianus of the third
century as a prophet who claimed to be descended from
ancestors who were prophets.) The work on the part
of the building financed from his grant was undertaken
by a team of workmen led among others by one Epigonus.
They had presumably contracted to complete the vaulting for some fixed sum, and may have found it more
tricky and laborious than they had calculated. Anyway
they evidently sought the authority of Apollo of Didyma to justify breaking their contract, putting the
query as alternative propositions. The god, however,
advised them to apply some ingenuity and the advice
of a good architect, adding the conventional recomm-
endation to invoke by sacrifices Athena the goddess of
technical skill and Herakles the deity who represented
physical strength. Otherwise, they were to use brains
and put their backs into the task. Presumably the
god's advice was adopted by Epigonus and his team and
turned out successfully. The vaulting was completed
and the inscription carved in the wall to record the
achievement with Apollo's help.
These seem to be the general lines. The notion
of wages or profits is not explicitly mentioned in
the document, but it is likely that it was at least
part of the problem. The stress instead seems to be
laid on the technical difficulty of construction. An
architect, Mnemophilus, is named as in charge of the
work, but perhaps we are to understand that the team
of workmen had lost confidence in his instructions.
However, no other architect is named: so presumably
he continued in charge till it was finished. In fact
Apollo may have meant that Epigonus should listen to
his directions, but with typical oracular caution he
puts no name on his "best man of good ability". Any

way in its oblique way the Apolline oracle seems to
have achieved its object by the use of common sense.

Also of the Hadrianic period in Miletus are two
inscriptions from the walls of the temple of Serapis.
Both probably record consultation of Apollo of Didyma
who is seen in them as supporting the cult of the
foreign god introduced from Egypt. The more detailed
of the two names a peculiar enquirer, apparently a
circus performer. "Appheion, also known as Heronas,
of Alexandria enquires, since at all times his
ancestral gods stand by him and you yourself also in
what work he carries off, on this account he begs
you, lord, if with good repute at all times he will
come off in his tip-toe dancing and training of bulls
and if he will serve with good repute.

The god of Didyma revealed his oracle:- Phoebus
and the swift eye of unutterable Serapis and Nemesis
who oversees the amphitheatres of athletes you will
have as helpers to your plans by prayer." (12)

Appheion of Alexandria had asked Apollo for
success in his peculiar profession. The somewhat
clumsy but intensely emotional phrasing of the enquir
is due no doubt to the performer himself and has not
been reduced by a priest to some conventional
paraphrase. His description of his act has caused
some trouble to the earlier commentators. As a passage in Aelian demonstrates, tame bulls were a favourite circus turn. "It seems that a special characteristic of the bull is its docility once it has been
tamed, and from being savage becomes gentle. At any
rate bulls remain quiet when harnessed to a litter,
or if you want them to lie still on their back or wit
their head on the ground or to sink down on their
front knees and carry a boy or a girl on their back.
And you will even see a bull bearing a woman on its
back or standing erect on its hind legs, while it
supports lightly the entire weight of its body on som
object or other. I have even seen men dancing on the
backs of bulls and the same men motionless there and
standing undislodged." (13) Presumably, Appheion's
act was something of this sort:- to stand on tiptoe o
a bull's back and make the animal go through various
tricks at his orders. The performance may perhaps
have seemed to be falling out of popular appeal. For
his enquiry is not aimed at the risks involved, but
at the question whether the reputation of the act wil
continue. Apollo is reassuring: he offers three deit
ies to protect the enquirer - himself, Serapis (no
doubt as his ancestral god in Alexandria) and Nemesis
who is described as specially taking charge of per-
formances in the amphitheatre. These three powers

were to be approached in prayer by Appheion, and it
implied he would continue his successful career.   In
gratitude he must have paid to have the enquiry and
Apollo's reply inscribed on the wall of the temple of
Serapis, to whom he had been told to pay worship.
    The other inscription in the Serapeum is of about
the same date, and though the oracle which it records
it not explicitly assigned to Apollo, it is probably
safe to suppose that it also was from the same source.
    "Carpus enquires if it is pleasing to Serapis for
him to accomplish his vow in the manner which he was
intended".
    "The Immortals rejoice at the well accomplished
honours of mortal men".
The enquirer who does not describe himself further
was probably a prominent Milesian of the Hadrianic
period - Ulpius Carpus, a member of the city council
and priest or prophet "of the holiest, most high
god".   He must have been active in municipal politics.
For he was honoured by inscribed altars set up by the
guild of gardeners and the guild of "razor-shell
pickers".   This record from the Serapeum shows him
as having made a vow to the god and then having enquired whether his proposed method of accomplishing
it would please the deity.   As we have seen already
it was usual to assume that Apollo knew the enquirer's
plans, even if he did not disclose them.   Also it was
quite in order to ask Apollo whether some other deity
would be pleased with the enquirer's deed.   Hence
there is no need to assume that the answer which is
recorded without the name of the oracle which gave it
came from anywhere else than Didyma.   The response is
very typical - a single hexameter sentence of pious
generalization: dignified and beautiful, but perhaps
rather unsatisfying.   However, Carpus also seems to
have been pleased enough to have it recorded on the
temple wall.
    Our next two oracles concern a famous personage
in the province of Asia, whose career lasted well
into the reign of Antoninus Pius.   He was Lucius
Cuspius Pactumeius Rufinus who attained the
distinction of the Roman consulship in 142 A.D.
He must have been possessed of huge capital, for in
the 150s he erected at his own expense the large
circular temple in the Asclepieion at Pergamum.
This was modelled on the Pantheon at Rome, and like
it had a facade with columns leading to a hall
which was roofed by a dome with a central opening.
This magnificent benefaction must have placed him
in a quite special position in relation to Pergamum.
Hence on his death arrangements were made to give

him a public tomb and possibly some form of cult as a hero. This is shown by a tantalisingly curtailed inscription found at Pergamum:-

> "When the people of Pergamum enquired of Apollo at Didyma where it was holy, that there should be buried the heroes Marcellus and Rufinus on account of the past excellence of their lives, the god gave as his oracle" -

At this point after the stating of the question, the response is lost. Clearly Apollo must have approved of some special arrangement or the text would not have been likely to have been officially inscribed at Pergamum. But no further information is available. It is even quite uncertain who is the Marcellus who is grouped with Rufinus and even named first. The only plausible conjecture is to identify him with an author and orator listed in the Suda as having written a book entitled "Hadrian or concerning kingship". This suggests someone of the right date. But why the Pergamunes would feel specially indebted to him, even if he was possibly a native of the place, remains unexplained.

In the reigns of Hadrian and Antoninus the old Roman prohibition against burials within the city boundaries were extended to the whole empire. So it is possible that the point at issue in the enquiry was to establish that Marcellus and Rufinus were not to be classed as ordinary mortals, but as heroes could be exempted from such restrictions and be buried in shrines within Pergamum. It would be entirely in keeping with the traditional function of oracles to declare whether a deceased person should be classed as a hero. (15)

Rufinus the subject of this enquiry may also have had his own relations with Didyma. Among the rather medley collection of oracular responses preserved in the fourteenth book of the Greek Anthology one of the few not attributed in the heading to the Pythia nor derived from any known literary source is described as addressed to Rufinus:- "Oracle given to Rufinus when he asked how he should take an oath from his sea captain." Thirteen hexameters follow which in style and diction might well have been composed in the mid-second century A.D. Also the fact that they are in this metre at least agrees with the possibility that they were delivered at Didyma. If so, they are the first example of a different style of response which was to become typical of the later period of oracular activity at Didyma and also elsewhere. They are rather wordy effusions of a consciously literary kind often dealing with questions of cult or theology. The subject of the enquiry was one which had frequently troubled the Greeks in earlier periods: how to devise an oath of such a kind that no one would dare to break it. It was sometimes wanted as a kind of self-enforcing contract whose infringement would carry a formidable penalty. At other times the purpose was retrospective - a man accused of a crime would be challenged to swear his innocence in a form which would invoke divine retribution. It is not clear here whether we are to picture Rufinus as wanting to bind his sea-captain to the performance of certain duties or perhaps more likely to challenge him to prove by oath that he had not been guilty of some malpractices.

The text runs:- "Whenever Titan at daybreak lifts his course above the earth after dissolving with his rays the offences of dark night, and shining Dawn sheds a new light, then lead the man to the sands and make him stand on the sea-washed beach, facing directly towards the light of the sun's ray. Let him keep his right foot within the surge and hold it in the eddies, while he plants his left foot firm on the land. With his hands also he is to touch in either direction, the sea with one, the dry land with the other. Then let him give his oath invoking as pledges the heaven and the boundless earth and the harbours of the sea and the life-giving leader of the ethereal fire. For such an oath they themselves do not dare to dishonour in their mouths the exalted dwellers in heaven." (16)

Ritual ceremonies at oath-taking are familiar throughout ancient literature. This particular one does not seem to recur elsewhere, but it is based partly at least on the earliest Homeric examples. In Iliad Book Three Agamemnon when swearing a truce on behalf of the Greeks invokes "the sun who sees and hears over all and the rivers and the earth and those who beneath it punish suffering men, whoever perjures himself". The principle underlying the invocation was to include in it all the parts of the world, though the Homeric example ends with the idea of punishment in the underworld. The oracular formula omits the underworld and substitutes for it the Aither, whose importance had developed greatly in contemporary thought. Also by this selection the four elements of philosophic theory are represented in the invocation. Otherwise the main feature of the response is a not very successful attempt to echo the conventional phrases of epic poetry. Apollo speaks in the grand manner.

Another illustration of the verbose oracle occurs in an inscription on a marble block found on the right bank of the Maeander facing Miletus. It appeared to have been part of an anta from a temple which had been reused. From the contents of the text one would suppose it had been a temple of Demeter, but the find spot was not likely to have been the original site. The text consisted of two oracular responses, one written on the front and the other on the side, in a completely similar hand. Hence the same enquirer was probably responsible for both, which were inscribed on the same occasion. (17) The text in front is evidently the start of the subject:-

"With good fortune.

The priestess of Demeter Thesmophoros Alexandra enquires - since from the time when she took over the priestes-ship, never have the gods in such a way been revealed in manifestations, whether by means of maidens and mature women or by males and young boys, why is this so and is it to be taken as favourable?
The god gave his oracle:-

The Immortals coming together with mortal men (of intelligence) reveal their purpose and what honour... "

Tantalisingly the first response breaks off at this point. The enquiry gives a somewhat pathetic picture of an anxious and conscientious priestess. This is not a query raised in an age of scepticism. It was instead, as we have pointed out, a time of increasing credulity. Hence the priestess's worry is rather that she found herself surrounded by stories of divine revelations through many different persons constantly occurring. So far from reassuring her these had produced alarm which was evidently causing her to feel some personal inadequacy as the reason. She uses the term "Epistaseis" for these manifestations which was the new and popular technical term. Apollo's reply is cut off too soon to show the real form of his answer, but he starts off reassuringly with what appears to be a general explanation of the principles behind divine revelations, and it looks as though the response would need a considerable continuation before the answer was completed. However soothing it may have been, the priestess appears to have returned to Didyma for a further consultation which was recorded on the side of the block. Unfortunately the question itself is missing and the lettering starts with the

reply. However from the content of this oracle it
is clear that Alexandra must have asked some question
which put in doubt the whole practice of worshipping
Demeter, since Apollo sets out to justify the cult.
One may presume then that the enquiry which called
for such a fundamental answer was on the lines that if
the goddess gave such manifestations, did she still
want to be worshipped.
    "The god gave his oracle:-

> Deo of the fair daughter, abounding in fruit, the
> mother of food dear to mortal men is bound to be
> honoured with sacrifices and good prayers by all
> the human race. For it is she who first sent up
> into the earth the fruit which bears wheat and
> thus stopped the heart of man from being fed like
> a wild beast and savage, at a time when dwelling
> under the natural roof of mountain caves with
> raw-eating jaws he had gluttonous food. Espec-
> ially ought the dwellers in the city of Neleus
> who fell by nis enemy's spear. For to them it
> is a token of their divine nobility that they
> perform mysteries of Deo and of Deo's daughter
> here. Therefore with your solemn honour as her
> servant who have been appointed to pursue the
> accomplishment of stability in life..."

The reply breaks off just at the point where Apollo
drove home his message to Alexandra herself. But the
general lines can be paraphrased. The worship of
Demeter was claimed to be an obligation on mankind
because by the invention of corn she had converted
men from being cannibals or at least raw flesheaters to
their civilised life. The Milesians, the dwellers in
a colony founded by Neleus, should be specially inclined to worship Demeter as they had the privilege
of performing her mysteries, a sign of their distinguished ancestry. Alexandra herself as priestess of
this goddess and one entrusted with the ritual of the
mysteries should learn their lesson of tranquillity.
The fragments of the last sentence beyond the point
where it can be translated seem to contain the name
of Eumolpus, the traditional founder of the Eleusinian
mysteries, and it is likely that the oracle ended by
pressing still further the thought that the privilege
of conducting this special ritual must not be neglect-
ed, and its teaching or reassurance must be learnt by
the priestess herself.
    Presumably Apollo's sermon was accepted by Alex-
andra, since the record on the wall of what was probably the temple of Demeter must have been set up at

her request. The poems in which the oracles were
expressed are of the wordy style which we have noted.
The first is only briefly preserved, but obviously was
starting in this style. The second when complete ran
to more than fifteen lines of verse. It is not epic
in diction, though this may be partly due to the
subject, but also it appears to contain a number of
neologisms, even if sometimes there is an uncertainty
in the reading.

A similar wandering stone with fragments of a
pair of cult enquiries was found in Maeander valley.
(18) Evidently some female enquirer had asked the
oracle for the proper ritual to deal with some situation and had been told to appease Hera, but had
found this answer not explicit enough. At this point
our text begins:-

> "...you said to appease Hera. What Hera is
> she to appease?

> The god gave his oracle:-

> Where for long time venerable antiquity had
> accustomed the exhausted bodies of old age to
> enjoy the baths, where girls uninitiated in
> wedlock set up the dance in rhythmic charm to the
> sweet euphonious tune of the lute, at the halls
> of an effeminate man pay worship first to Hera."

These rather clumsy and enigmatic paraphrases
apparently advised the female enquirer to worship Hera
in a eunuch's house situated near a long established
bath for men and a girls' school of dancing. Presumably all these buildings actually stood together somewhere; perhaps in Miletus. The oracle was contrived
to authorise the setting up of a shrine to Hera on
this particular site. It is not such a lengthy effusion as some of those which we have considered, but it
has the same elaboration of style.

Toward the end of the second century a lengthy oracle
was issued from Didyma about a priestess of Miletus, which
is preserved on a monument to her erected by her sons. (19)
They were Marcus Aurelius Hermeias and Marcus Aurelius
Minnion who record that their "sweetest mother" was
"priestess for life of Athena Polias in front of the
acropolis, chosen by the most truthful god, Apollo of
Didyma on account of her sound character and dignity
by means of his divine oracles and praised thus". The
response which follows was delivered at the time when
their mother, Saturnilla, was a candidate for the
priestes-ship. Evidently her appointment had been
delayed over the technical fact that she was not a

maiden, as priestesses of maiden goddesses usually were, but was a wife and mother, though possibly widowed. Apollo had decided in her favour by means of this oracle:

> "Late in the day you have come, inhabitants, to call on the gods for a prophetic omen concerning the priestess of the goddess born from the head (of Zeus), who broke the top of her reverend progenitor and skipping danced among the immortals a dance in armour. Hence it fell to her lot to control the acropolis of many a city, a good defender, and handy in skills as an overseer of famous craftsmen. It was necessary that a female from the blood of the nobly born should receive the priestly office of the goddess who revealed herself, but since she has already chosen as her lot in life the goddess born from the seafoam - and Cypris is hostile to the maiden Athena - for she in uninitiated in love and the marriage bed, while the other has rejoiced in marriages and the joyful noise of the wedding shout - still obeying the Fates and Pallas make Saturnilla your reverend priestess in her holy duties."

This long and complicated oracle is difficult to translate without a running commentary to explain its allusions. For whoever composed it was not content to give a direct answer to the question whether Saturnilla should be appointed priestess, but worked his way round to the subject by elaborate digressions on the birth of Athena and her name and functions. The old legend that she was born from the head of Zeus is used to justify the practice of putting the temple of Athena on the top of cities. Her name Pallas is alluded to by the description of her dancing in armour when she leaped from her father's head. For by means of the Greek word for "shaking" (pallein) as applied to her dancing movements a derivation for Pallas was invented in late philology. The problem of a married priestess is treated as a conflict between Aphrodite and Athena in which Saturnilla had chosen too soon to support Aphrodite. But after all this periphrasis the oracle in the end comes our unequivocally for her appointment.

There may, however, be more behind the enquiry than this paraphrase conveys. The response starts rather dramatically with an echo of a Delphic oracle of mythological date. This serves to emphasise the point that the "inhabitants", evidently the city of

Miletus, have been dilatory in approaching Didyma.
This may not merely mean that the appointment had been
postponed because of an argument over Saturnilla's
eligibility. More likely Miletus in filling the
priestessship of Athena Polias was already experienc-
ing that difficulty for which there is frequent evidence in Asia Minor in the late second and third
century A.D. The aristocracy from whom the magistrac-
ies and priesthood were traditionally filled were more
and more unwilling to undertake office. This was
chiefly because of the economic stringency and inflat-
ion which made it more and more difficult for cities
to pay enough to the holders of offices, and the expenses of the office which were traditionally met by
the incumbent were becoming more and more crushing.
The priestessship of Athena Polias must have been
founded at the establishment of the Ionian city and
hence no doubt it had an aura of great antiquity. But
we do not know how far the aristocratic holder may
have been expected to contribute to the maintenance of
the cult and in return may have had only some perquisite from the victims offered, which might provide
no material compensation. Hence it may have been that
in the latter years of the second century, when a
vacancy had occurred in the life priestessship, no
qualified applicant of unmarried status could be
found, and the issue was shelved for some time until
at last the only solution was to appoint a widow of
considerable means, who perhaps for prestige was prepared to accept the onus. Even so such an unorthodox
appointment could not be made without the sanction of
the gods and this involved the problem of putting the
question to Apollo. Happily, the priesthood of Didyma, though generally conservative, were prepared to
authorise this innovation. Their sanction was framed
in this elaborate piece of quasi-theological erudition, which owes something to the allegorical interpre-
tations of Stoicism.
    The priesthood of Athena in Miletus was not the
only public office of the kind which it was difficult
to fill. Early in the 3rd century A.D. the shortage
of such candidates led to a tendency for the same
person or members of the same family to come round
again and again like a stage army. The prophetship
of Apollo at Didyma was already so little the object
of competition that instead holders, such as Aelianus
Poplas, record that they had voluntarily undertaken
the task, implying that if they had not volunteered
the post might have remained unfilled. Poplas himsel
is recorded as holding eight public offices and was
probably the individual whose consultations of the

oracle on two occasions are recorded in a late source. (20)

As the century went on the prophetship became even more the perquisite of a small group of related families, and the behaviour of the holders became more and more idiosyncratic. About 245 A.D. a kinsman of Aelianus Poplas inscribed a remarkable oracle given in his own honour. He was Titus Flavius Ulpianus, who described himself as pious and a prophet who had offered himself for the post. He also recorded that he was descended of ancestors who were prophets, listing his father and his grandfather and three uncles, one of whom was Aelianus Poplas. He even went on to mention his cousins as those who completely performed public services and were benefactors of the state and first citizens. This led up to the statement that Ulpianus was the man to whom also the god by divine oracular utterances often had borne witness in visions and now in the oracle-centre·had addressed him on account of his good piety as follows:-

> "Like to a spreading tree you hold out thriving branches and you pasture fleecy sheep beneath your tapering boughs(?). Therefore when you enquire yet again it is right for me to give an oracle... But you yourself, confident in our oracles, growing into piety with a mind that believes in God by means of the former commandments and former prophecies have placed your care on minding the sacrifices about my altars." (21)

The inscription breaks off where Ulpianus was just proceeding to record a second oracular tribute to himself. The monument was rather erected <u>ad majorem gloriam Ulpiani</u> than to the greater glory of Apollo. In recording the first of the two responses Ulpianus omitted to mention what the question was and the space left vacant in the middle of the hexameters indicated where he had left out the particular answer of Apollo. All that he reproduced on the monument was what referred to himself. The whole document breathes the spirit of the time - the immense pride in the family and the self-consciousness of the small minority of wealthy aristocrats who monopolised the civic and religious posts of distinction. There is also the reference to visions as well as oracles. It was an age when the pious expected the gods to reveal themselves often and in striking ways. Again the antiquarianism implied in the reference to "former commandments and former prophecies" corresponded to their erudite approach to religion. It was not enough for a prophet to go through a conventional ritual: he should be properly versed in the records of the past so as to maintain or restore the ancient traditions. In the case of Ulpianus one does not feel confident that there was much reality of spiritual feeling behind all this verbiage.

Titus Flavius Ulpianus was not unique among contemporaries in his proud and boastful record of his prophetship. A much more fragmentary record also survives of a prophet, Ulpius Athenagoras, who after describing himself too as having offered himself for the post, and presenting a similar record of his family's services to the temple and the community, adds the extraordinary statement that the god had given him a prophecy spontaneously. This kind of honour whereby the oracle addressed an enquirer immediately on his entry to the sanctuary before his question had been put is more a legendary happening than one of authenticated history. It is recorded from Delphi for such personages as the founders of colonies, such as Battus of Cyrene, or for Lycurgus, the Spartan lawgiver. An address of this sort to Cypselus the tyrant may be genuine, and it was made the model for a similar address to Attalus I of Pergamum, which is probably mythical. This last is the only example falling within fully historical periods. Possibly Didyma had its own legends of similar spontaneous addresses, but if so, they have not survived. Nowhere does a parallel exist for Apollo greeting his own prophet with a spontaneous oracle. The idea seems to be a fantastic piece of self-advertisement on behalf of Ulpius, even if he contrived or connived at some actual performance of the sort. Unfortunately the inscription is too fragmentary for the text of the oracle to be reconstructed; at most it is clear that it was in hexameter verse. (22)

To the period before 250 A.D. also belong some responses which are preserved in literary sources. For instance Porphyry wished to show that some gods were servants of others and took as an example the relation of Pan to Dionysus as recorded in an oracle of "Apollo at Branchidae". He briefly and obscurely describes the circumstances of the enquiry. Nine men were found dead. So those living in the field enquired the cause and the god gave as his oracle:-

"Golden-haired Pan, the servant of dignified Dionysus, walking along the wooded mountains with a rod in his mighty hand, and with the other he was grasping the polished pipe, uttering a shrill note, and was charming the heart of the

Nymphs. But as he blew a sharp whistle from
his pipe he struck with fright all the wood-
cutters and amazement seized them as they gazed
at the chilling body of the Daemon rushing in
frenzy. Indeed the ending of chilly death would
have grasped them all if it had not been that
Artemis the Huntress, holding a terrible rage
within her breast, stopped him from his powerful
might. Then you should pray to her that she
become your guardian." (23)

There is no reason not to treat this as a perfectly authentic response of the Didymaean Apollo.
Also the circumstances as recorded by Porphyry are
correct enough as far as they go. The enquirers in
the plural were evidently some community concerned
about the unexplained cause of death of some wood-
cutters. The number of the dead as nine is not
derived from the response and is probably part of the
correct tradition, but the response also indicates
that others escaped. From such limited data it is
impossible to reconstruct a rational account of what
happened. The interesting point is that the oracle
of Didyma, when faced with a mysterious disaster in
the woods, attributed it to Pan - a god who was not
worshipped in Miletus nor generally in the Greek East.
He had emerged as a favourite figure in Hellenistic
and Roman art in pastoral scenes and similarly in
literature. Here it is likely that the composer of
the response had been inspired from literary sources.
The reply itself has a very scholarly flavour. Generally it uses a highly correct epic diction and even
goes so far as to lift half a line from the Iliad.
But the choice of words seems rather cramped. The
verb "to grasp" and the adjective "chilly" each occur
twice in this limited passage and in rather different
senses. Also the epiphet applied to Dionysus does
not seem to be used in its normal epic sense, but in
a meaning only found in late literature. So though
the occurrence in Porphyry would not preclude this
response from having been given centuries before his
time, it probably belonged to the same general period
as those which we have been discussing.

A similar subject for a response is preserved in
Aelian's Nature of Living Creatures (24) where he is
discussing the question whether Tritons exist. He
suggests that the problem is settled by the impeccable
evidence of Apollo of Didyma. Evidently the god had
been asked to explain some naval disaster, and from
what was probably a longer response Aelian cites for
his purpose the two hexameters:-

> "The nursling of Poseidon, a watery marvel,
> the loud-sounding Triton, as he swam in a rush
> encountered the smooth ship."

In this instance again an unexplained disaster is
accounted for by the prophet, who attributes it to a
literary figure of mythology rather than a normal
object of worship. Again the response, which might
have come from the same hand, aims, though not
entirely successfully, at an epic diction. It is
possible that if we had the full text of the reply it
might, like that on the subject of Pan, have ended by
advising the worship of some familiar deity as a
protector. As Aelian published his work in the first
half of the 3rd century A.D. he gives a <u>terminus ante
quem</u> not greatly different from Porphyry's. Can
one ask whether these consciously literary responses,
derived in diction from the epic and in subject matter
from mythology, represent the ideal expressed in
Ulpianus' monument - the use of "former commandments
and former prophecies"?

The other response which Porphyry attributes to
Didyma is less literary and less interesting. He
cited it as an instance of an oracle which described
the functions assigned to the different deities and
his quotation fits this purpose perfectly. (25) But
curiously he also recorded the enquiry - if one is
bound to give an oath to the man who requires it of
one. The problem put to Apollo was another aspect of
the same piece of traditional ritual which we have
discussed already in connection with the response giv-
en to Rufinus. Here the quotation has no apparent
relevance to the enquiry. The explanation must be
that it is an extract from a much longer response in
which the list of deities and their functions was
brought round in some way to connect with taking an
oath. Perhaps the oath was expected to be in the name
of the appropriate deity. Anyway the list runs as
follows:-

> "To the mother of the blessed gods, the Titaness
> Rheia, flutes and the rattle of drums and the
> throng of women are of interest, while to Pallas
> of the good helmet struggles and the strife of
> Enyo. The maiden daughter of Leto. cares with
> dappled hounds to hunt the mountain-roaming
> beasts along the steep-cliffed ridges, and to
> Hera of the melodious sound belongs the gentle
> sprinkling of the moist atmosphere. To tend the
> well-nourished fields which yield the grain is
> the duty of Deo, while Isis from Egypt beside

the fruitful streams of the Nile must seek for
her fair husband Osiris with the rattle of her
sistrum."

All these six goddesses were probably worshipped
somewhere in Miletus. We have already come across
Athena, Artemis, Hera and Demeter in Didymaean responses. In the context Rheia is likely to be a poetic
name for Cybele, and Isis had no doubt long been
accepted from Egypt. In this way the list differs from
the two previous responses in that it is not concerned
with literary or mythological personages. Also its
style is noticeably different in that there is scarcely any attempt to reproduce an epic colouring. This
may suggest that it was produced later than the previous examples, but the evidence of the datable instances does not prove that there was any consistent
pattern in this matter. The descriptions of the goddesses' offices are fairly conventional, except that
the connection of Hera with air was a typical Stoic
theory based partly on a fanciful derivation. The
whole is a characteristic product of the Roman period
with its concern to produce a systematic theology for
paganism.
Porphyry may also be the source of another consultation assigned to Didyma. An enquirer named Pol-
ites asked whether the soul remains after death or is
dissolved. The reply ran:-

"The soul, so long as it is held in bonds to the
corruptible body, being itself without passion,
yields to the body's pains. But whenever after
the decay of the mortal body it has found swift
release, it is carried entire to the upper air,
as it is ageless for ever, and remains for all
time unharmed. This is the ordinance which the
firstborn divine Providence established." (26)

This is the kind of question and answer which
would never have been found in the classical or even
the Hellenistic period of oracular enquiry. But one
need not assume that it is unauthentic. In the third
century A.D. this kind of problem was more open to
general debate, and oracles were expected to give a
ruling on this type of philosophical question. It was
the occurence of such matter that led to Porphyry's
search into "the philosophy to be derived from oracles."
The content is usually, as here, borrowed loosely from
Stoicism, the philosophy which most accepted oracles
as divine manifestations and in whose teaching the
prophets of oracular centres will have found their

most fitting expression.

Besides these responses actually attributed to Didyma there is one interesting oracle which mentions the place with evident knowledge of local legends. Porphyry quotes it in connection with the problem of the decline of oracles - the subject on which Plutarch had written one of his essays. It appears as if the enquirer, whose question is not recorded, must have asked what oracles were still capable of utterance. The first lines of the reply may be missing. As extant it begins:-

> "Concerning Pytho and the land of Claros, the oracles of Phoebus, my voice will speak prophetic omens. Countless oracle-centres of the gods have gushed out on the back of the earth, springs and eddying breaths of vapours. Some the gaping earth herself has received back again beneath the bosom of the ground: others the myriad ages of time have destroyed. Alone in the eye of the illuminating sun there still are in the vales of Didyma the inspired water of Mycale, and on the foothills of Pytho beneath the cliff of Parnassus, and the rocky land of Claros, the harsh voice of Phoebus' prophecy." (27)

When asked what Apolline oracles survive the prophet begins by stating that he will have to mention Delphi and Claros; - that he would have to mention his own sanctuary was too obvious to need stating at this point. Then he goes on to give the usual quasi-rationalistic explanation of oracles as produced by springs or vapours, and ceasing when these sources failed. He ends by naming the three surviving oracle centres, starting with his own.

To date the prophecy is difficult. It is likely that no significant oracle of Apollo except Delphi survived on the Greek mainland into the 3rd century A.D. Even Delphi is very little in evidence in that century, but if, for example, we accept as authentic the elaborate poem on the soul of Plotinus, it must have still operated occasionally as late as 270 A.D. and after. In Asia Minor it is quite likely that the local oracles, except for Didyma and Claros, had dwindled away by 250 A.D. or earlier. So the prophecy could appropriately have been produced about the middle of the third century A.D. (28)

Chapter Six

THE IMPERIAL ROMAN PERIOD: THE DECLINE

At this period Didyma had probably in some ways fallen
on hard times. The economic and social state of the
empire had severely declined. The cities, including
Miletus, had for long found it increasingly difficult
to fill municipal and religious posts owing to the
inflated expenses involved. In addition Miletus itself may have begun to suffer from the effects of the
alluvial deposits on the Maeander, which had already
ruined the cities situated farther up the gulf, which
had formerly existed. The construction of the temple
had probably been finally abandoned. This need not
have meant that it lacked any of the practical facilities of the original plan. It simply amounted to
leaving incomplete the height of the great curtain
walls in part at least and other similar external details unfinished, such as the channelling of some columns at the sides and rear of the building. One must
not, however, equate a time of great political stress
and economic stringency with any decline in the practice of the religious ceremonial. Laumonier has shown
from the contemporary inscriptions that the great inland shrines of Caria at Panamara and Lagina were
flourishing institutions at this retrograde period.(1)
So one must picture at Didyma a somewhat reduced body
of religious enthusiasts continuing to maintain or
striving to maintain the traditions of the past.
    Then just after the mid-century Miletus and Didy-
ma were struck by a new terror. The Goths, who had
for some years been inflicting severe damage on the
Roman empire along the line of the Danube, took to the
sea and proceeded to cross into Asia Minor and ravage
the Mediterranean coast. The exact year in which they
came as far south as Miletus is uncertain, but it is
usual to assign the event to the reign of Gallienus in
263 A.D. (2)   The Milesians had had sufficient warning of the threatened invasion to fortify the town

afresh. Also at Didyma sensational precautions were taken to meet the emergency. The temple itself was converted into a castle by blocking the entrance on the east front, and the residents in the neighbourhood of the shrine were received for shelter inside the walls of the adyton. When adequately provisioned the Didymeion must have presented a formidable obstacle to a Gothic raider. Its walls of solid stone rose some sixty-five feet sheer above the topmost step of the peristyle and the whole building stood on its basement quite separate from the surrounding sanctuary. Without the use of sophisticated siege apparatus the Goths would scarcely hope to storm the place, and their main object in these raids was quick plunder rather than the capture and occupation of strong points. The one great weakness of the defenders was shortage of water. Apart from the sacred spring, which was probably a very feeble source, there was no other supply within the walls. However, this difficulty was solved in a way which was later regarded as a miracle.

Our information on this event does not come from literary sources (which are very scanty and inadequate for this period), but from a remarkable group of poems preserved on an inscription. In the floor of the Byzantine basilica there was found a re-used stone, which must have come from some other site in the adyton, where it had stood as a stele inscribed with three separate sets of verses. (3) By the lettering they could be dated to the reign of Diocletian. The three poems, one in iambics and two in elegiacs, are all on the same theme - the erection of a fountain by the proconsul Festus. Either one poet had chosen to show his virtuosity by producing three variations on a single subject, or perhaps it is more probable that there was a competition in which these are the three qualifying entries. Translated they run as follows:-

1. "Previously this was a miracle of the Pythian god, a spring bubbling with golden-flowing streams at his command, when the barbarian God of War imprisoned the citizens together. When they were worn out with the pangs of thirst, Apollo saved them by having unfolded this vein. Now it is the miracle of Festus, who shares his throne with golden Justice. For he has surrounded it with a polished decoration and brings so great a gift of the god to memory, while he preserves the citizens by the nymph's flow, imitating the Delphic association with Castalia. For the gift of prophecy is dear to the

nymphs through whom the inspiration of the gods is poured to the prophets.

2. Once upon a time in war Apollo saved his citizens by revealing this spring when they were tormented with thirst. A second time Festus as consul of famous Asia in golden peace for the inhabitants has made this a decoration to the city, after he has ornamented the fountain with a building, so that it is pretty to look on and for life a cure from every form of death.

3. I am the water of Apollo. The god of the golden lyre gave me as a present to the citizens in the Scythian war, when, as Ares had pressed hard round the temple, the son of Leto himself saved his suppliants. For water alone was failing and the mighty multitude were tormented. Then hearing their prayers he rescued them from death. From below the Lord sent up the dark-blue water, myself whom you see, and from that day I flow on. But now when I was in trouble by the wickedness of mortal men, once more His Excellency Festus has given me to flow. He who is the proconsul of all Asia has toiled to make this decoration which you behold. Offspring of Leto and Zeus, reward the famous man, I pray, who saved me again by means of a shrine when I was perishing."

These wordy and rhetorical exercises have given rise to two misinterpretations. Some scholars had failed to grasp that Festus was not contemporary with the Gothic war. But Rehm has shown by means of other inscriptions from Didyma that his proconsulship can be dated within the period between 1st April 286 and 1st May 293: roughly twenty-five years after the military events. The restoration and decoration of the fountain was evidently part of a general revival in this period under the influence of Diocletian.

The second point on which the interpretation of the inscription involves doubt is the identity of the fountain itself. Most scholars have chosen to regard Festus' fountain as a renovation of the sacred prophetic spring itself. But this leads to considerable difficulties in meaning. For instance, the clear statement that the bursting out of the spring during the Gothic war was a marvel can then only be justified by supposing that the oracle itself had lapsed before 263 A.D. for some considerable length of time, sufficient for the source to have gone completely out of use

and been filled in by neglect. But this is utterly
inconsistent with the evidence which we have already
examined, which points to the oracle being active and
prosperous well up to the middle of the 3rd century
A.D. Rehm, who saw this difficulty, attempted to
evade it by the hypothesis that at some unknown date
previously the procedure of the oracle had changed
from the use of the prophetic fountain to other methods and so had allowed the fountain to lapse without
suspending oracular activity. But apart from its use
as an explanation of these poems this hypothesis has
no evidence in its support. The more plausible explanation is that Festus' fountain was a new discover-
made under the pressure of the Gothic raid.

What must have happened then was that at the news
of the menace of the Goths precautions were taken by
fortifying the temple as a refuge. As the invaders
approached, the populace living round the sanctuary
and in the neighbouring country streamed into the
building and camped under the trees in the adyton. So
long as the Goths were not within reach, it would be
possible to carry water for them from the large well
outside the temple, but when the building was infested
by the enemy - and the inscription implies that the
Goths came so near - the only source of supply already
existing would be the sacred spring, whose use would
have been objectionable on religious grounds, and also
it may well have been quite inadequate in its yield.
So presumably when faced with this emergency, if not
earlier, the authorities will have set about searching
for an alternative supply. Digging elsewhere in the
adyton produced sufficiently quick and plentiful results for the priests to be able to hail it as a miracle of Apollo. The poems imply that the new spring
was a spontaneous manifestation, just as it had been
announced in 334 B.C. that the sacred spring had re-
emerged by divine action. But in neither instance
need we exclude some human initiative. The fresh
source of water sufficed to enable the occupants of
the temple to last out the siege. But also it continued to exist and even to be used.

When the Goths retired unsuccessful in 263 A.D.,
the inhabitants of Didyma may have felt great relief,
but no security for the future. The enemy had not
been driven back defeated. It was not till six years
later that Claudius Gothicus at Naissus in Thrace in-
flicted a serious blow on them, and even that victory
did not put a final end to all Gothic raids. So the
emergency fortifications appear to have remained in
place on the temple as a measure of security, and one
may wonder whether all the squatters once admitted

were as easily induced to evacuate their camp. The
Goths may well have destroyed some of the former homes
of the refugees. In any case the inscription implies
that there were still twenty-five years later inhabitants who used the new spring, though it also suggests that until Festus stepped in the installation
had deteriorated. Perhaps the priestly authorities
were willing enough for the new spring to fail again
in the hope that this would discourage those who used
it. However, in the years after 286 A.D. Festus on
becoming governor of the province of Asia intervened
and caused a new fountain-head to be erected at his
expense. The building was evidently designed to be
both ornamental and practical, and the occasion was
taken to celebrate the new erection in an effusion of
verse epigrams. The implication seems to be that by
that time the adyton had a certain population of permanent residents needing to use Festus' fountain. If
they did not live within the walls, we have the rather
improbable picture of a string of women regularly
traversing the extensive temenos in front of the temple with water pots on their heads, climbing the temple steps and negotiating awkwardly the narrow low-
roofed passage to reach a well in the adyton. The
alternative which seems more reasonable is to suppose
families living within the adyton's walls.

All this must have had a very prejudicial effect
on the working of the oracle. Those who identify
Festus' fountain and the sacred spring have to suppose
an even more difficult situation for the prophets.
But, as we have suggested, that interpretation is
probably incorrect. When the poet referred to the
"association" of drinking water and prophecy, citing
the example of Castalia, he meant only to suggest that
there was nothing profane in a fountain in association
with a sanctuary. Provided the families were kept
away from the naiskos itself and the sacred spring
immediately adjacent to it, presumably the rites could
be maintained, though it is possible that elaborate
ceremonial, such as processions, may have become impossible to organise. That the oracle did not simply
relapse into silence is certain. Some inscriptions
continue to record enquiries and responses which must
date from the last years of the third century A.D. and
some literary sources indicate the same. But how
these related to the ups and downs of the period cannot be precisely shown.

A turning point, however, probably came in the
earlier part of Diocletian's reign. For Festus the
proconsul not only left his mark in the adyton by
erecting his fountain-head, he was also responsible

for setting up two statues which prove a new interest
in the shrine on the part of the Emperor. The evidence is contained in the somewhat fragmentary texts
of duplicate inscriptions preserved from two statue
bases.(4) These record the figures of "Zeus and Leto
together with the twin gods" (i.e. Apollo and Artemis
were dedicated to Apollo Didymeus by Diocletian and
his co-emperor, Maximian. The work of erecting them
was under the care of Titus Flavius Festus, the proconsul. One is to picture a pair of bronze statues
designed as a group, showing Zeus on the one side and
Leto with the youthful twins in her arms on the other.
The prominence given to Leto is not very typical of
the cult of Didyma, and suggests a rather bookish
erudition of research, which had revived the priestly
myth that Didyma had been the scene of the union of
Zeus with his beloved. Anyway the choice of Zeus as
the chief figure in the group came with great approp-
riateness from the Emperor who had identified himself
as Jovius. The fact that the Caesars are not named
in the inscription is a probable indication that it
dates from the earlier part of the reign before their
nomination in 293 A.D. Ancient authors and inscriptions both show that Diocletian made it his regular
policy to restore the ancient religion, and Didyma is
one example of this principle at work.

It is, therefore, likely that we should assign
to the latter years of the third century A.D. three
inscriptions which by their lettering appear to belong
then and in their content reflect a similar atmosphere
of rather self-conscious and emotional piety. The
longest and most elaborate is a pair of enquiries made
by a prophet, Damianus, not otherwise known.(5) His
record takes the form of an address to the god.

> "Your prophet Damianus enquires. Since in your
> holy encirclement of the altar which belongs to
> all the gods he does not yet see set up an altar
> of your most sacred sister, who is the goddess
> of his ancestors, the Maiden Saviour, and as he
> loves the gods, such a thing grieves him. He
> begs you, Lord, Didymaean, Sun-god, Apollo, give
> an oracle to him if you allow him to set up be-
> side the altar of Demeter the Fruitful an altar
> of her daughter."

> The god replied:-

> "Perform the honour of encirclement of the altar
> for the Maiden Saviour."

"Your prophet Damianus asks: since by your divine oracle you permitted him in your holy encirclement of the altar to set up an altar of the
most sacred goddess of his ancestors, the Maiden
Saviour, beside the altar of the most reverend
Demeter the Fruitful, he begs you also yourself
to give him a law concerning the auspicious
address to her suitable for hymns."

The god replied:-

"Let us call on her as Saviour in good and holy
cries to come to meet us always in mercy together
with her mother Deo."

Evidently this was the charter from the oracle
of Didyma for the local establishment of a cult of
Persephone under the special title of the Maiden Saviour. But there is a great deal more to the document.
As L. Robert has pointed out, the fact that Damianus
twice describes Persephone as a goddess of his ancestors seems to show that he was not in origin Milesian,
but that his family hailed from some city where Persephone was specially prominent under the title Saviour. Robert suggests Cyzicus as likely. In any case
a family devotion to this cult would help to explain
Damianus' deep feeling on the subject, which must be
taken as completely sincere. But a further question
concerns what he was actually proposing to do. The
words used in the text and in the first response which
are here translated by "encirclement of the altar" are
unique in Greek documents and evidently refer to some
special institution at Didyma, whose nature can only
be conjectured from the literal meaning and the context. It implies some grouping of the altars of numerous deities in one encircling gathering. The fact
that it is described as "of all the gods" shows that
it was meant to be comprehensive and further explains
Damianus' enquiry when he noted the omission. Where
this group of altars was set up is not known. The
inscription itself occurs on an altar-shaped marble
base found in front of the south-east angle of the
temple. As it is not previously mentioned, one can
perhaps assume that this pantheon was created as part
of the revival under Diocletian. The move towards
combining the cults of different pagan deities was
typical of the spirit of the time and may also have
been influenced by the pressure of Christianity against paganism. This is further illustrated by the syncretism which caused Damianus to address Apollo as the
sun. It is likely from the legend about Branchus'

birth that the original deity at Didyma, perhaps before he was called Apollo, was identified with the
sun. But this idea was generally foreign to Greek
thought, and there is no sign that the Branchidae in
the late archaic period or the prophets of the Hellen
istic revival had accepted this identification. In
the third century, however, under oriental influences
the worship of the Unconquered Sun was spreading over
the Roman empire, and here we find the Milesian
priesthood had accepted this new description of their
Apollo.

A recently discovered inscription also refers to
this "encirclement of the altar" in a rather similar
way and adds to our evidence on it. (6)

> "Hermias the treasurer enquires: since the altar
> of Tyche in the sanctuary has been shut in the
> so-called Paradise by the houses which have been
> built round it, and on this account it is not
> seen and visited by many, whether it is better
> and more good and pleasing to the goddess that
> this altar should be included in the encirclement
> together with the rest of the gods or not."

The god replied:-

> "One ought to honour and reverence all the gods.

Evidently Apollo here agreed to the transfer of
another deity to the "encirclement", a meaning this
time conveyed by the use of the corresponding verb in
the enquiry. The goddess of Good Luck (Tyche) had
already been worshipped in the precinct of Apollo, but
her altar was suffering from a housing development,
which was making access difficult by surrounding it.
Hence a transfer to the "encirclement" would restore
the opportunity for worship of the goddess. But what
are we to make of this "so called Paradise"? It was
evidently somewhere in the sacred precinct, where
previously the altar of Tyche had stood in an open
space. Now it had been occupied by buildings, and the
words used imply private residences. So in any event
one must suppose a new housing estate erected on the
territory of Apollo.

Already as early as the beginning of the Imperial period, Strabo had described "the circuit of the
sacred enclosure" as containing a settlement, and that
there was a magnificent sacred grove inside and outside it. So the new houses may have been in some
tree-lined area adjacent to the sanctuary. But can
it even have been inside the walls of the temple,

where, as we have seen, Festus' fountain was built for
the use of the inhabitants? In the Hellenistic period
the word "Paradise" could be used of a public park
which was to be converted into a sacred precinct.
Hence it would not be an unsuitable word for the tree-
covered open spaces in the adyton. It may seem
strange that at a time of religious revival the temple
of Apollo would be subject to this degree of secular-
isation. But Diocletian and his governors recognised
that they lived in changing times, and the restoration
of the old religion was not inconsistent with a ratio-
nalisation of its practices. If the people had to
be housed in the adyton originally for security and
later had persisted in their residence, one may
presume that their squatters' encampment was then converted into dwellings, even if they were simple
structures of wood or mud brick. This development
might have been a factor in encouraging the plan to
move the altars of the gods from their casual scattered locations and assemble them in one complex, possibly outside the temple, round the main altar of
Apollo, thus creating the "encirclement".

Also at this time Apollo himself could express
views on the way in which his worship should be
revived. One of the inscriptions from the Prophets'
House records in a late imperial script of painful
correctness a lengthy poem in thirteen hexameters,
which is presumably an oracle of the god, addressing
his Milesian worshippers. (7) The form of enquiry to
which it was a reply, as it is not recorded, can only
be conjectured, and the text lacks the first two or
three words of every line, so that it cannot be restored with complete confidence, but the general sense
is not in doubt. The god rejects hecatombs and statues as unnecessary, but expresses his liking for offerings of music, particularly of an old-fashioned
style. A translation of the most plausible reconstruction so far suggested runs as follows:-

"[Sons of Neleus,] what concern have I with
bountiful hecatombs of cattle and [bright]
statues of expensive gold and images tricked
out in bronze and silver? The immortal gods
indeed have no need of possessions nor [of the
service of mortal men,] with which their hearts
are warmed. For you [it is seemly] to sing a
hymn in my sanctuaries as afore when the axon
was about [to reveal] a word from the innermost shrine. I rejoice over every song [when
it is solemnly performed,] but chiefly if it
is old. [What pleases me more] is much better

for me. For this pleasure my gratitude will always be unfailing [from the time when] I drove off the painful plagues after I had put to shame the [baleful] Fates with their griev- ous threads."

This poem is an elaborate and sophisticated pro- duction with considerable literary echoes. As Hommel has pointed out, it is not to be taken as meant par- ticularly to appeal for economy in offerings. Choirs of two or three dozen singers, which were the usual performers of hymns, were expensive to train and pro- duce. But the trend of worship may have been in that direction. We have seen already how Damianus, when authorised to worship Persephone, enquires how she should be addressed in hymns. Asia Minor had a stron native tradition of music in Phrygia, Lydia and even in Caria, and elsewhere besides Didyma in the third century A.D. one finds it prominently employed in pagan cults. For instance, at Lagina a choir of thir children was maintained, who sang a daily service to the goddess Hecate. From Claros, as we shall see, there are abundant records of choirs sent on pilgrim- age to perform before the local Apollo. So the god c Didyma's request, though expressed remarkably force- fully, was not out of keeping with the time and the place. Yet is is rather curious that he should be made to reject hecatombs and statues when asking for hymns. This critical attitude seems to need some special relevance to justify it. The obvious conjec- ture is that either Apollo had been asked whether he wished to be presented with a statue and a hecatomb or else whether he was pleased with a statue and a hecatomb already presented. This again seems to coin cide curiously with Festus' dedication of the imperi gift of statues in the <u>adyton</u>. They are the only instance for which evidence survives of such a dedic- ation in the relevant period. It is, of course, impossible to prove that this response was given ex- actly at this time or in this connection, and it may be argued that the prophet of the period would not d anything to flout imperial patronage. But the appar ent coincidence remains. The statues of Zeus and Let were of bronze and may well have been tricked out wit silvered or gilded accessories - such as a thunderbo and a bow and arrows. Is it possible that, though th prophetic authorities might have preferred choirs to statues, they had also another motive for feeling ho tile to Festus' activities?

As we have seen, Festus' fountain gave formal recognition and practical support to a permanent sec

ularisation of part of the <u>adyton</u> at least by supplying a water supply for the <u>laity</u> and thereby facil-
itating their residence there. The priesthood may
very well have regarded this as an intrusion in their
traditional rights and the sacred use of the place.
At the same time, Festus' action may have been popular
enough with the common people, who by this time, even
at Didyma, may have included some Christians. Rehm
has pointed out that in 262 the organiser of the defence of Miletus was called Makarios and his wife's
name was Eucharia, both typical names for Christians.
So it is probable enough that the new faith was making converts even within the Milesian aristocracy.
The local inhabitants of Didyma itself may have been
less open to conversion, but one cannot tell even
there what strange under-currents of religious and
social dissidence existed. So perhaps one should picture Festus as walking a diplomatic tight-rope. On
the one hand, he pleased the emperor and hoped to
appeal to the priests by new expensive statues. On
the other hand, he won the approval of the populace
by a highly unorthodox water installation. This may
explain the emphasis in the poems on Apollo as providing a precedent for Festus' benefaction and on
Castalia as a partnership of prophecy and utility.
     The response also contains two other features of
interest. The reference to the time when Apollo rescued people from the plague is not very clear, but its
purpose is to suggest how long the god has enjoyed
hymns. So the best interpretation is not that it
alludes to some recent deliverance, but rather to the
legendary example when Branchus purified the people
and made them sing a mysterious incantation. If so,
it is another example of the literary antiquarianism
typical of this period. (8)
     The other interesting passage is the reference to
the performance of hymns when the oracle was functioning. The restoration of the text is uncertain, but
the word <u>axon</u> which occurs in the sentence is best
supposed to refer to a piece of apparatus, which
Iamblichus almost contemporaneously mentions as one of
several possible methods used in the procedure of consultation. The response seems to imply that the choral service at this point in the ceremony had ceased;
which in view of what we have seen of the disturbed
condition of the <u>adyton</u> is very possible. (9)
     The oracular response which we have just examined
could be regarded as indicating a more spiritual attitude to religion than the classical practices of
burnt offerings and images. In the latter years of
its activity, the oracle of the Didymaean Apollo

issued or had attributed to it a number of responses
dealing with theological or philosophical questions of
a sort which never appear in the classical period. As
we shall see, Claros at the same period was also
notable for this sort of production. Individually
these responses present a difficult problem. They are
never datable, except by the limiting point of the
authors, pagan or Christian, who quote them. Also
owing to their abstract content and lack of particular
context these documents could be easily fabricated.
So it would be unsafe either to assign them individually to particular dates or to assert that they must
each of them be authentic. But they are best taken as
a group representing correctly enough the spectrum of
one branch of the oracle's activity at a late period.
    Lactantius writing his <u>Divinae Institutiones</u> in
the early years of the fourth century tells how the
"Milesian Apollo" was consulted whether Jesus was a
god or a man, and replied as follows:-

> "He was mortal in the flesh, a wise man of mir-
> aculous works, but he was convicted by Chaldaean
> justices, and nailed to a stake he fulfilled a
> bitter end."

Unlike some alleged Delphic oracles quoted in
Christian authors, this response is obviously not a
Christian's forgery created to suggest that even pagan prophecies had recognised the true God. It ack-
nowledges the miracles and the crucifixion, but describes Jesus as mortal with no suggestion of the incarnation, and it does not express any direct condemnation of the Jews for his death. Lactantius himself
was unwilling to accept at its face value the denial of
Christ's divinity. He ingeniously argues that Apollo,
who for his purposes was a demon, with devilish cun-
ning was deceiving his worshippers. When he described
Jesus as "mortal in the flesh", the implication, as
Lactantius suggests, was that he was God in spirit,
and so the demon masquerading as Apollo Didymeus had
borne witness to the dual nature of Christ. This
interpretation by Lactantius no doubt never occurred
to those who originally framed the response, even
though the notion of oracular ambiguity was of traditional antiquity. Instead it is best taken as an authentic attempt of the prophets of Apollo to define
their position with regard to the claims of Christianity.
    Another response quoted by Lactantius seems to
show a much more respectful attitude towards the God
of Israel on the part of Apollo. Only a few verses

are quoted, but they run:-

> "...and to the god who is king and to the be-
> getter of all things at whom both earth and
> heaven and sea and the depth of Tartarus tremble,
> and demons are chilled with fear." (11)

Lactantius states that this was the response of
the Milesian Apollo when asked concerning the religion
of the Jews, and quotes it to prove against pagan
philosophers that God is to be feared. Later St. Augustine cited what was evidently the same response
which he translated into Latin. According to him the
question had not been concerning the religion of the
Jews, but "which is better, the Word, otherwise reason,
or the Law". According to Augustine, this was only a
relevant extract which he gave from a longer text of
the oracle and his source was Porphyry's book which we
have mentioned above. He gave an additional line not
found in Lactantius, but fitting with his description
of the enquiry:- "those of whom the Law is father,
whom the very consecrated Jews honour". Augustine
contents himself with referring the response to Apollo
in general, leaving it uncertain whether Porphyry, his
direct source, had actually attributed it to Didyma,
or whether Lactantius derived this attribution from
his intermediate source.

It may seem strange that Apollo should speak in
a respectful way of the God of the Jews and of the
Law. But there had for long been considerable settlements of Jews in Asia Minor, and the trend of religious development among the Greeks was towards a quasi-
monotheism, in which the supreme god could be identified with any of a series of deities. This is a
practice which we shall find illustrated even more
clearly by the oracle of Claros in one of its responses. So far as the Jews were concerned, this tendency
is shown by the spread among pagans of the cult of
"The Highest God", sometimes identified with Zeus,
but more often left nameless and therefore open to
identification with Yahweh. (12) If this response is
authentic, and not a theological fiction, it must be
explained as part of that syncretism, which was evidently affecting Didyma in late periods. If Porphyry
is the source, it must date before the mid-third
century A.D. In any case, one can believe that the
prophets of Apollo of that period would find it easier
to come to terms with the transcendental monotheism
of the Jews than with the Incarnation and Crucifixion
of the Christian faith.

These religious attractions and oppositions had

been developing throughout the third century A.D.,
but the climax which came with the Great Persecution
under Diocletian had actual associations with Didyma.
If we can trust Lactantius, the particular episode
following upon which the persecution began was very
relevant to the practice of oracles. (13) At a sacrifice performed in the presence of Diocletian and
his Caesar, Galerius, the priests whose function it
was to obtain prophetic signs from the victims search
ed the entrails in vain, and this failure was repeate
on the second attempt. The chief augur explained tha
the gods had not answered because of the presence of
Christians who had crossed themselves surreptitiously
to avert demons. Diocletian was furiously angry, and
commanded that all the members of his court should
sacrifice and that the army should be ordered to appl
the same test to its members. There is no evidence
that this instruction was applied at this time system
atically in the palace or in the legions. But Lactan
tius evidently believed that episode was the starting
point of Diocletian's hostile measures against Christ
ianity. The presence of Christians in high positions
at the imperial court is interesting and otherwise
attested. Also it is typical of the period that even
pagans could credit them with the power to disturb
religious ceremonies by their influence.

The climax came in the winter of 302-3 A.D. when
the emperor and his Caesar were in Nicomedia, and
Galerius, who was strongly hostile to Christianity,
was pressing his senior colleague to issue an officia
edict against those who practised this religion.
Diocletian hesitated for long and consulted different
advisers. Finally, according to Lactantius, he decid
ed to refer the issue to the gods and sent a sacred
embassy to Apollo of Miletus, who "replied like an
enemy of the holy religion". (14) This response removed the last justification for Diocletian to resist
the proposals of Galerius and the edict was sent out,
though in a milder form than what the Caesar would ha
chosen. At the time when these events were happening
Lactantius was attached to the court as a professor o
Latin. So there is no reason to doubt the general
truth of the picture while recognising that he would
not have had access to the inner imperial council. H
does not reproduce the words of the oracular response
but only alludes bitterly to its hostile meaning.
Perhaps he had never heard the actual text of Apollo'
answer.

A more detailed, though less reliable, record come
from a strange source. The future emperor Constantin
was also in Nicomedia at the time - 'a mere boy', as

he afterwards recalled; probably about twenty. In 324/5 some twenty-two years later he recounted the occasion in a rather extravagantly worded manifesto, which Eusebius reproduced in his Life of the emperor:- (15)

> "They said that Apollo then from some cavern and darksome recess, not from a man, issued his oracle: that the Just on earth were an obstacle to his speaking the truth and on this account the prophecies of his tripods were made false. This then was the lament which the priestess uttered, having let her hair fall down loose and driven by madness. But let us see to what end it crashed. On Thee now, God Most High, I call. At that time while I was still quite a boy, I heard how he who held the first rank among the Roman emperors (Diocletian) - a miserable fellow, truly miserable - deceived in mind, enquired in meddlesome curiosity from his courtiers, who were the Just on earth. Then one of the priests of his entourage replied: 'The Christians, I suppose.' Then the emperor swallowed the answer like so much honey and stretched out the swords devised against wrongdoing as a threat against blameless holiness."

It is difficult to decide how far to trust this rhetorical outburst. Constantine does not name the particular oracle, but simply speaks of Apollo. His description of the details would not at all fit Didyma. There was no cavern there, and though the subterranean shrine at Claros could be so described in an ancient author, its responses were given by a man. So neither of the great Apolline oracles of Asia Minor suits with the literal account. But this is probably because Constantine (or the secretary who wrote his speech) seems to have chosen to insert a purple patch modelled on the traditional pictures of a legendary consultation of the Pythian Apollo. One need not suppose that Delphi, not Didyma, was actually consulted. It is most likely that it was already extinct as an oracle before 300 A.D. Still Constantine supplies at least an independent witness that an Apolline oracle was consulted by Diocletian, and his sudden relapse into the first person singular introduces what was, as one must suppose, a personal recollection of the gossip in palace circles about the words of the oracle and the emperor's reaction to them. If not entirely fictitious, it looks as though the prophet of Didyma had lived up to the ancient traditions of Apolline ambiguity and had

not named the Christians explicitly, but had used som
periphrasis, whether ironic or not, to describe them.
But as it stands, the references to the Christians as
the Just and Apollo's own oracles as made to lie are
not very plausible. It is perhaps best to suppose
that in the process of transmission through the
Christian emperor the original response had been distorted so as to correspond to the popular legend of
Apollo as admitting that his oracular powers had bee
vanquished by Christianity.

There is, however, yet another independent piece
of evidence, which points once more to the consultation of Didyma by Diocletian. This is a very fragmentary, though lengthy, inscription of a script appropriate to the period of the Tetrarchy. (16) It belong
ed to the Prophet's House, and so, though apparently
written in prose, is likely to have recorded or referr
ed to an oracular consultation. Unfortunately, only
stray words and phrases survive, but these are strange
ly significant. They include "the Emperors" (in the
plural), "the Christians" and "the god". Otherwise
it is too fragmentary to allow for any satisfying
restoration, but can be taken as pointing to some
consultation in this period involving Diocletian and
the Christians. So while it is not safe to suppose
that we can reconstruct from literary and epigraphic
sources the form of enquiry and the reply, it is reas
onable to believe that Diocletian was finally induced
to order the Great Persecution in consequence of
consulting Apollo of Didyma.

Historically it was a most remarkable event. Th
Roman state had consulted Delphi occasionally during
the Second Punic War. But once the Greek world was
dominated by the Republic, the use of Hellenic oracle
for state purposes ceased. An emperor or a member of
his family as a very distinguished visitor might enquire as a courtesy like Hadrian at Delphi or Germanicus at Claros. But for the emperor actually to refe
a major question of policy, even religious policy, to
the guidance of Apollo, was unprecedented. It is
perhaps partly to be explained by the very individual
character of Diocletian himself, but also it fitted
with his archaising policy. He may have consciously
felt that he was acting like Croesus or Seleucus and
following the tradition of the ancient rulers of Asia

The consultation of Apollo of Didyma by Diocletian may have been a great honour to the sanctuary at
a time when it was in decline, but it did not lead to
any great change in the popularity of the oracle. Al
by producing a response hostile to Christianity the
prophet had committed Didyma to an extreme position

in what was to be the bitter feud of the next quarter
century. If one can trust Sozomenus, the Church historian, (17) there was one later enquiry made by an
emperor. Licinius, when about to engage in his final
struggle with Constantine, diverged from toleration
of Christianity to a renewed persecution, and consulted sacrifices and oracles in a revival of paganism.
He enquired of Apollo of Didyma concerning his prospects of success in the war, and received as a response, not an original composition, but two lines quoted
from the Iliad:

> "Old man, indeed youthful warriors torment you,
> and your force is weakened, and grievous old age
> has come upon you."

This quotation could only be regarded as a dis-
couragement of a sort improbable for an oracle to
address to an emperor. The implied comparison with
Nestor could be regarded as a compliment, but in the
context it was no help to the cause of Licinius. As
for the practice of substituting a quotation for an
original composition as a response, there are some
doubtful analogies for it in the history of Delphi in
the period of its decline. Certainly the adoption of
the same method by Didyma, if it were authentic, would
be a symptom of the oracle's loss of skill.

With the triumph of Constantine there could be no
more question of emperors consulting Didyma. He issued an edict declaring sacrifices and divination
illegal, but the enforcement seems to have been left
to the initiative of local governors. However,
Christians were not prevented any longer from
bringing pressure against their pagan oppressors.
Eusebius mentions that he had heard that "a prophet
who was also a philosopher at Miletus" had been convicted of fraud and punished. (18) So it would appear
that the Christians were able to contrive some legal
charges to avenge themselves on the source of their
persecution. But Apollo may not have remained silent.
Julian the Apostate twice quotes from a response issued
from Didyma, which refers in scathing terms to those
who ill treat priests:- (19)

> "All those who act in folly against the priests
> of the immortal gods by their presumptuous wick-
> edness of purpose, and plot against their priv-
> ileges with plans that show no fear of the gods,
> no longer will they traverse the whole path of
> life in so far as they have violated the
> blessed gods whose honour of a reverend

office these priests held."

Besides quoting this twice, in one place Julian
goes on to refer to another response (apparently also
Didymaean), of which he cites one obscure opening
line, that the god threatened to impose a penalty on
behalf of his servants. The emperor was applying
these oracles to contemporary situations and arguments
but clearly derived them from some earlier occasion
whose circumstances he does not explain. By their
turgid style and use of prosaic abstract nouns they
are obviously productions of a late period, and it is
improbable that at any date before the fourth century
Apollo would have had occasion to protest against what
was evidently a concerted attack on his priesthood.
In both instances, even where Julian quotes six lines
of verse, we probably have not got the whole of the
response, and the enquirer and his question, if there
was one, are not recorded. Perhaps the oracles were
supposed to be spontaneous utterances of the god, an
interpretation which could be put on Julian's words.
One may doubt whether this kind of protest produced
much effect at this period.

The Christians had also another legitimate method
of tormenting pagan oracles, besides prosecuting their
priests. This was to transfer the relics of Christian
martyrs to shrines erected in the immediate neighbourhood. For just as it was believed that by crossing
himself a Christian could upset the operation of pagan
divination, so also the functioning of an oracle could
be disturbed by the near presence of a martyr's cult.
The most famous example of this procedure was at
Antioch where the shrine of Saint Babylas was set up
near Apollo's temple at Daphne. When Julian had intervened to have these relics removed, he heard,
according to Sozomenus, that there were houses of
prayer in honour of the martyrs near the temple of
Apollo at Didyma. So he wrote to the governor of Caria
that, if the buildings had a roof and a holy table, he
was to burn them down with fire, but if they were half
built, he was to dig them up from their foundations.
Whether these instructions were actually carried out
is doubtful, as Julian fell in battle within nine
months. (20)

How far, if at all, the oracle had managed to
function in this last period is uncertain. Julian
himself accepted the office of prophet, which must
have conferred some patronage and prestige on the place
though Julian did not, so far as is known, visit it.
He mentions his prophetship in the letter in which he
quotes the Apolline response. There he charges a

governor with having been influenced by Christians to
ignore the beating of a pagan priest and denounces him
for this neglect. But unfortunately as the beginning
of the letter is lost, there is no clue to show where
the outrage occurred, and one need not suppose that
it was at Miletus.

There are no inscriptions about responses from
Apollo Didymeus which can certainly be dated to the
period of the Julian revival, but two examples have
been conjecturally assigned to that time. One stone
belonged to an altar of Poseidon found at Miletus and
is inscribed with the record that it was consecrated
"in accordance with the oracular utterance of the god
of Didyma, Apollo the sun". It might date to any
period from the late 3rd century onward. Also the
base of a statue of Apollo at Didyma is inscribed
with a poem recording that it was dedicated by the
Rhodians, "since to them, when they enquired, he always
uttered true omens on many occasions from his un-
deceiving tripods". Rehm thought it probably belonged
to the reign of Julian. More interestingly none of
these many consultations by the Rhodians are preserved
in our evidence. This only serves, if necessary, to
demonstrate how scanty and inadequate any modern
attempt at a survey of the activity of the Apollo of
Didyma must be. (21)

Julian's revival of the oracle must have been
brief. It is not even recorded that he consulted it
on the outcome of his Persian expedition, as he is
alleged to have attempted to do at other oracular
centres.(22) With his death there was a final reaction
against Apollo culminating in the edict of Theodosius
which prohibited any form of consultation of the pagan
gods. If Didyma lasted till then, it may well have
been entitled to claim the longest period of activity
of any Apolline oracle in Asia Minor.

PART II

CLAROS

Chapter Seven

IN THE ARCHAIC AND CLASSICAL PERIODS

It would be hard to find two sites more different in
their setting than those of Didyma and Claros. The
ancient shrine of the Branchidae stood on the top of
a bare stony ridge overlooking the sea. The temple of
Claros was in the deep trough of a river valley amid
rich alluvial soil. But the two points that they had
in common were that each was situated at a spring
whose waters were regarded as possessing special properties, and neither sanctuary was immediately in the
neighbourhood of a city. The Branchidae lived some
sixteen kilometres from Miletus and were probably not
originally under its control. Claros was within easy
reach of two towns. On the coast some two kilometres
distant at the river mouth was Notion; inland up the
river valley at a distance of some twelve kilometres
lay Colophon. The oracle of Apollo was fated to be
controlled by the government of these cities. But
probably Claros, like its sister oracle at Didyma, was
originally independent of them and dated from before
the coming of the Hellenes. At least legend suggests
this picture and, in the case of Claros, as we shall
see, legend is curiously confirmed by archaeological
evidence in one particular.
     Branchus, as we have noted, was scarcely admitted
to the Greek heroic tales. But Claros, though not
mentioned by Homer, found a strong place in the Epic
Cycle.(1) In the Epigoni which told of the capture
of Thebes by the sons of the ill-fated Seven, it was
described how they sent a tithe of their spoils to
Delphi, including Teiresias, the great Theban prophet,
and his daughter Manto. Teiresias died on the journey
and was buried at Telphusa, but Manto was duly presented to the Pythian Apollo. In accordance with a motif
familiar in Delphic legends Manto was instructed by the
oracle that she was to marry the first man whom she
met on leaving the temple, who proved to be Rhacius,

the son of Lebes, of Mycenae. Together they journeyed
to Colophon, where Manto, despondent at the destruction of her native land, burst into tears, and the
place was named Claros, because of her weeping. (The
Greek derivation of Claros from klaio, a verb meaning
"to weep", is very far-fetched.) The Epigoni is not
quoted as continuing the story, but from the Nostoi
and Hesiodic poetry it is clear that the epic tradition was that Manto settled at Claros and had a son,
Mopsus, who inherited from her the ancestral gift of
prophecy.
    This legend of Manto and Claros is compounded of
traditional Delphic motifs.(2)   The dedication of
captive peoples as a tithe to the Pythian Apollo
occurs in several other legends and may have had some
basis in ritual practices of prehistoric periods.
The theme of the "first met" recurs in all sorts of
forms in Delphic mythology. Also the notion that an
enquirer on another subject might be sent willy-nilly,
to found a colony occurs elsewhere. We are not told
that the story in the Epigoni contained any instructions for Manto to found a colony at Colophon. This
version did occur in later authors who made her find
her future husband, Rhacius, there instead of at
Delphi. (3) Also in this different version he is a
Cretan, not a Mycenaean. Probably the original story
did not name Colophon at all. The mention of it may
have been inserted by the scholiast who paraphrased the
Epigoni for us, because he knew of Colophon as the
place where Claros was situated in his day. The primitive form of the legend was evidently simply invented
to account for the two facts, that there was a famous
oracle, and that it was situated at a place called
Claros. (4) If as is possible the sanctuary of Apollo
was there before the founding of Colophon, this legend
in some form could go back to the founding of the colony. The particular version which we have in the
Epigoni was evolved by the time when Delphi was already well known as an oracle centre. But this would
be acceptable enough for an Epic tradition in view of
the Homeric references to Delphi. (5)
    Hesiod carries on the story. (6) After the fall
of Troy one contingent of the Achaeans consisting of
Calchas the prophet and Amphilochus, the son of
Amphiaraus, and, as some authors added, Leonteus,
Polypoetes and Podalirius with their followers started
on their return by land. This divergence from the
Homeric picture in which the heroes all appear to sail
away from the Troad evidently caused difficulty to the
ancient commentators. But as usual they were able to
get round the problem by finding the right text in the

Iliad on which to pin an explanation. Since Homer
makes Agamemnon in one speech mention that owing to
the nine years which have already passed in the war
their ships' timbers are rotten and their cables
loosened, the commentators suggest that some of the
heroes found their vessels too unseaworthy, and had to
set out by land. At any rate, it is evident that a
tradition not found explicitly in Homer brought a band
of Achaean warriors to Colophon, where they met Mopsus, the son of Manto.

According to Epic chronology this was barely
possible. Homer made Diomedes and Sthenelus, sons of
two of the ill-fated Seven, fight at Troy after their
capture of Thebes. So presumably there was just
enough time for a son to have been born to a captive
from that city and to grow up in time to meet heroes
returning from the Trojan war. Of those mentioned in
our sources as arriving at Colophon Calchas, of course, and also Leonteus, Polypoetes and Podalirius all
appear in various places in the Iliad. But curiously
Amphilochus, the son of Amphiaraus, who is prominent
in the Hesiodic stories, is not recorded by Homer as
present at Troy, though known to him in the Odyssey
as a member of a prophetic family. Of course, the
commentators had not failed to notice this omission,
and one of them conjectured that Amphilochus arrived
late at Troy; presumably after the actions described
in the Iliad were over. (7)

The encounter of Calchas and Mopsus was to prove
fatal to the former. For Calchas had received a
prophecy that he was doomed to die when he met a
prophet greater than himself. A contest took place
between the rivals which was described in various versions by our sources. But Hesiod and his successors
all give it a feeling of earthiness suggesting an origin in folk-lore. According to Hesiod Calchas challenged Mopsus to state the number of figs on a specially prolific fig-tree. "Wonder holds me at heart
how many figs this wild fig-tree holds, small though
it is. Could you tell the number?" Mopsus' reply
was:- "Myriad they are in number, but in measure a
bushel. Yet one remains over which you could not put
inside it." Hesiod ends the story abruptly at this
point: "so he spake, and the true number of the measure was seen by them. Then indeed the conclusion of
death enveloped Calchas." One feels that the folk-
tale was so familiar that it only needed to be told in
outline.

An even more rustic version of the contest occurred in Pherecydes, the early fifth-century Athenian
mythographer. (8) According to him Calchas proposed

the query how many piglets a pregnant sow was carrying, and Mopsus answered three, of which one was female. When this proved correct, Calchas died of vex-
ation and grief in accordance with the oracle. But
other variations of the story existed. For instance,
that both tried to tell the number of figs and Calchas
got it wrong, when Mopsus got it right. Or again that
Calchas set Mopsus the problem of the fig-tree, which
he solved, but that when in return Mopsus set Calchas
the problem of the piglets he was wrong and Mopsus
right. It might be an interesting speculation to
follow Immisch in discussing which of these versions
was the original form and how the variants arose, but
for the purpose of the present enquiry this is not
very relevant. The importance of the legend is that
it was evidently created to glorify the founder-proph-
et of Claros and so by implication his successors.
Also it may have been occasioned to some extent by the
presence at Colophon of a tholos tomb of the Mycenaean
period which could be arbitrarily identified as that
of the defeated prophet. (9)
    The legend of Manto provided a pedigree for the
prophets of Claros, and the legend of Mopsus and
Calchas vouched for their credentials. Of the figures
concerned, Manto is obviously invented as a link to
connect Claros with the mainland of Greece and the
great traditions of Hellenic mythology. Her name is
merely a feminine form of the word for 'prophet', and
is clearly that of a fictional character. Mopsus is
more of a puzzle. The name occurs elsewhere as be-
longing to one of the Argonauts, the son of Ampyx, a
Lapith, who figures in most of the legendary actions
associated with them - the Centauromachy, the Calydon-
ian hunt, and the funeral games of Pelias. (10) But
he was also a famous prophet, skilled in understanding
the omens from birds and even their language. Hence
it is not surprising that he is connected with Dodona.
The name Mopsus has no obvious derivation and is probably not fictional, but simply a personal name of the
Mycenaean epoch. This is confirmed by its occurrence
in Hittite documents and on a Linear B tablet from
Cnossos. There is a possibility that the name is
Luvian in origin. It evidently had associations in
the Epic tradition with the gift of divination and was
a suitable name for a prophet. The Lapith should be
chronologically the earlier, but we cannot be sure how
the traditional figure of Mopsus as prophet originated. (11)
    At this point, however, Mopsus undergoes a trans-
formation, and like such heroes as Amphiaraus and
Helenus the Trojan he proves himself just as capable

in warfare as in divination. Callinus of Ephesus, the
elegiac poet of the early seventh century B.C., knew
the story of Calchas' death at Claros, and followed it b
telling that Mopsus 'led a host of peoples over the
Taurus; some of them stopped in Pamphylia, others
split up and settled in Cilicia and Syria and even as
far as Phoenicia'. (12) In this great expedition he
was accompanied and partnered by Amphilochus. In the
Roman period Mopsus was claimed as founder by such
places as Aspendus and Perge in Pamphylia, but he lef*
his chief mark in Cilicia. There in the plain were
towns which in the historic period bore his name:-
Mopsuestia ('Hearth of Mopsus') and Mopsucrene (Spring of
Mopsus'). But his chief centre was Mallus, said to have
been founded by him and Amphilochus. The legend ran
that Amphilochus handed over his share of the kingship of Mallus to Mopsus and returned to his native
Argos, but after quarrelling with the people there,
he came back to Cilicia prepared to take up his right*
again. But Mopsus shut him out of the city, and the
dispute became a war which ended in a duel between th*
two chieftains. They killed each other and were buri*
in the neighbourhood. But so that the rivals might not
see each other, their graves were placed on opposite
sides of the hill. (13)

This legend, modelled to some extent on that of
Eteocles and Polyneices, was evidently created to explain the presence in historic times of two shrines
where heroes were worshipped under the names of Mopsu*
and Amphilochus. Also they continued to be rivals,
for each had a considerable reputation as an oracle-
centre even in the Roman period.

It has not been usual for scholars to treat thes*
legends very seriously, even though they evidently
went back to epic and elegiac traditions of the seventh century B.C. and earlier. At most it was though
that the later Greek settlers in the Cilician plain
had tried to invent mythical predecessors of the heroic age. But in the nineteen-forties Bossert, when
excavating Karatepe, the summer palace of a local
king, situated in the hills overlooking the Pyramus
valley in Northeast Cilicia, found a lengthy inscript
ion in Hittite hieroglyphs and Phoenician, in which
the king about 700 B.C. refers to himself as a 'descendant of the house of Mopsus'. It is evident that
this native Cilician tradition is quite independent o
the Greek legends, and proves that the connection of
Mopsus with the kingship of Cilicia is not simply a
Greek fiction. Archaeological support can be found
in the discovery by Hetty Goldman at Tarsus of an in-
trusive Mycenaean settlement (Late Helladic III B to

C) dating from about 1200 B.C. It cannot be proved
that these Mycenaean settlers came to Cilicia by way
of Claros, but a plausible context for such a movement
can be conjectured on other evidence. (14)

On the walls of his funerary temple at Madinet-
Habu Ramesses III recorded in grandiloquent phrases
the victory which he had won in the eighth year of his
reign (c. 1190 B.C.) over the invading Peoples of the
Sea. 'The foreign countries made a plot in their
islands, and the lands were dislodged and scattered
by battle all at one time, and no land could stand before their arms: Khatti (the Hittites), Qode, Carch-
emish, Arzawa, and Alashiya (Cilicia).' (15) This
vast migration which overthrew the Hittite empire and
swept through Cilicia, Syria and Palestine to the bor-
ders of Egypt, could well be the occasion when Mopsus
and his people moved from Western Asia Minor. The
Denen who appear in Ramesses' list of invading peoples
may well be the Danaoi of the _Iliad_.

In so far as Mopsus in Greek legend was a prophet
and in Greek cult in Cilicia was a giver of oracles
he appears to be the originator of the oracle at
Claros. Ancient authors who mention him often refer
to Colophon, but this is probably because our sources
date from the time when it was the dominant city. The
rare statement that he actually founded Colophon can
be disregarded, in so far as it might imply the
archaic and classical Greek city. Evidently the Ionian
colony could not have been founded by the son of a
Mycenaean settler and was not established before the
Trojan war. Instead, it is chronologically plausible
that, if Troy fell in the late 13th century, Mopsus'
migration took place about 1190 B.C. When he left
Claros, presumably the traditional practices of the
oracle, whatever they may have been, were continued
under some un-named successors. It is significant
that, though the legend of Mopsus at Claros was
strongly established in Greek literature, we never
hear of the later prophets there as Mopsidae. While
Branchus, probably a non-Greek, held no place of importance in Greek legend, but was the eponymous ancestor of a powerful family, Mopsus was famous in mythology, but founded no family of prophets in Ionia. Instead he was the ancestor of a dynasty of kings in
Cilicia.

The Hellenic colonies in the neighbourhood of
Claros present a historical problem. Colophon was one
of the twelve cities of the Panionion, the religious
league of the Ionian colonists. Notion, in spite of
doubts to the contrary, was one of the twelve Aeolic
cities. The evidence for this statement is the list

of the Aeolic twelve given by Herodotus, which contains the name Notion. (16) Its classification as an Aeolic city is at first glance amazing, as it lies far south of the group of Aeolic colonies which originally ran from Smyrna northward. But it would be unreasonable to assume on a priori grounds that an Aeolian colony could not be founded among the main group of Ionian settlements. Magnesia on the Maeander, which lay inland from Ephesus, was always recognised as not a member of the Panionion. Again Phocaea was an Ionic colony with Aeolians around it. Though the two groups of dialects and tribes mostly settled according to a distribution by separate districts of Aeolis and Ionia, the arrangement was not completely systematic. The very fact that Notion bore a name which literally meant "southward" may perhaps be due to the fact that it was much the most southerly of the Aeolic colonies.

If the statement of Herodotus is to be discounted, it cannot well be supposed that he made a mistake. To make up the number for the Aeolian cities, Notion needs to be included. To suppose that he referred to an otherwise unknown Greek colony whose name duplicated that of the town at the mouth of the river Ales is absurd. If there had been two towns called Notion Herodotus would have distinguished by some phrase which place he meant, just as he did with Cyme in the same list. Similarly the Athenian tribute lists record one Notion separately with no distinguishing epithet. So the only reasonable supposition is that at least in the fifth century and evidently for some time previously there had been two Greek cities within some eight miles of each other; Notion near the mouth of the river Ales and Colophon in the hills further up its course. The positions in such close proximity and linked by a river valley were highly peculiar in this respect, and this did not pass unnoticed in the ancient world. Aristotle in the Politics remarks that 'sometimes cities are at variance because of their situations, when the country is not conveniently disposed for the creation of one city", and cites as his second example 'the men of Colophon and the men of Notion'. (17).

How the situation first arose is never explained because our ancient sources give no account of the foundation of Notion. This is not surprising since in the end, as we shall see, Colophon absorbed it and so its early history was eclipsed. Whichever city is assumed to have been founded first, a certain difficulty remains in imagining the circumstances. If Colophon was already established, one may be surprised that the Colophonians allowed the Aeolians to land at the river-mouth and occupy a position which in effect controlled their nearest access to the sea. If Notion was already founded, one would expect them to be able to resist effectively the landing of an Ionian expedition there. The fact that Notion survived the foundation of Colophon proved that it was not conquered in the operation. So it remains to suppose either that the Ionian settlers negotiated their rights of passage up to their inland site or more probably that they reached it originally up one of the other river valleys. Colophon stood on a watershed which covers not only the upper course of the Ales, but also two tributaries of the Astes which flows into the sea somewhat further west. It is possible that this gave a route bypassing Notion to reach a site already known from Mycenaean settlement.

There is, however, another line of argument based on the early legends of Claros. It is significant that these are not Ionian, but Aeolian in connection. Manto appears as the daughter of Teiresias and is linked with the fall of Thebes. Similarly in the story of the contest with Calchas not only is Amphilochus linked with Aeolian legend, but also all his companions, Leonteus, Polypoetes and Podalirius, are located by the Homeric Catalogue in Northern Thessaly and so are Aeolians. The reasonable supposition seems to be that all these legends are derived from the colonists of Notion and that Claros which lay within two miles of that city passed into their control as soon as the first Hellenic colonists arrived.

The traditions of the founding of Colophon appear to involve a contradiction. The earlier account of the Ionian settlers is preserved in a fragment of Mimnermus, a native of the city, writing in the late seventh century B.C. He named the founder Andraemon and told of the colonisation:-

> "We left the steep city of Neleus, Pylos, and came by ship to charming Asia. With overpowering might we settled at lovely Colophon, leaders of grievous haughtiness."

Mimnermus is writing rather loose history, but he certainly implies a direct migration from Messenia to Colophon. A later tradition introduced two Athenians, Damasichthon and Promethos, sons of the Athenian king Codros, as leaders of the expedition. This form of the legend implied an intermediate stage in Attica and was probably part of the assimilation of the Ionian cities to Athens as its colonies which took place in

the sixth and fifth centuries. Herodotus himself
noted that in one respect the people of Colophon did
not show that they were derived from Athens: they
failed to observe the Athenian festival of the Apaturia. But he was prepared to accept that there was a
special explanation for this fact. (18).

Colophon, settled inland and facing north, developed itself as a land power. Its cavalry were famous, and the wealth of the citizens must have been
based on the great inland plain between Colophon and
the mountains of Lydia. This will have led to a constant warfare with their Asiatic neighbours, in which
Colophon may have been originally successful, but according to Herodotus Gyges, the leader of the new
militaristic dynasty of Lydia, captured the lower tow
of Colophon. (19). In the Cimmerian invasion which
followed, the Lydians will have lost their hold on it
again, but warfare between the two powers continued.
Unlike Miletus, Colophon seems never to have come to
terms with Lydia. Also, unlike Miletus, it did not g
in for large scale colonization overseas. If, as we
have suggested, it did not at this time control the
mouth of the river Ales, this will have been one factor against it. Also the rich acres of inland plain
satisfied any land hunger of the Colophonians. Aristotle remembered them later as the remarkable example
of a Greek city where the majority of the citizens
possessed large landed property.

Significantly their only colony of importance wa
Siris, founded on the arable land of South Italy,
whose settlers are described by Strabo as 'fleeing
from the rule of Lydia'. Presumably about 675 B.C.
when Gyges won his victory, many Colophonians, who ha
temporarily lost their land, decided to settle in
Italy. The city of Siris flourished for a century
till it was overwhelmed in war by its Achaean neighbours. In that period they had managed to import the
legend of Calchas into Italy, and his tomb was shown
there. It is also worth remarking that while most of
the Achaean and Dorian colonies in South Italy had
traditional legends of oracular responses from Delphi
which were the occasion of their foundation, no such
story about Siris survives. This is probably not because of its destruction, but because in 675 B.C. one
can imagine that the Colophonians would not consult
the Pythian Apollo, who had shown himself a supporter
of Gyges. Instead they may well have been guided by
a response from Claros.

We have suggested that at this period Claros was
in the control of Notion, which must have remained a
small Aeolian town dominated by its more powerful in-

land neighbour, but also protected by it against the threat of Lydia. Notion itself was not big enough to send out colonies on its own. Its oracle probably had only local importance, but the cult of Apollo there managed to secure a small mention in Greek literature. The ninth Homeric Hymn is a charming address to Artemis "who has made her horses rise from the river Meles, deep in rushes, and drives her chariot all of gold swiftly through Smyrna to vine-clad Claros, where Apollo of the silver bow sits awaiting the far-shooting goddess, who delights in arrows". (20) This account of the journey of Artemis to Apollo's temple at Claros, as the commentators saw, has some precise reference, and the meaning was explained by Louis Robert's excavations. On the north side of the Hellenistic and Roman temple of Apollo he found the ruinous remains of a small Ionic temple which was evidently dedicated to Artemis Claria. For in front of it stood a small altar beside which was found a very early life-size kore. This female statue was inscribed: 'Timonax, son of Theodorus, consecrated me to Artemis, having been the first priest.' Thus the dedication of the temple was revealed and also a late-seventh century date established, judging from the style of the kore and its inscription. Following Louis Robert we can safely identify the Homeric Hymn as a special composition produced for the festival held at the consecration of the temple. Why Artemis should be pictured as coming to the ceremony from Smyrna is not so certain. But probably there was already a cult of Artemis there, and, as Smyrna was at this time linked with Colophon, it may have been the source from which the cult was introduced. The poet pictures Apollo as awaiting his sister at Claros, since her temple was built beside a shrine of Apollo, which was already there.

Besides the ninth Homeric Hymn two other passages in early Greek poetry contain the name of Claros. It occurs in the Homeric Hymn to Apollo in a long list of places all round the Eastern Aegean visited by Leto in search of a spot where she could give birth to her son. But it has no special significance in the context, except to prove that Claros made no claim to Apollo's birthplace. (21) The other passage is in a hymn to Apollo by a little-known poet, Ananius. He invoked the god by his favourite shrines:-

'Apollo, who dwell in Delos or Pytho or Naxos or Miletus or holy Claros, come to the temple....'

The lines must have been well-known to fifth century

Athenians, for Aristophanes uses them for some comic business in the <u>Frogs</u> (405 B.C.). But otherwise Claros is not mentioned, and we can only assume that it went through the same political history as the rest of Ionia. Croesus will have acquired some degree of mastery over it in the mid-sixth century, but it is not included in Herodotus' list of the oracles to which the king applied his famous test. The present writer believes that this story was a Delphic myth, and that the absence of Claros simply indicates that from the late -sixth century, when the story was invented for the glory of the Pythian Apollo, Claros was not reckoned a serious rival as an oracle.

Persia conquered Colophon and Notion on the fall of Croesus, but there is no record that they put up any special resistance. Similarly they are not recorded in the Ionian revolt. As that was largely based on the naval power of Miletus and her allies, it is possible that Colophon, which did not appear to have had an important fleet, played little or no part in it. In fact, Colophon, whose wealth depended on the cultivation of the inland plain may well have been unwilling to jeopardize it by rebellion (22).

Both cities joined the Delian league where Notion is listed separately. Colophon paid three talents a year compared with five from Miletus and six from Ephesus. Notion was only assessed at one third of a talent. But the Colophonians were not enthusiastically loyal to the League. About 447 some of the citizens had called in the Persians, and Colophon was only recovered after a revolt and probably an Athenian expedition. Once more during the early years of the Peloponnesian war in 430 B.C. Colophon called in the Persians. This time Notion was involved in the revolt, for the pro-Athenian Colophonians fled for refuge there. In 427 a Spartan fleet coasting round Ionia briefly appeared 'at Claros,' as Thucydides writes. Presumably they put in at the beach west of Notion. But as they feared Athenian pursuit, they did not linger. When the Athenian fleet following them arrived, its commander, Paches, found Notion split between two factions, one of which had called in a garrison of Greek mercenaries under Persian command. Paches ruthlessly reinstated the pro-Athenian party, and later the Athenians sent a settlement of their own citizens and collected any sympathizers among the Colophonians into Notion. Colophon itself proably remained independent until in 409 the Athenian general Thrasyllus landed at Notion and marching inland caputed the city. Notion with its rear thenceforth secured was used by the Athenians as a base. It seems to have remained

free of Colophon even after the defeat of Athens and
the end of the Peloponnesian war. For in 403/2 B.C.
the Athenians passed a decree in which among other
votes they thanked the citizens of Ephesus and Notion
for receiving hospitably the pro-Athenian refugees
from Samos. (22)
   At last at some date in the first half of the
fourth century the Colophonians absorbed their weaker
neighbour. The circumstances are not recorded in our
literary sources. Only we find that Theopompus,
writing about 340 B.C., described Notion as 'a place
(chorion) lying in front of the city of Colophon'.(23)
By this time, then, if not previously, the sanctuary
of Claros must have fallen into the control of the
Colophonians. Already as early as their first coinage
at the end of the sixth century, they had put the
head of Apollo on it as their symbol. But this may
merely have been a tribute to the importance of the
sanctuary at Claros without indicating that it was
already under their control. From the mid-fourth century the symbol of the tripod becomes usual on their
coins and with its association with prophecy, even if
not the method used at Claros, makes a more positive
reference to the oracle. But the earliest precise evidence for Claros controlled by Colophon occurs in a
lengthy inscription dated to 307/6 B.C. From the ritual prescriptions of this document it is shown that
there was among others an altar in the old agora dedicated to Apollo of Claros. Athena Polias as usual
was the patron goddess of the colony, but in the contemporary ritual Apollo of Claros had become the leading deity. This was the final outcome of the incorp-
oration of the Apolline sanctuary in the territory of
Colophon. (24)
   Judging by its coinage Colophon had deteriorated
economically in the disturbed years of the latter part
of the fifth century, but showed a considerable revival in the fourth century. Under the King's Peace its
relations with the Anatolian hinterland will have been
friendly and the acquiring of Notion will have provided
a satisfactory communication with the sea. How the
inhabitants spread over the combined area of Colophon
and Notion is not known from our literary sources and
unfortunately the very limited amount of archaeological
exploration of civic sites which has so far taken place
has not done much to elucidate the problem.
   A French expedition to Notion in 1921 determined
the line of its fortifications, running a distance of
some four kilometres, but did not fix their date. The
main temple was sufficiently excavated and proved to
be Doric in style and of Hadrianic date in its surviv-

ing form. It had formerly been conjecturally identified as a temple of Apollo, but it proved, much more
in accordance with the practice of early colonies in
Asia Minor, that the city goddess was Athena and that
Apollo had his shrine outside. (25)
    An American expedition to Colophon in 1922 ex-
plored the extensive site and began to excavate, when
it was interrupted by the change in the political
situation. Cemeteries of the Mycenaean, Geometric and
Hellenistic periods were identified, but no necropolis
of the fifth century. A tholos tomb, rifled, but still
containing Creto-Mycenaean sherds, was excavated. The
acropolis had no habitations later than the fourth
century, but elsewhere buildings of Roman date were
observed, and one house site was traced which had been
occupied from the 7/6 century to about 250 B.C. (26)
The results of one season's work were enough to suggest what immense possibility the site might hold.

Chapter Eight

CLAROS UNDER THE HELLENISTIC MONARCHS AND THE
AUGUSTAN PRINCIPATE

The Hellenistic world was a difficult place for the
city-states, particularly in Asia Minor. Even a powerful city, such as Miletus, as we have seen, was subject to recurring pressure this way and that from the
contending monarchies. Colophon, while less important
strategically, was also much weaker to stand this
stress.
    The city fathers of Colophon in the last years of
the fourth century may have rightly appraised the
situation. The lengthy inscription of 307/6 B.C.,
which we have already mentioned (1), showed them ar-
ranging for the erection of a great new system of fortifications so as to enclose within one wall "the old
city" and the contemporary fourth-century city. The
necessary funds were raised by means of subscriptions.
Some four hundred subscribers with their contributions
are recorded and this may only represent half the original list. Unfortunately, for lack of archaeological
exploration, it is not known how far this scheme was
ever put into execution. It is not likely to have
been completed. For in 302 B.C., only some four years
later, Colophon was taken by Prepelaus, the general of
King Lysimachus, in the course of establishing a base in
western Asia Minor for the war against King Antigonus. When
the war ended on the death of Antigonus, Lysimachus retained his control over the territory, and about 286 B.C.,
while engaged in enlarging the city of Ephesus, he transferred the inhabitants of Colophon and of her neighbour,
Lebedus, to the new settlement. Ancient authors write as
if Colophon was depopulated by this act, and Phoenix, a
native poet, composed a lament for his city. But
actually coins of Colophon continued to be struck,
though the issues dwindled. So no doubt a remnant at
least remained on the old site and also on the site of
Notion, and after the death of Lysimachus and the
collapse of his empire in 281, there may have been no

restriction on former citizens of Colophon who wished
to leave Ephesus and return to their old homes. The
communities of Notion and Colophon seem to have continued for some time to retain some degree of distinc
ion between them, for a document shows that they were
organised as a _sympoliteia_ - a shared citizenship of
two city-states. The name Colophon covered both part
and they were distinguished as "those who dwell in th
old city" and "the Colophonians from the sea". Probably the centre of importance shifted gradually to th
latter, so that by the Roman period the name of Notio
dropped out of use completely. (2)

So far the history of Claros and of its two neig
bouring cities has not included any specific examples
of enquiry at the oracle. It is one of the odd features of the sanctuary's traditions that no inscriptio
al or literary records survive which mention any particular response before the time of Alexander. This
is part of the general loss of the history of Ionia
except for what is preserved by Herodotus, and he, as
we have seen, mentions Colophon and Notion, but never
refers to the oracle at Claros.

The lack of early evidence for oracular function
ing had led such a nineteenth century scholar as
Buresch to argue that the practice of divination was
only developed at Claros in Hellenistic times. (3)
But this is to discount the significance of the rich
store of legendary references which date from the
seventh century B.C. at latest. It is impossible to
believe that these stories would have grown and attached themselves to Claros, if it was simply a temple
of Apollo with no oracular functions. On the other
hand, the fact that Claros is not included in the lis
of oracles alleged to have been tested by Croesus
suggests, as we have noted, that Delphi did not recko
it among its serious rivals towards the end of the
sixth century.

It is best then to suppose that from very early,
probably prehellenic periods, Claros had been the sit
of an oracle, but the extent and frequency of its act
ivity remain quite uncertain. Even the earliest recorded response, that connected with Alexander the
Great, is of somewhat doubtful historicity. The stor
is told by Pausanias: the king was the founder of the
contemporary city of Smyrna in accordance with a visio
in a dream. "They tell that Alexander was hunting on
Mount Pagos, and when he came from the hunt he reache
a sanctuary of the goddesses Nemeseis and happened
upon a spring and a plane tree growing above the wate
in front of the sanctuary. As he slept under the
tree, they say that the Nemeseis revealed themselves

to him and commanded him to found a city there and
bring to it the Smyrnaeans after he had made them
remove from their previous city." The Smyrnaeans
therefore sent sacred ambassadors to Claros to enquire
concerning their present circumstances and the god
gave them an oracular response:-

> "Thrice blessed shall they be and four times
> blessed again, the men who shall dwell on Pagos
> beyond the holy river Meles."

So they voluntarily removed and adopted a cult of two
Nemeseis instead of one. (4)

The story of Alexander's dream was evidently popular in Smyrna in the mid-second century A.D. For
besides Pausanias, Aelius Aristides mentions it no less
than three times in his works. Also the scene of the
two goddesses appearing to Alexander under the plane-
tree was represented on a succession of coins minted
in Smyrna starting in the reign of Marcus Aurelius.
If, however, one looks into the historical evidence
for the story, some weaknesses emerge. No trace of
the legend, not even a suggestion that Alexander was
concerned with refounding Smyrna, appears in any of
the histories of the king. The day's hunting on Mount
Pagos would have to be fitted into the programme of
his march from Sardis to Ephesus when he was hastening
to cut off the Persian forces in Asia Minor in 334 B.C.
Alexander's interest in hunting was well known, but,
while it is just possible that he indulged it, even at
this time of critical military action, it is not very
plausible. It is even more significant that a century
and a half before the story appears in Pausanias,
Strabo mentioned the restoration of Smyrna as due
first to Antigonus and then to Lysimachus. (5) This
would date it to the last years of the fourth century
and beginning of the third, a very likely period for
this kind of action on the part of these two kings.

If Antigonus was the real founder of New Smyrna,
his decision need not have been influenced by any
previous intention of Alexander motivated by a vision.
On the other hand, the legend about Alexander's hunt
is a romantic embellishment of the sort which might
have been created locally in Hellenistic or Roman periods and have found its way into literature by the
second century A.D.

If we look back at Pausanias' story, it is seen
to fall into two very loosely connected parts. The
enquiry of the Smyrnaeans is couched in the most general terms and contains no reference linking it with

Alexander's dream. The two lines of oracular respons
are a typical enough answer to those wishing to found
a colony on a new site. The god gives his blessing a
names the place - on Mount Pagos on the opposite side
of the local river from the old site of Smyrna. Thei
is no allusion to the vision of the Nemeseis. Yet
one would expect Apollo to confirm that their message
to Alexander was a divine command, which must be obey
ed. But though brief the response as quoted seems to
be complete. Pausanias is the only author to quote i
and he had a particular weakness for hunting out and
quoting unfamiliar oracles which he had encountered i
his extensive reading in this field. He may well hav
derived it from some other source and tagged it on to
the legend of Alexander's dream. The only connectior
is that it explains the willingness of the inhabitant
to remove at the king's order. But this does not nee
justification.

Therefore, the enquiry of the Smyrnaeans "concerning their present situation" may just as well hav
been made on the occasion of the foundation of the
city by Antigonus without any preceding divine manife
tation. It was an old custom that newly established
poleis should have an oracular response as a sort of
charter. While one must admit that the lines quoted
by Pausanias could easily have been forged, it is
most unlikely that, if so, they would have been so
simple in form with no reference to Alexander or the
Nemeseis. So one is probably entitled to judge from
this specimen that the oracle of Claros shortly befor
300 B.C. issued its responses in hexameter verse and
so corresponded in practice with Delphi and Didyma.
What its usual form had been in the classical and
archaic periods is not otherwise evidenced.

Excavation conducted by Louis Robert has proved
that at the end of the fourth century B.C., about the
suggested date of this response, work had begun on
constructing a temple at Claros which was to remain
in general plan the building down to the end of its
history. It had no doubt been preceded by some form
of temple since the seventh century. For it is too
unlikely that at the time when the archaic temple of
Artemis Claria was erected Apollo had no building in
the precinct. But the large-scale rebuilding of the
Hellenistic period has prevented the recovery of any
plan of earlier structures on the site. Even the
fourth-century plan was to be greatly altered in the
Augustan period. But the one basic feature which pe
sisted was the special adaptation of the shrine for
the purpose of oracular consultation. (6)

As laid out in the closing years of the fourth

century, the temple was externally of a normal classical type. It had the usual peristyle of a Doric
temple with six columns on the front and eleven on the
sides. That the Doric style was chosen in preference
to the local Ionic is perhaps somewhat surprising. In
area it was just a little larger than the famous Ionic
temple at Priene and far smaller than the temples of
its rival oracle centre at Didyma or its near neighbour at Ephesus. It was divided internally into a
<u>pronaos</u>, and a <u>cella</u>, but no <u>opisthodomas</u>. The <u>pron-
aos</u>, as in the Ionic temples of Asia Minor, was very
deep from front to back, and this gave opportunity
for the insertion of an elaborate system of basement
passages beneath the level of the floor. For as at
Didyma, the architect was faced with the problem that
if he erected an elevated temple on the primitive
site, he must provide access to a sacred spring at the
original ground level. At Didyma Paeonius had opted
for an open courtyard to act as the <u>adyton</u>; the anonymous architect of Claros chose instead to provide
his temple with a basement, much of it roofed over,
though the holy of holies itself may have been left
open to the sky. The details of the internal arrangements are best left to describe in their final form as
reconstructed in the Augustan period. But two points
remain to stress here:- the early Hellenistic plan was
fully designed to provide for the functioning of the
oracle, and it was laid out on such a large and complicated scale that one must suppose it had an active
business with many enquirers.

This is interesting because from after its capture by Prepelaus (302 B.C.) it seems unlikely that
Colophon could have undertaken to finance such a project. Immediately before, the city had been occupied
in raising contributions to fortify itself. So it had
at least one other major building project on hand at
the time when it undertook the rebuilding of the temple. It may have been some burst of prosperity following on Alexander's conquest of Persia which encouraged the Colophonians to commission the design for
the building, and then the development of the struggle
between the Diadochi had impressed the need for fort-
ification. Anyway, Colophon had probably taken on
more than it could immediately carry through, and
there is no sign that any of the Hellenistic monarchs
emerged as a benefactor to the sanctuary. So while
the construction of the temple may have begun before
300 B.C., it is likely to have progressed very slowly,
perhaps depending at times on what could be collected
from worshippers. The first stage was the construction of the elaborate basement and then the walls

129

above; the peristyle was probably left to be added
later.

No other responses are quoted or referred to
during the Hellenistic period, but there is evidence
to identify several prophets or other functionaries
attached to the oracle-centre. The best known is
Nicander of Colophon, two of whose poems, the
Theriaca (on venomous reptiles) and the Alexipharmac
(on antidotes to poisons) are extant. The titles of
many more books attributed to him are preserved, and
the fragments in quotation show that besides hexameters - the metre of the surviving poems - he also wrot
in elegiacs. Nicander described himself as one "whom
the snowy town of Claros nourished". (Why he should
have called Claros "snowy" is a puzzle. It does not
seem an appropriate epithet for the climate of the
Ales valley. Pausanias says that the river's water
was the coldest in Ionia and that Ionic poets sang it
praises on this account. So perhaps in an affected
manner typical enough of Hellenistic verse Nicander
intended an obscure allusion to this fact.) Again he
ends the dedication of his Alexipharmaca by writing
that he "is sitting beside the Clarian tripods of
Apollo". So the ancient biographers were justified
in describing him as "a priest of the Clarian Apollo,
having inherited the office from his ancestors".
Tradition made him a contemporary of the last king of
Pergamum, Attalus III, and quoted in support lines
from a lost poem, but so far as it goes it could have
been addressed to any of the Attali. However, judgin
by style, it is the most likely date for the author
of the extant poems. (7)

The chronology of Nicander, however, has been
confused by the excavation at Delphi of an inscriptio
giving a decree in honour of a "Nicander of Colophon,
an epic poet". dated probably to 258 B.C. (8) The
most plausible explanation is that there were actuall
two poets of the same name from the same city, but
separated by a century or more in date. The Nicander
of the extant poems described himself as "the son of
Damaios", while the poet honoured by the Delphians is
called "the son of Anaxagoras". It might, of course,
be explained away on the hypothesis that there had
been a case of adoption in mature years. But the
simpler supposition is that there were two poets, who
were probably related. If the position of prophet at
the oracle of Claros had descended in the family, bot
may have held it in different generations, though it
is only proved for the second-century Nicander. Similarly, some of the lost works whose titles are preserved may really belong to the earlier poet.

Claros under the Hellenistic Monarchs and the
Augustan Principate

A hereditary tradition of versifying for the
oracle is very likely, and it is interesting that one
of the works attributed to Nicander was "On the poets
from Colophon". So he may have been consciously the
heir of a poetic heritage. Certainly, it is remarkable how many earlier poets are known to have sprung
from this one city:- Mimnermus, Xenophanes, Antimachus,
Hermesianax and Phoenix. But only Nicander is known
to have been connected with the oracle. His concern
with the subject may have been demonstrated in another
lost work, if one can trust the title "About all
oracle-centres, in three books". The intention of the
word "all" in the title may have been to emphasise
that, though practising at Claros, his books were much
wider in scope. Unfortunately, not even a fragment
has survived. The only passage where he is otherwise
quoted as mentioning Claros, apart from the allusions
to it in personal contexts, is a rather charming pair
of elegiac couplets which tell how Apollo had made
the place free from all noxious creatures:-

"No adder, no hateful spiders, nor the scorpion
that wounds deeply dwell in the groves of Claros,
since Phoebus laid a grassy floor, and covered
the deep glen with ash-trees to keep off vicious
creatures."

For once Nicander strikes a note of poetic beauty,
which is rare indeed in his crabbedly erudite verse.(9)
The influence of Nicander can be traced in one
Greek legend. Ovid in the Metamorphoses is telling
the tale of Ceyx, a king of Trachis in Central Greece,
who to satisfy the requirements of the story had to
be drowned at sea. So, to provide an occasion, it is
described how he set out on a voyage to consult the
Clarian Apollo, and the explanation is inserted parenthetically, that he could not go instead to the neighbouring sanctuary of Delphi, because at that time it
was occupied by the godless Phlegyans. This ingenious
motive might have been credited to Ovid's imagination,
but a scholiast records that he is following Nicander.
So one can recognise the introduction of Claros in the
legend as the work of the priestly poet, who had chos-
en to substitute a version involving his local sanctuary in place of the other versions of the story.
Except for this instance, the Clarian oracle-centre is
not made the scene of any legendary consultation. (10)
An inscription found at Notion records another
scholar who was once attached to the oracle-centre.
He was Gorgos, who is unknown to our literary tradition and cannot be dated more precisely than that his

period fell after 200 B.C. The monument is his
epitaph describing his qualities and recording that
he was buried in Attica.

> "Gorgos was a guardian of many books derived from
> every form of research, a venerable scholar, who
> had plucked the pages of the bards. In his great-
> hearted mind he loved wisdom and was a servant
> of the tripod of the Clarian son of Leto. The
> dust of Cecrops' land hides him in its bosom.
> But for the sake of his piety he has gone after
> death to the place of the pious."

Clearly like Nicander he was a functionary at the
oracle-centre, but the vaguely bombastic phrases of
eulogy leave undefined his actual office and do not
reveal precisely what his forms of scholarly activity
were. Mutschmann supposed that his work was a collection of mythology, and Jacoby, accepting this interpretation, included him in his Fragments of the
Greek Historians under the classification of mythographer. This is probably correct, but it remains
unclear whether Gorgos wrote prose or verse. (11)
    Louis Robert has also discovered in an unpublish-
ed inscription at Claros the evidence for a third
functionary of the Hellenistic period - a "chresmologe",
summoned from Smyrna to preside over the oracle. This
evidence is seriously inconsistent with the picture
which we get from Nicander of a native family of
scholarly and poetic prophets, but it is paralleled
by a statement of Tacitus, which we shall later encounter, about prophets fetched from Miletus. More
detailed and precise information about this Smyrnaean
would be valuable. (12)
    If one could work out the pattern of ups and
downs in the history of Claros and Colophon during
the Hellenistic period, it might be possible to explain the apparent changes in the character of the
prophetship. But our evidence only supplies a limited
number of obvious points in the relations of Colophon
and its overlords. In 219 B.C. they submitted to
Attalus I, but later fell under the renewed influence
of the Seleucids, as shown by the fact that a statue
of Antiochus, son and co-ruler with Antiochus III
(209-193 B.C.) was set up at the corner of the temple
at Claros. On the Roman invasion of Asia Minor Colophon must have been prompt in joining them, as a
fragment is preserved of a letter from the brothers,
Lucius and Publius Scipio, recognising the sanctuary'
rights to asylia. Later the Attalids were their patrons, when Nicander the prophet dedicated a poem to th

last of the dynasty. (13)

Two opposite poles may be represented by the
erection of the <u>Propylaea</u> in the second century and
the plundering by the Pirates in the first. The
<u>Propylaea</u> was a very handsome building of marble
decorated with Doric columns. It was erected on the
south side of the sanctuary, showing that the main
approach was from the former site of Notion and from
the sea. It led to a sacred way lined at first on
both sides and then on the west side only by a succession of monuments. (14) The Pirates' raid is only
known from our literary sources. The attack on the
temple is recorded first in Plutarch's list of outrages and the sacking of the city of Colophon was one
of the few examples named by Cicero. So the French
excavators may be right in supposing that serious
damage was done to the sanctuary buildings. The great
restoration and alterations which followed in the
Augustan period make any traces of the destruction
hard to identify. (15)

The monuments on the sacred way are in themselves
an interesting illustration of Colophon's policy.
There was a statue of Pompey set up by the Ionian
League - an appropriate tribute on this spot to the
man who had rescued the coastal cities from the scourge
of the Pirates. Otherwise the monuments were not
erected by outside authorities but by the Colophonians
themselves. They are conspicuous for including a
number set up in honour of the Roman governors of the
province of Asia. The series of proconsuls commemorated is remarkable, including Lucullus, Valerius
Flaccus and Cicero's brother Quintus in the Republican
period, and Sextus Appuleius under the Principate.
Compared with this number Didyma has yielded only one
example of a proconsul of the period honoured by a
monument. This difference cannot be explained merely
by the accidents of preservation. Evidently while
Miletus maintained a strictly correct attitude of
loyalty, Colophon went out of its way to flatter the
Roman authorities. (16)

Sextus Appuleius was a particularly striking
example: he was actually hailed on his inscription as
"second founder". As a half-nephew of the Emperor
Augustus, being the son of his half-sister Octavia,
who was the daughter of Augustus' father by his first
wife, he was a specially significant object for flattery. Though he achieved all the traditional honours
of a senatorial career and appeared to have been
trusted by the emperor as a military commander, he
avoided any unwise prominence in the dynastic struggles of the court. So as a man of wealth and influence

Claros under the Hellenistic Monarchs and the
Augustan Principate

Colophon could safely choose him as a suitable target
for their adulation. But even allowing for the hy-
perbolic languagr of such eulogies, he could scarcely
have been described as "second founder" if he had not
made some considerable contribution to the material
welfare of Colophon. What this was can be conjectured. (17)

The excavation of the temple has shown that unde
the Augustan principate it was furnished with a new
set of cult images carved from marble on a colossal
scale. These represented the conventional triad of
Apollo, Artemis and Leto. Apollo was seated with a
bough of bay in his extended right hand. One arm and
a leg from above the knee are preserved, and from the
it can be estimated that the height of the figure was
some 7 to 8 metres. Artemis and Leto stood on his
right and left, and as they will have reached to
approximately the same height, were proportionately
on a smaller scale. The principal statue is reproduced on a new series of the coins of Colophon struck
in the reign of Augustus. The city evidently thus
expressed its pride in the new cult image. (18)

The installation of these new marble statues of
immense size had also occasioned some structural difficulties. The Hellenistic building, as we have already mentioned contained a complicated arrangement of
passages and rooms in the basement and the far west
end, where the statues were to be placed, may have
been open to the sky from the substructure. The
early cult image, perhaps dating from the archaic per
iod and of no more than human scale may have been
housed in a small naiskos, standing in a paved court
on the level of the stylobate. To adapt this setting
to the new statues involved sweeping away much of the
Hellenistic shrine and roofing over the basement with
stone vaulting strong enough to sustain their weight
superimposed. The whole undertaking of adapting the
temple and furnishing it with new cult figures must
have involved very considerable expense. Though one
can suppose that Colophon like the other cities of
Asia experienced a new prosperity in consequence of
the peace produced by the Augustan principate, it is
probable that one can detect the hand of a particular
benefactor behind this costly restoration. The Hellenistic temple had never been completed. It may stil
have lacked or only imperfectly possessed its colonnade. Also, the sanctuary may still have shown dis-
tressing signs of the Pirates' devastation. The new
classicizing spirit of the Augustan age would appropriately call for a restoration involving something in
accordance with the taste of the time and on a scale to

134

suit the temple. One may therefore suggest that
Sextus Appuleius while he was proconsul of Asia was
persuaded to contribute handsomely towards the expense
of the undertaking and give it his patronage. As
Apollo was Augustus' favourite deity, the persuasion
may have been easy. He will thus have earned not
entirely inappropriately the title of "second founder".
   This connection with a prominent member of the
Imperial family may also have some responsibility for
the fact that at this point for the first time Claros
emerges frequently in Roman literature in the later
poetry of Ovid. Of course the poets of the late Republic and the Principate would have known of the
sanctuary of Apollo from the mentions in Nicander's
works, even if they did not read the early poetry and
classical prose which referred to it. But evidently
its name was not originally popular as a decorative
noun or adjective in association with Apollo. Before
its emergence in Ovid there is only one allusion extant - in Vergil's _Aeneid_, and even Ovid did not
mention it in the _Amores_. It appears first in the
Ars Amatoria (completed by 1 B.C.). Again it figures
twice in the _Metamorphoses_; once in a brief list of
Apollo's domains and the second time in a more complicated passage, based on Nicander, which we have already discussed. The _Metamorphoses_ was nearly completed by the time of Ovid's exile in 8 A.D. Finally
the revised dedication of the _Fasti_, addressed to
Germanicus, must have been written between 14 and 17
A.D. It contains the remarkable lines:-

> "A page is dispatched which will undergo the
> criticism of a prince, like a message sent for
> the Clarian god to read."

The purpose is to introduce a flattering comparison
between Germanicus and Apollo, but the remarkable
features are that Ovid should think of Apolline oracles
as being consulted by letter and should choose Claros
in particular as the place for this practice. These
passages in Ovid, particularly the last two, show an
interest in Claros which is not found among previous
Roman poets. One may suggest that, if this was not
simply a personal quirk of Ovid's mind, which had
developed subsequent to his writing the _Amores_, it may
have been inspired by the patronage which Sextus
Appuleius had bestowed on the shrine. This may have
created at Rome a certain interest in Apollo Clarius
in those circles of the Imperial court to which Ovid
is known to have had access before his exile, and there
may even have been a contemporary fashion among upper

class Romans of sending enquiries to Claros by letter. (19)

It is perhaps a further consequence of this new
interest that soon after Ovid's death Claros received
a visit from an even more distinguished member of the
imperial family then Sextus Appuleius. This was no
less a person than the object of Ovid's dedication,
Germanicus Caesar, son of the favourite stepson of
Augustus, adopted son and heir apparent of Tiberius.
In 18 A.D. after a succession of campaigns in Germany
which had been made the subject of exaggerated eulogies and a triumph, this ambitious prince was dispatch
ed to the East with the powers of vice-regent. His
journey took on the character of a royal progress
while he visited in turn the most notable sites of
Greece and Asia Minor. He was accompanied on his
journey by his no less distinguished wife, Agrippina
the elder, the granddaughter of Augustus. Their
selection of ports of call was guided by what Tacitus
described as "a passionate desire to get to know
antique sites made famous by their repute". So for
instance Germanicus attempted unsuccessfully to land
on Samothrace so as to visit the sanctuary of the
Great Gods. After going to Ilion to pay respects to
the traditional origin of Rome, he put in at Colophon
on purpose to consult the oracle of Apollo at Claros.
One will not suppose that his motive was a serious
need for the guidance of the god. It was at best
sincere interest in the ancient tradition of the place
Apart from the possibility which we have already considered that through Sextus Appuleius the imperial
family may have acquired a certain connection with th
temple, Germanicus himself might have particular motives in the matter. He was not merely a patron of
literature, like some other members of the Julio-
Claudian house; he had also written an original work
on omens foretelling the future, which was in the
tradition of the didactic verse of the Hellenistic
poets. All these activities would incline him to be
interested in the operation of such an oracle as
Claros and in the scene of the career of such a poet
as Nicander.

Tacitus, partly no doubt for his own literary
purposes, made Germanicus' visit to Claros the climax
of his narrative of the prince's tour and devoted mor
space to the occasion in his account than to any
other site. This may have been because he expected
the traditions of the place to be novel and interesting to his Roman readers, but also it gave convenient
scope for his typical lines of rhetorical emphasis -
a colourful description of exotic happenings and a

somewhat cynical appraisal of conventional beliefs in
the supernatural. Also, as has been suggested by
Syme, the passage was probably written soon after
Tacitus had himself been proconsul of Asia and had had
an opportunity to visit the sanctuary and observe its
activities with a cool gaze. It is noteworthy that
when he turns to describe the procedure of the oracle,
he momentarily lapses into the present tense and evidently tells what happened in his own day, nearly a
century after Germanicus' consultation.

We are not told what was the form of Germanicus'
enquiry, which perhaps he was not called on to express, but it would appear to have been about his own
future, perhaps with special reference to his mission
in the East. The account runs: "There, unlike at
Delphi, it is not a woman, but a man, selected from
particular families and usually summoned from Miletus,
who acts as priest. He hears only the number of the
enquirers and their names. Then after departing into
a grotto and taking a draught of water from a hidden
spring, though generally ignorant of poetic literature, he produces replies in set forms of verse on the
subjects which each enquirer had conceived in his
mind. It was told that to Germanicus in ambiguous
phrases, as is the custom of the oracles, he forecast
in verse that his death would be premature." (20)

The episode as recounted by Tacitus is less important to modern scholars for the enquiry and the
reply than for the occasion which it gives for a
description, however brief, of the procedure of consulting the oracle. One can only wish that a historian had had similar occasion to give an account of the
method of consultation at Didyma. Even Delphi has no
single description of its procedure as precise as this.
Tacitus did not deign to reproduce the words of the
prophet, even in paraphrase, and his use of the phrase
"it was told" (ferebatur) sufficiently conveys his
suspicions that the version in circulation may have
been doctored after Germanicus' death, or else re-
interpreted to provide a prophecy of it.

But even though written in comparatively clear
and simple phrases Tacitus' description of the typical
consultation occasioned doubt and misunderstanding to
scholars until recent years. The word specus, which
we have translated "grotto", could mean either a natural or an artificial cavern; hence an uncertainty
whether the prophet entered a hidden subterranean part
of the temple or else a cave in some natural location.
The problem was not made any easier by the fact that
Pliny the Elder, writing some fifty years after Germanicus' visit and fifty years before Tacitus wrote,

137

used the very same word "specus" to describe the
place entered by the prophet. He is listing all the
fountains with remarkable properties and records:-
"at Colophon in the grotto of Apollo Clarius is a poo
by drinking of which marvellous prophecies are produced, but the life of the drinkers are shortened." (21)
Pliny will have derived his information from some
previous writer, but who it was is not known. The
point of his narrative is quite different from anything in Tacitus. Both agree that the oracle was
produced by drinking from a sacred fountain in a grot
to. Tacitus stresses the wonder that the inspiration
makes the prophet speak in verse and that he can answer the unspoken questions of those consulting him.
To Pliny the remarkable feature is the penalty of the
shortening of their life which the prophets incurred -
a circumstance not elsewhere recorded. Both left the
nature and situation of the grotto unexplained.

When in the late nineteenth century it was recog
nised that the site of the temple must lie in the fla
valley bottom of the Ales, the cave was sought in the
rocky face of the hills overlooking it, and a conspic
uous cavern there was actually excavated in 1911, whe
it yielded some not very significant traces of human
occupation. It was not till L. Robert at last found
the temple and exposed its structure, that the specus
could be identified as an artificial construction in
its basement. The building above the level of the
pavement had been almost entirely laid flat by some
earthquake in the Middle Ages. But the substructures
were preserved practically intact and had been engulfe
in alluvial mud. Consequently, L. Robert has been able
to disclose the "grotto" and all its setting. (22)

About 13 metres from the facade and just inside
the antae of the pronaos two stairways of four steps
descended on either side of the temple into the subterranean interior. They gave access to two passages
which turned at right angles towards each other and
united into a single corridor which ran down the middle of the temple, till after reaching the area under
the cella it divided again into two branches which
led round through a sort of antechamber into either
end of a central vaulted room. These passages through
out were only 2'4" (70cm) in width and so could only
be traversed in single file. Also the ceiling, which
was also the floor of the temple and was carved below
in the fashion of a vault, was so low - 5'10½" (1.79m
that a tall man could not walk upright. The inner
room contained a marble bench and from it a final
passage led centrally to a similar, but smaller vaulted chamber. This passage will have been traversed on

the occasion of consultations by the prophet alone,
leaving behind him in the previous room the enquirers
seated on the marble bench and such other officials
as had conducted them through the maze of corridors.
In the innermost shrine he found to his left a well
from which he could draw his inspiring draught of
sacred water. The spot where the prophet drank was
appropriately the most holy in the temple, for vertically above the back of the room was the base of the
cult statues in the <u>cella</u>. The vaulting was an Augustan development, also the well to the side of the
room. In the Hellenistic period there had been a
pavement all over this area of which remains were
found at a depth of more than a metre below the Aug-
ustan-period floor. Also in the Hellenistic arrangement the sacred water had been contained in a trough
lying along the base of the west wall and divided
from the pavement by a raised rim. But these changes
did not imply any basic alteration in ritual. The
general plan of passages, rooms and sacred fountain
had been the same since the end of the fourth century
B.C.
     What the building on the site had been like be-
fore that date cannot now be traced, so that it is
impossible to establish what constructions it might
have contained for the functioning of the oracle. But
it can be presumed that from the end of the fourth
century the method used was in general such as Tacitus
described.
     There is no evidence that Germanicus' visit to
Claros was followed by any benefaction to the sanctuary. In fact, it might not have influenced the history of the oracle at all, if it were not for two
rather doubtful examples of subsequent consultations.
     Pausanias, when discussing the giants of mythol-
ogy, raises the question whether they had snakes in
place of feet as legend suggested and as they were
conventionally represented in Hellenistic art. To
prove that the notion was ridiculous, Pausanias cites
an instance to the contrary. "The Syrian river Orontes
does not flow entirely in level country to the sea,
but is carried against a sheer cliff and down a steep
course from it. The Roman emperor wished it to be
navigable by ship from the sea to the city of Antioch.
So with toil and expenditure of capital he excavated
a reservoir at a convenient point on the inland voyage
and diverted the river into it. When the ancient
channel was dried up, there was found in it a coffin
of earthenware more than eleven cubits long, and the
dead body was great in proportion to the coffin and
human throughout all its body. This body the god at

Claros under the Hellenistic Monarchs and the
Augustan Principate

Claros, when the Syrians came to the oracle-centre,
stated to be Orontes, and that he belonged to the
race of the Indians." The response satisfied Pausanias, who found it appropriate that India, which
produced such huge beasts as elephants, should in
primeval times have produced colossal men. (23)
    Though the story as told by Pausanias has fan-
tastic features, it is likely that it had some foundation in fact. The engineering project on the cours
of the Orontes is probably not a complete fabricatior
though it is described in rather exaggerated terms.
The finding of fossil bones in the river bed may be
quite authentic. If so, one need not suppose that
they were really in a coffin of earthenware or were
actually human. All we need suppose is the remains o:
some large prehistoric animal resting in a clay bed.
A find of this sort would at once suggest a giant's
grave. But the correct procedure, as analagous instances show, would be to consult an oracle for an
identification of the discovery. The interesting
point is that the distant sanctuary of Claros should
be chosen. There was the neighbouring shrine of
Daphne, outside Antioch. Also in the copious evidence
which Louis Robert has found to demonstrate the widtl
of Claros' contacts, even in the late second century
A.D. when they were at their most extensive, they do
not seem to have included links with Syria.
    It is unfortunate that Pausanias made no attempt
to date the discovery by naming the Roman emperor cor
cerned. If we have to suppose his personal presence
at Antioch, only Trajan and Lucius Verus had any
length of stay there before Pausanias' time. But a
consultation of this sort in Trajan's day seems unlikely. In the time of Verus Claros was already rising to fame in Asia, and so it would be more probable
but, if so, it is strange that Pausanias did not mention a contemporary ruler with greater precision.
More probably his description simply means that it wa
an imperial project with the emperor's personal approval, and a likely enough time for such an undertaking would be during Germanicus' eastern viceroyalty.
This also would fit with a possible reference in
Philostratus to the same discovery of giant's bones.
If so, the otherwise unexplained choice of Claros as
the oracle to consult may be attributed to the
influence of Germanicus. He had lately enquired of
the oracle there and may well have suggested to the
authorities of Antioch that they should put the problem to the same authority. The answer was of a conventionally safe kind; to identify the remains found
in the river as the body of the giant who gave it its

name. Also to call him Indian added a suitably exotic
colouring. Pausanias, who was a specialist in the
subject of oracles and prophets, had found this story
in some out-of-the-way source and recorded it for us.

One later occurrence of the name of Clarian Apollo
in Tacitus'<u>Annals</u> may show that some special devotion
to that sanctuary persisted among members of the
Julio-Claudian court. In 49 A.D. Agrippina the younger having succeeded in achieving marriage with her
uncle Claudius, proceeded to avenge herself on a former rival, Lollia Paulina. She trumped up accusations
that Lollia had been guilty of the treasonable offence
of seeking to obtain prophecies about the emperor's
future, particularly about what interested her, his
matrimonial prospects. In Tacitus' phrase the accuser
brought up against her "astrologers, wizards and an
image of the Clarian Apollo questioned about the emperor's marriage".(24) Attempts have been made to explain away or amend the sentence but it is best taken
literally, rather than to suppose that a message sent
to Colophon is meant. Instead it implies that Lollia
possessed an image dedicated to the Clarian Apollo -
probably a miniature copy of his cult statue - and by
the use of magicians was alleged to have tried to extract from it a divination about Claudius. Such magical inspiration of statues to produce prophecies was
a familiar process in the second and third centuries
A.D. It is less usual to find evidence in this period, but this does not make it implausible. The interesting point is that once more we encounter the
Clarian Apollo as favoured in Julio-Claudian circles.
It is the last instance of this kind and one may suppose that with the death of Nero and the advent to
power of Vespasian this fashion lapsed.

Chapter Nine

THE LATE-FLOWERING OF CLAROS

Claros in the Julio-Claudian period had benefited by
a restoration of its cult statues and its adyton. It
had also been distinguished by the visit of Germanicus. But the temple was still not completely built.
The facade for instance was not finished. Also the
method of enquiry which pleased Tacitus by its sim-
plicity and wonder may not have charmed others to an
equal degree. We find instead another picture of the
effects of consulting the Clarian Apollo very different in some ways from Tacitus' account, but not necessarily inconsistent with it.

Oenomaus, a Cynic philosopher, had been born in
Gadara, the out-of-the-way town of Transjordania,
which some two centuries before had produced the famous love-poet and anthologist, Meleager. (1) The date
of Oenomaus' activity is uncertain, but he appears to
have spent his last years in his native place in the
reign of Hadrian. His works would scarcely be known
if it were not that Eusebius, the great Christian
apologist, found in this obscure predecessor a weapon to
attack the pagans in what was one of their favourite
strongholds, their oracles. Oenomaus had published
a book entitled "Exposure of Cheats", which was an
assault on the credentials of Greek oracle-centres.
This venomous work seems to have been occasioned by a
succession of episodes connected with Apollo of
Claros, which had so disillusioned and infuriated
Oenomaus that he wrote his "Exposure".

As he narrated the happenings, he had enquired
on some subject connected with commerce and received
in answer three verses in trochaic tetrameters.

"In the land of Trachis lies the fair garden of
Herakles containing all things in bloom for all
to pick on every day, and yet they are not dim-
inished, but with rains continually their

142

weight is replenished." (2)

This vague picture of an earthly paradise combined with the place-name Trachis (which suggested to Oenomaus some connection with the Greek word "rough") seemed to promise in symbolic phrases, which were appropriate to the style of prophecy, bountiful rewards for his labours. But Oenomaus was seriously put out when he was told by someone in the crowd that they had heard exactly the same response given to one Callistratus, a merchant from Pontus. Further investigation on his part suggested that this stock reply had been issued to numbers of enquirers in all walks of life, who had all experienced the toil, but none of whom had found the beautiful garden.

Two subsequent enquiries of Oenomaus at Claros had no better results. One of the two responses, at least as preserved in our manuscripts, is unintelligible without emendation, and as the example was cited by Oenomaus for its absurdity, it is impossible to establish a correct reading. The other response, also presumably meant to be interpreted allegorically, ran:-

"From a widely whirling sling a man shoots stones and slays with his throws geese huge and fed on grass."

On this final instance of an obscure oracle Oenomaus pours his ridicule. He had some justification, if, as one is apparently meant to assume, the prophet simply repeated a selection like this from a series of allegorical verses and fitted them to each enquirer almost at random.

Oenomaus is, of course, at best a somewhat prejudiced witness. He was presumably already a convinced Cynic before he consulted Apollo at Claros, and his enquiries were not strictly sincere, but were meant to test the oracle. Actually, the Cynic philosophy need not require its members to be utterly sceptical of oracles if, as Julian the Apostate pointed out, Diogenes their founder believed that his life had been guided by a response of the Delphic oracle. So perhaps Oenomaus would have maintained that before his detection of the fraudulent character of the oracle at Claros, he had had an open mind on the subject. But significantly in Plutarch's approximately contemporary dialogues the Cynic interlocutor is chosen as the typical sceptic on this subject. The "Exposure of Cheats" was clearly a very one-sided document, and leaves the same uncertainty as is produced by the other

second-century satirist, Lucian. One wonders how far
the account may have been distorted by exaggeration
or even invention. Still it is significant that the
method of 'prophecy' pictured by Oenomaus could lie
behind Tacitus' sober description of the oracle's
procedure. A priest, untrained in literary composition, might produce as required one of a number of
stock answers in verse. They might mostly not have
been as absurd and open to scorn as those which Oenomaus quoted, and if the priest had been challenged he
might have maintained that his method was not more
unjustifiable than the method of drawing written responses by lot, which was a favourite form of oracle in
Asia Minor. The prophetic inspiration consisted in
fitting the right response to the enquirer by intuit-
ion.

Such an almost mechanical method of divination,
if one accepts it as at one time practised at Claros,
does not explain how the oracle could ever achieve a
permanent reputation for excellence. Yet in the period from the mid-second century A.D. for a hundred
years or so Claros is regularly mentioned in conjunction with Didyma as one of the two leading oracles of
Asia Minor. The temple itself also has furnished
abundant numbers of inscriptional records showing that
embassies from many different cities in the Greek
world came to pay homage. Also within this same period, we have contemporary evidence from a number of
widely scattered places for a quite different style of
oracular response from that attributed by Tacitus and
Oenomaus to the prophets of Claros. They are lengthy
poems sometimes composed in a variety of metres and
obviously designed to answer a particular enquiry on
behalf of a community on one occasion only.

The easiest supposition to explain these phenomena is to conjecture that at some date, probably in
the later years of Hadrian's reign a reformation may
have taken place in the functioning of the oracle at
Claros whereby the procedure was improved and applied
with a new strictness. It may partly have been influenced by a general movement of thought and social
custom such as we have already observed in the history
of Didyma. But also there may have been some particular factors at work locally leading to changes in the
ritual of consultation such as we have no reason to
suppose for Didyma. It is unlikely that the criticisms of Oenomaus had anything to do with it, nor need
we suppose alternatively that his attacks had any adverse effect on the oracle's popularity. Though one
cannot be certain, it seems probable that Oenomaus'
book did not attract much attention or win any wide

circulation. It is never cited until about 315 A.D.
when Eusebius was writing his 'Preparation for the
Gospel' at Caesarea in Palestine. He then appears to
have rediscovered Oenomaus' work of nearly two centuries previously. It may have been preserved in the
great library collected by Pamphilus, to which
Eusebius had access. As Oenomaus of Gadara had lived
on friendly terms with the Jews of Tiberias and was
remembered with great respect in their tradition, one
can suppose that it would have been possible to obtain
copies of his work in Galilee. Eusebius found in it
a useful weapon against the pagan claims based on
their oracles. To employ against them one of their own
philosophical writers was a specially effective blow.
The only later author, apart from Lexica, to cite
Oenomaus was Julian the Apostate. He will have encountered him in Eusebius, and in two of his polemical
pamphlets against the Cynics he attacks him bitterly.
As a philosopher who was used by the Christians
against the pagans he was particularly odious to the
apostate emperor. (3)

One other feature about Oenomaus' book is worth
noting. When he set out to show up the ambiguities
and absurdities of oracular responses, apart from the
three given to himself, which we have already mentioned, he quotes no examples from Claros, nor for that
matter from any other oracle centre except Delphi.
The explanation must be that he could not find in
general literature instances where responses of the
Clarian Apollo were quoted verbatim. His only plentiful source of prophecy would be the Pythia. This
situation is even more likely if we picture him as
writing in his native Gadara. If he had been a
scholar working in Alexandria or one of the other
great centres of learning, he might have been able to
delve in obscure specialist authorities. As it was,
he used mostly the responses familiar from classical
literature which he probably found assembled in some
collection. (4)

The date of Oenomaus' consultations at Claros
cannot be determined with any precision. If he wrote
in Gadara after his return to his native place and was
on friendly terms with Rabbi Meir, whose <u>floruit</u> fell
in Hadrian's reign, he may plausibly have consulted
Claros in the later years of Trajan or the early years
of Hadrian; otherwise, about the same time when Tacitus as proconsul of Asia may have visited the place.
The reformation of the oracle, which we have conjecturally assumed, may have taken place some ten or more
years later. The only other allusion to Claros which
falls in the twilight period before the new dawn occurs

in Dio Chrysostom (c.40-120 A.D.). In a rather flip-
pant passage in a speech about his birthplace he sur-
veys the various cities which claimed to be the birthplace of Homer and remarks: "One does not take much
account of Chios or of Colophon, though the latter
presents Apollo as no worse poet than Homer." This
is apparently meant as an ironical reference to the
verse responses emanating from Claros. Dio seems to
have expected his audience in Bithynia to know that
Apollo Clarios produced answers in verse of a not
very distinguished quality. (5)

Such then was the situation at Claros about the
end of the first century and the first quarter of the
second when it suddenly rose with the "great flowering
of the oracles of Asia". Louis Robert found one piece
of evidence which pointed to what may have been a major factor in the change. The stones of the entabla-
ture of the temple were excavated and proved to contain an inscription in fine characters across the facade naming the emperor Hadrian in the nominative
case. Evidently he was described as dedicating the
temple to Apollo, and this can be taken as proving
that by some imperial benefaction he paid for the completion of the peristyle and the front of the building
which had been left unfinished since the Hellenistic
period. The inscription by the titles must date between 135 and 138 A.D., but work on the building may
have been started much earlier. Actually half a century later Pausanias could write of both Didyma and
Claros as uncompleted. This statement was proved to
be true of various details at Didyma, and it would not
have detracted from the justification of Hadrian's impressive inscription at Claros if there still were details left undone. (6)

The official undertaking of the temple by Hadrian might of itself have caused an upsurge of popularity and prestige. The earliest indication is in
the first datable record of an embassy to the sanctuary, sent from Amisos in Pontus in 132 A.D. This was
to be the commencing of an immense series of such records of embassies from cities (proskynemata). (7)
Already, however, it refers to a developed form of
ceremony which was to be typical of this new period in
the oracle's activity. The ambassadors "had been initiated and had made their entrance". The "entrance"
was presumably the formal approach to the hall of consultation by means of the basement passages. The initiation is a new feature, which had not been mentioned by Tacitus or Oenomaus. As Nock suggested, the enquirers "underwent a rite, possibly purificatory," as
a preliminary to the ceremony of consultation. The

second century A.D. was a period when mysteries and
initiations as features of religious cults were
achieving a new popularity. So it is appropriate if
at Claros a greater sophistication was introduced into
the proceedings. This is confirmed by the record that
there was no longer just one priest, but three offi-
ciating ministers, a priest, a singer of oracles and a
prophet. The unlettered official of Tacitus' narrative, if he still functioned, was backed up by a professional singer of verse.

The next writer to mention enquiries at Claros is
a friendly witness, very different from Oenomaus.
Aelius Aristides was a most distinguished orator of
the Second Sophistic movement. His home was in Asia,
and his copious stock of orations and other works
show him to have been a man of deep, and even superstitious, piety and also a very introspective neuras-
thenic. He would not have doubted the genuineness of
oracular prophecy as a phenomenon, but he felt himself
so frequently the object of direct communication from
the gods by dreams or omens that he did not often call
on official divination to help out his own private revelations. However, he records one such instance when
he was lying ill in Lebedos. "When I had recovered a
little, the thought occurred to me to consult the god
at Colophon both on the subject of my present symp-
toms and about my general ill-health. Colophon is not
far from Lebedos, and the sacred night happened to be
impending. Having decided what to do, I sent Zosimus
(his foster father), and when the night arrived the
following oracular response referring to me was given
to him:-

> 'Your illness will be healed for you and you will
> be cured by Asclepius, who honours the famed city
> of Telephus, not far from the springs of the
> Caicus.'" (8)

This reply is very different from those given to
Oenomaus. The meaning is plain and simply expressed
without obscure ambiguities, and it answers directly
the question put by Aristides. Of course, it might be
true that these verses were the stock reply given to
enquiries from invalids. To assure them that Asclepius at Pergamum would heal them was a rather obvious
solution for the problem, since his temple at this
period contained the most famous and elaborate sana-
torium in Asia Minor. But one need not assume that
Apollo of Claros used exactly this same formula to
other enquirers. It is probably a fair sample of the
kind of response given at this period to private

questions; the form used for public questions presented by embassies from cities was, as we shall see, much more elaborate. One notes, however, that as in the case of Oenomaus, the prophet did not use hexameters. This time the metre is iambic tetrameters. Also by his reference to the "sacred night" Aristides' narrative seems to indicate that enquiries could only be made on certain occasions, which would not in itself be surprising, but also that the consultation did not take place in day time, but by night. There is no suggestion of this in Tacitus' account of Germanicus' visit, and it looks as though this may be another instance of the changes introduced into oracular procedure at the time of the reformation. Initiation and a nocturnal ceremony would go well together and both help to increase the solemnity of the occasion.

Aristides' other reference to Claros is of a more general character. He mentions an earthquake which shook the province of Asia when Albus was pro-consul (probably in 149 A.D.). "The people of Ephesus and Smyrna ran about among themselves in a panic. At one time they sent to Claros, and the oracle-centre was the scene of a struggle to enquire. At another time with symbols of supplication they went round the altars and the marketplaces and the circuits of the cities, nobody having the courage to stay at home, and generally they exhausted themselves in making supplication". The motive behind Aristides' picture of these hysterical scenes was to contrast it with his own sober and dignified form of sacrifice. But for our purpose it serves to confirm the view that by the mid-second century A.D. Claros was becoming a greatly recognised centre for divination. From this time it is not unusual for it to be mentioned in company with Didyma in general contexts. The first example is in Lucian's diatribe against Alexander of Abonuteichos. He represents this false prophet as sometimes advising those who consulted him to put their enquiries instead to the Apolline oracles of Claros or Didyma or to Amphilochus' shrine at Mallus in Cilicia. To illustrate the practice Lucian quotes the hexameter line in which Alexander's deity, Glycon, a reincarnation of Asclepius, was supposed to give his instructions:-

> "To Claros hie now, that you may the voice of my father (Apollo) hear."

Later in the same essay Lucian represents someone as interrogating Glycon on the authenticity of oracles and referring to Claros together with Didyma and Delphi as the examples. This sort of association

of these three or of Didyma and Claros became usual
in subsequent literature whether it was favourable to
their oracular claims or whether instead it was a
Christian writer attacking them as spurious. (10)

Another illustration of the importance attached
to Claros in the later second century A.D. can be
taken from the romance of 'Anthia and Habrocomes'
(1,6). If its author, Xenophon, was an Ephesian, as
stated in the Suda, he would have been well-placed to
know the practices of Claros. The starting scene of
the novel is set in Ephesus, from where the parents
of the love-sick couple send to that oracle-centre to
enquire about their ailment. The response consists of
nine lines of hexameter verse in a turgid style with
no attempt to reproduce the diction of epic. Instead
it contains two unique compound adjectives. Xenophon
gives no local colour to the consultation of the
Clarian Apollo, and as has been noted, his account of
happenings in Ephesus also does not fit with a close
knowledge of the city. So though he probably wrote
somewhere in Asia Minor between 150 and 200 A.D., it
is reasonable to suppose that he only knew of Claros
and its responses by hearsay, and simply chose to make
use of that oracle-centre for the convenience of his
fiction. However the fact that Claros, like Didyma,
was borrowed for the plot of a contemporary novel,
shows that it had a popular reputation in the later
Imperial period.

It is in the latter half of the second century
A.D. also that for the first time we come across
inscriptional records of the responses of the Clarian
Apollo. They resemble the contemporary replies from
Didyma in one respect only. Like them they are wordy
and elaborate, which presumably suited the expectat-
ions of the time. But they differ in so far as they
are normally written in other than epic metre. The
preference for iambic or trochaics shown in the earlier brief examples preserved in literature continues
to assert itself in the inscriptional records. Also
in one way our sources curiously differ from those of
Didyma. The main examples preserved from that oracle
were inscribed in the sanctuary itself or in the
territory of Miletus. Didymaean responses are not
usually found in the cities of those enquiring. The
reverse is true of Claros. While Louis Robert found
very numerous records of sacred embassies and choirs
attending at the sanctuary, he did not find there a
single text of an answer delivered. On the other
hand, a wide selection of verse responses of Clarian
Apollo have been found in various towns which had
enquired at the sanctuary. This may be merely an

accident of survival, but it looks more probable that
while the priests of Claros may not have approved the
dedication there of inscribed texts of responses, the
may have encouraged enquirers to inscribe the answers
locally to the honour of the god.

No less than five of these consultations of which
the answer is preserved in whole or part concern the same
subject - plague. Traditionally the great epidemic
took place in the reign of Marcus Aurelius and was
first encountered by the Roman soldiers when they penetrated as far as Seleuceia in Mesopotamia in the year
165. As the army retreated, it was said to have carried the plague with it and so spread it through the
Roman empire. Unfortunately, none of the inscriptions
containing these oracles are datable by any internal
reference. So it cannot be proved that they actually
refer to this outbreak. But the highly emotional and
horrific language used in some of the responses could
only be appropriate on the occasion of some unusually
severe epidemic. In general style they would be
plausibly assigned to this period, and the strong resemblances in form and content between them suggest
they they are an inter-related group. Of course, they
may have been spread over quite a number of years, as
references in our literary sources suggest that the
initial outbreak was followed by recurrences of the
disease. (11)

One of the most striking responses comes from
Caesarea Troketta, a very unimportant little town in
the mountainous interior of Lydia. It was inscribed
on the base of a statue of Apollo the Saviour, which
had been set up in accordance with one of the instructions contained in the oracle. The first line is
missing, but it must have been part of an address in
the vocative case to the embassy of enquiry, whose
subject was evidently relief from an attack of the
plague. It continued:

"...You who inhabit Troketta beside snowy Mount
Tmolus, honoured by Bromios and the most mighty
son of Cronos, why indeed now in amazement do
you wend your way to my threshold, desiring to
approach the pavement of truth? To you in your
care I shall shout a prophecy all of verity.
Woe! Woe! A powerful disaster leaps onto
the plain, a pestilence hard to escape from, in
one hand wielding a sword of vengeance, and in
the other lifting up the deeply mournful images
of mortals newly stricken. In all ways it dis-
tresses the new-born ground which is given over
to Death - and every generation perishes - and

headlong tormenting men it ravages them.
    Such are the evils which are intended at
once...
But, Ionians who are eager to see an escape from
these things in accordance with divine law, who
indeed have contrived to come near to my aid,
from seven fountains strive to provide pure liq-
uid. Fumigate it from afar and draw it off eagerly and sprinkle the houses at once with nymphs
who have become pleasant.
    In order that unstricken the men who are
left behind on the plain may achieve to their
fill the fair things out of the blessings which
are revived again, straightway provide that you
set up Phoebus in the midst of the plain, with
one hand wielding (a bow)..."

This is a very elaborate and ecstatically worded
composition whose precise meaning in places is difficult to determine. But basically it is simply an
expansion of a traditional pattern of reply. The god
begins by greeting the embassy and expresses surprise
at their coming. Then he describes in horrific terms
the plague which is the subject of their appeal. At
this point, there is a gap in the text, but it continues with the next main section - the god's remedies.
These consist of a ritual lustration and fumigation
for the houses and the setting-up of a statue of Apollo
in the fields to ward off the attack.
    The whole is also an elaborate metrical composit-
ion. It begins with three lines of formal address in
hexameters - the traditional metre of most oracles.
This changes into iambic tetrameters as the god expresses his surprise. The pestilence's attack is described in iambic trimeters, and the metre is altered
again for the remedies. The lustration is prescribed
in anapaestic tetrameters; the erection of the statue
in trochaic tetrameters. Presumably the whole response was sung by the Thespiodos, who must obviously
have been a versatile performer of high professional
ability. It is interesting that so elaborate an
effort was expended on the answer given to one very
minor embassy from an unimportant town. It suggests
an entirely different attitude to enquirers from that
which enraged Oenomaus. Of course it is impossible
to prove that some of the matter is not conventional
and reused. But the whole content of the response
suggests otherwise. We shall see that some features
in the prescription are paralleled elsewhere, but this
particular expression of them appears to be unique
and well adapted to the needs of a small isolated

agricultural community.

A very similar style of oracular response, but surviving in a much more fragmentary condition, was inscribed on a stone found on the promontory of Gallipoli at the site of the ancient Callipolis. (13) When complete it ran to some thirty-two verses; so it must have been on much the same scale and pattern, and like the Troketta response it was composed in a series of different metres. The strong resemblances in form are supported by similarities in content. Also it would be likely enough, as the proskynemata from Claros show, for towns in this neighbourhood to have relations with that oracle. So though the name of the Clarian Apollo is not now preserved in the record, the prophecy can reasonably be assigned to his shrine.

It begins with four lines of hexameters addressing the city, followed by four lines of anapaests criticizing the citizens. Then the horror of the pestilence is described in twelve lines of iambic trimeters, beginning as in the Troketta response with the exclamation "Woe! Woe!" With the change to the subject of remedies the metre becomes iambic tetrameters ending again with hexameters. The variation of pattern throughout the two responses is similar, but apart from using hexameters for the opening address the particular metres chosen for the various sections differ. Hence it does not appear that the Thespiodos had one metre and melody, for instance, for prescribing remedies.

The cure ordered in this instance is first a holocaust sacrifice and then a statue as required from Troketta:-

"If you are anxious to behold an escape from grief, sacrifice to the gods beneath the earth, heed the libations on each occasion. To the god of the fine locks of hair (Hades) slaughter a he-goat and to the goddess (Persephone) a sheep, both victims black. ...When the black blood has entered the pits, then pour in the loose earth from above together with crowded remedies (?). But as for the victims let the flame consume them together with perfumes and sweet-smelling frank-incense. Also one must consecrate the pyre with sparkling wine and grey sea-water, and besides set up (a statue of) Phoebus, plague to men, bearing his bow, who is the driver-away of the epidemic. If another hateful distress should come nigh to the people, pityless, subduing men, then hereafter a remedy will follow it."

The final instruction to erect a statue is
exactly as in the Troketta response. Why the one town
should be required to conduct a lustration and the
other an atoning sacrifice is perhaps not to be explained, but may have been according to the impulse of
the Clarian prophetes. If any rational motive lies
behind the difference, it may be that the town in
Thrace had a local cult of Persephone known to the
priestly authorities.

Somewhat different from this pair of responses in
varied metres are another pair of responses on the
plague which are composed entirely in hexameters, but
are laid out on a similarly generous scale. In one
the enquirer was the city of Hierapolis (Pamukkale)
in Phrygia. The response was one of several miscel-
laneous oracles which had been inscribed on some
building in the late second century A.D. by a private
individual, who recorded in a heading that he did this
"in accordance with the command of the founder-god
Apollo for his own sake". The content of this response shows clearly that it was given by the Clarian
Apollo in answer to an enquiry from the city seeking
a remedy for the plague. The first lines containing
the address to the embassy are lost. Apollo begins by
explaining that the epidemic is due to the wrath of
the Earth Goddess, apparently because of the slaying
of her off-spring, Python. The first complete sentence of the text starts:-

"But you are not alone in being injured by the
destructive miseries of a deadly plague, but many
are the cities and peoples which are grieved at
the wrathful displeasures of the gods. The painful anger of the deities I bid you avoid by libations and feasts and fully accomplished sacrifices.

Firstly then to Earth the mother of all
bring a cow from the herd into her hall of four
measures, and sacrifice it with sweet-smelling
incense and then ravage it with fire, and when
the flame has consumed it all, then sprinkle
around with libations and a mixture of honey and
soil all together. Secondly sacrifice an un-
feasted offering to the Aither and to the gods of
the heavens, all sweet-smelling with incense.
To Demeter, as your custom is, and to the gods of
the underworld, perform rites with victims free
from pollution, and to the heroes in the ground
pour drink-offerings in accordance with the
precepts, and continually be mindful of Apollo
Kareios. For you are descended from me in family

and from Mopsus, the city's patron.

Also around all your city gates consecrate
precincts for a holy statue of the Clarian Phoebus equipped with his bow, which destroys diseases, as though shooting with his arrows from
afar at the unfertile plague.

Moreover when after you have wrought
appeasement and the evil powers have departed,
I instruct your boys with maidenly musicians to
come together to Colophon accompanied by libations and hecatombs in willing spirit. For indeed often I have saved you, but I have not received a share of fat to gladden my heart. Yet
it is right not even to be forgetful of men who
have done you benefit. If you perform what it
is seemly for godfearing men to accomplish,
never will you be in painful confusions, but with
more wealth and better safety..."

The remainder is missing, but cannot have contained
much more.

The prescriptions given by Apollo for the immediate cure are partly familiar - the statue of Apollo
with a bow at the gates - and partly a variant on the
instructions in the Gallipoli inscription - holocaust
sacrifices - but this time to the elements (the earth,
the heaven and the underworld). It is unfortunate
that the initial sentences of the response are lost as
they appear to have explained the plague in terms of
the wrath of the Earth Goddess, and therefore provided
some motive for a ritual of atonement.(15) This is in
contrast to all the other oracles about the plague, in
none of which, so far as their sometimes fragmentary
condition allows, is there any trace of an explanation
of the disaster. It is simply taken elsewhere as a
fact. Incidentally, in none of these inscriptions is
there any confirmation of the picture given in our
literary sources of an epidemic carried from the east
Perhaps one may suppose that the immediate impression
made on contemporaries was of a blow from heaven
rather than of a spreading infection.

The response, however, contains a more remarkable
feature in its instructions for the thank-offering to
be sent to Claros after the cessation of the attack.
It was to take the form of a sacrifice and libation
accompanied by a choir of boys and girls performing a
hymn. This was one of the proskynemata, which are
plentifully recorded in inscriptions all over the
sanctuary at Claros. In some instances these records
contain a statement that the ceremony was performed
in accordance with an oracular command, but this is

the only example of such a verbatim instruction being preserved. Also it is particularly interesting on this occasion for the illustration which it gives of the relations between different temples of Apollo. The inscription itself was found built into the walls of the temple in Hierapolis, where Apollo, as the heading shows, was reckoned the founder of the community, and the response itself reminds the citizens that they are descended from the god and from Mopsus. This probably alluded to the genealogy found in later authors that Mopsus was a son of Apollo. (16) No doubt this was not regarded as inconsistent with the older legend that his mother Manto was married to Rhacius. The Clarian Apollo bids the citizens of Hierapolis always be mindful of their local god, Apollo Kareios, but also claims their gratitude for averting the plague and calls for an offering in forceful terms. It may have been because, as our other inscriptions suggest, the Clarian Apollo had acquired a special reputation for averting plague, that Hierapolis had appealed to him rather than trusted for help to their local Apollo. Anyway the Clarian priesthood took occasion to adopt a politely patronizing tone toward Apollo Kareios, while insisting on their own prerogative.

The other response dealing with a plague, which was composed entirely in hexameters, is addressed to the city of Pergamum. (17) It is easy to imagine that this dignified metre was specially chosen because of the importance of this embassy. That the Clarian priesthood were conscious of this point is also indicated by the fact that no less than nineteen lines are spent in welcoming the ambassadors with a formal address. The heading also records that they had gone through the ritual of initiation. So clearly this consultation was treated as an important occasion. Apollo contented himself with prescribing an elaborate ceremony of choirs and sacrifices to be performed for seven days at Pergamum. The mystic number is the same as that of the seven fountains from which the men of Troketta were to draw their water. But there is no instruction about setting up a statue of Apollo, nor any demand that offerings be sent to Claros.

The text reads:-

"To the sons of Telephus, who dwell in the land of Teuthrania honoured more than others by Zeus the king, the son of Cronos, and by the offspring of Zeus the loud thunderer, and by Athena Atrytone the war-sustaining, and by Dionysus who brings forgetfulness of care and produces life,

and also by the healer of grievous diseases,
Paieon; among whom the sons of Uranus, the
Kabeiroi, above the peak of Pergamum, were the
first to wonder at Zeus the lord of the lightning
flash, as he was being born, when first he loosed
his mother's womb - to you I would truly speak a
safeguard in oracles without lies in order that
the people of the sons of Aeacus may not long
be worn down by a wretched pestilence. For that
will be pleasing to my son (Asclepius). Therefore I bid you, leader of the pilgrimage to the
shrine, divide into four the young men who wear
a military cloak beneath the divine citadel and
place four leaders over their bands. Of these
one with a hymn will sing the son of Cronos,
another Eiraphoites (Dionysus), a third the maid-
en Tritogeneia bold with the spear, and the
fourth Asclepius, my dear son. For seven days
let them sacrifice the limbs of victims on the
altars: to Pallas offering the meat of a two-year
heifer without blemish: to Zeus and Zeus Bacchus
of a three-year bullock and similarly to the son
of Coronis of the accustomed bull. When offering
the limbs prepare a feast, young men, robed in
cloaks all of you and not without your fathers.
At each libation as you pour it pray for a good
remedy for the pestilence from the mortal gods,
that far off to the land of the enemy it may
advance into the distance...."

The response broke off incomplete at this point,
but it may not have extended much further as the general sense would be satisfied by what is preserved.
The composition is carefully arranged. Pergamum is
correctly described as beloved by Zeus, Athena and
Dionysus, whose great sanctuaries on its acropolis are
well known, and also by Asclepius, whose imposing precinct faced the city on a neighbouring hill. The
choirs and sacrifices are also arranged in a fourfold
pattern corresponding to the deities. The response
also refers parenthetically to a local myth that
Pergamum was the place where Zeus was born, and links
this with the mystery-cult of the Kabeiroi. For the
rest the oracle is of a quite conventional kind in so
far as the hymns and sacrifices prescribed contain
no abnormal features. (18)

If one asks why the form of ritual prescribed for
Pergamum was so different, for instance, from that for
Troketta, while one cannot be certain of the reason,
it is obvious that the Pergamenes will have had a large
and well trained body of ephebes who could be expected

to perform the somewhat complicated ritual required.
Troketta could not have mustered enough participants
for such an elaborate ceremony. One may also ask why
the sacrifices on Gallipoli and at Hierapolis were to
be holocausts expressive of atonement, while Pergamum
would have the satisfaction of seven days' feasting.
Cynically one may wonder whether Claros found it
easier to adopt a minatory tone to these cities, but
could only address the great capital of Pergamum in
respectful terms and with authority for a celebration.
Also Pergamum is the one instance where no statue is
prescribed unless it came in the lost final sentences.
Perhaps Pergamum was known already to contain statues
of Apollo the Averter of Evil.

The last instance of a consultation of Claros on
the subject of a plague is only known from indirect
evidence. An epitaph in verse in a cemetery at
Odessos (Varna) honoured the memory of a citizen who
had been on an embassy to Apollo and had driven away
the disease (evidently through the success of the
oracular remedy which he had obtained). (19) No details of the procedures enjoined by the oracle are
preserved, but it serves to illustrate yet again the
important part played by the Clarian Apollo in this
connection.

About the same time Claros may also have given
instructions for dealing with another form of public
danger - piracy or brigandage. In the town of Syedra
on the easternmost coast of Pamphylia, Bean and
Mitford found an inscription in hexameter verse of
imperial date. It is evidently an oracle delivered
to the citizens, but the source is not stated. However Claros is very likely, in spite of the fact that
the metre is a conventional hexameter, since as L.
Robert has pointed out, these cities of Asia Minor
which were not specially Hellenic in tradition, tended
to consult Claros rather than Didyma. (20)

The text runs:

"Pamphylians of Syedra inhabiting a land in the
bordering territory of the people of mixed race,
set up an image of Ares, the blood-stained slayer
of men, in the midst of your town and perform
sacrifices beside it, while holding him in the
iron bonds of Hermes. On the other side let
Justice giving sentence judge him, while he himself is like to one pleading. For thus he will
be peacefully disposed to you, after he has
driven out the unholy mob far from your native
land, and will raise up much-prayed-for prosperity. But also you yourselves together put your

> hand to the hard task, either chasing them or
> manacling them in unloosable bonds, and do not
> give to delay the terrible vengeance on the
> plunderers. For thus you will escape from im-
> pairment."

One can see a certain similarity of underlying
principle between this and the responses about a remedy for the plague. The recipe is to institute a new
cult centred on the erection of an appropriate statue
In the case of pestilence this was Apollo; in the cas
of war it is Ares. The particular purpose in this
instance is to be fulfilled by the erection of a pec-
uliarly complicated group of figures. Ares is to be
shown in chains, held convicted by Hermes, while
Justice delivers sentence over his suppliant form.
This might be rather difficult to picture as actually
carried out in religious sculpture, if it were not fo
the fact that the group is several times illustrated
on the coinage of Syedra - a fact to which Louis
Robert has called attention. It was usual for the
cities of Asia Minor in the imperial period to employ
cult statues as the subjects on their coinage. Syedr
showed the group first in the reign of Verus, and
struck the design again nearly a century later under
Decius and some of his successors. This proves that
the oracle cannot be later than the responses about
the plague, which have been assigned to Verus' reign.
Probably, they were all approximately of the same
period.

What the exact trouble was which beset Syedra is
not clear. The word used for "plunderers" could be
equally applied to brigands by land or pirates by sea
The situation of Syedra on the border of Rough Cilicia, as indicated in Apollo's address, laid it open to
brigandage in the passes of the Taurus and piracy fro
the notorious haunts on the coast immediately to the
east of it. Of course, Syedra was not an independent
community, and the Roman government had the ultimate
duty of keeping the peace, but a certain amount of
responsibility for policing and maintaining public
order fell on the cities, and so it was quite appropriate for the Syedrians to enquire on the subject and
for Apollo to warn them in somewhat forceful terms at
the end of his reply that the solution depended to
some considerable extent on their own initiative.

Evidently the city of Syedra set up the group of
statues and presumably also established the cult.
Indeed they were so impresssed by the institution tha
they used this group as a design on their coins. We
have assumed that this first instance was probably

contemporary with the fulfilment of the enquiry. The
revival of the type under Decius might have corresponded to the disturbed conditions and dangers produced
by the invasion of the Goths, when the ritual recom-
mended by Claros nearly a century earlier might have
been revived.

This practice of enjoining the erection of cult-
statues as a remedy for difficulties is peculiar to
the oracle of the Clarian Apollo in contrast to that
of Didyma. No example exactly parallel occurs in the
Didymaean responses. In fact in one late instance the
god expressed his personal scorn for such offerings
in comparison with choral hymns which he enjoyed. (21)
Claros undoubtedly accepted and encouraged the worship
of visiting choirs, but it also showed this conspicuous approval of statues as the local centres of cult.

An inscription from near Hadrianopolis (Ederne)
in Thrace gives positive evidence again for this
practice. A group of Thracian ladies recorded that
they had dedicated "the ordained images of the gods in
accordance with the oracles of the Lord Apollo of
Colophon". (22) Who the deities were or what was the
motive of the dedication is not made clear, but at
least it can be listed as another instance in the late
second or early third century A.D. when Claros prescribed the erection of statues. It is possible that
a further example is to be detected behind a reference
in Pausanias. He is giving a quick survey of the
Agora in Corinth and lists in passing a statue of the
Clarian Apollo, but gives no further details or explanation. It is significant that the inscriptions
of the proskynemata show that the ancient cities of
Greece did not send embassies to Claros, but the Roman
colony of Corinth - the only recent foundation - did.
(23) The statue of the Clarian Apollo in their market
place may have been simply a spontaneous mark of their
devotion, but also it could have been enjoined by the
oracle on some official approach by the Corinthians.

In its practice of requiring the erection of
statues Claros may have exhibited a special line of
religious policy, but during the third century A.D.
it also exhibited several tendencies in oracular
responses which parallel developments which we have
already traced at Didyma. The three most conspicuous
are the grouping together of all gods and goddesses,
the rise in importance of the sun-god involving his
identification with Apollo and the acceptance of a
supreme god as behind and above the manifestations of
particular deities. In all three of these aspects
there is striking evidence for Claros' attitude, and
the dating, so far as ascertainable would suggest the

possibility that it may have led Didyma in some of
these developments.

The evidence for Claros sponsoring a pantheon of
deities is based on a highly peculiar and unexpected
collection of inscriptional records. For the first
and only time five votive memorials, all in the same
phrases, occur in the western half of the empire
and written in Latin. The best known of these comes
from Hadrian's Wall at the fort of Vercovicium
(Housesteads), where it was erected by the first
auxiliary cohort of the Tungri. (24) It reads:-

> "To the gods and goddesses in accordance with th
> interpretation of an (or the) oracle of the
> Clarian Apollo,"

followed by the title of the military unit. Inscriptions in exactly similar phrases, but without a ded-
icator's name have been found in Corinium (Karin) in
Dalmatia, at Nora in Sardinia, in a far inland site
in Numidia (Ciucul, Djemila) and at Volubilis in
Mauretania. There are many features about this evidence for an utterance of the Clarian Apollo which are
peculiar. First of all, the recurrence of the same
wording in five such widely scattered places is quite
unparalleled with any other oracular response and points
to some common origin behind all the inscriptions, which
needs to be explained. Secondly, the places themselves well off the main trade-routes of the empire,
exclude the possibility of separate personal enquiry.
One cannot picture, for instance, the cohort of the
Tungri being allowed to send an embassy from Hadrian'
Wall to Asia to consult Apollo. Even an enquiry by
letter, though physically not impossible, is extremel
improbable. In the Augustan period a member of the
Imperial court might have sent a written request from
Rome, but a couple of centuries later a detachment of
German auxiliaries on the furthest northwest frontier
of the Empire would be most unlikely to address a
communication to Claros. One would have to assume
that the same procedure was also adopted by unknown
individuals in the Adriatic, in Sardinia and at two
places in North Africa, and that all four produced
exactly the same answer as that given to the Tungri.
We have seen in earlier periods that the Clarian
Apollo might have repeated the same verses to different people consulting him. But it would be remarkabl
if the only evidence from the West for the oracle of
Claros all happened accidentally to contain identical
replies and express its meaning in the same words.

Nock was prepared to accept that the origin of

these inscriptions, as Picard had suggested, was in
some corpus of responses of general application cir-
culating under the name of the Clarian Apollo. (25)
One has then, presumably, to picture that copies of
this corpus were distributed to North Britain, Numidia, Mauretania, Sardinia and Dalmatia where they were consulted by five different parties needing guidance. On
looking up the appropriate passage they each found
and carried out instructions to set up a dedication
"To gods and goddesses". This is not impossible, but
it would be an extraordinary coincidence if only one
instance of this kind of use of a corpus of Clarian
oracles is extant, and yet that is preserved in five
identical examples. It looks more plausible to suppose that a single consultation lay behind these
parallel instances.

This line of argument leads to the proposal put
forward by Eric Birley that these dedications were
all occasioned by an enquiry of the Emperor Caracalla.
An emperor was the only authority whose writ could
run simultaneously in Britain, Dalmatia, Sardinia and
across North Africa. Also Birley shows that the Housesteads inscription supplied evidence for dating the
event. It could only have been set up when Tungri I
were there early in the third century. The occasion
of the enquiry was probably in 214 A.D. when Caracalla
visited the eastern provinces in preparation for his
war against the Parthians. He was a psychopath with
a morbidly superstitious nature. Dio Cassius, a
contemporary, describes how in 213 he had applied una-
vailingly to gods for a cure for his ills of body
and spirit. (26) On the occasion of his eastern journey he was still suffering severely from ill health,
and on landing in Asia proceeded immediately to Pergamum, where he stayed using the treatment provided
at the Asclepieion. It would be a likely occasion
for the emperor to have consulted Apollo at Claros.
He need not, of course, have attended in person, but
can have sent an embassy. Also his enquiry need not
have been confined to his health, but perhaps was
about his campaign against Parthia, or even about the
prosperity of the empire as a whole. One can suppose
that Apollo's answer, which may have been long and
wordy, contained what could be interpreted as advice
that it would be better to pray to the gods and goddesses in general. An instruction based on this
"interpretation" was then circulated to the military
commanders and the imperial procurators. The consequence was the setting up of a number of votive inscriptions, five of which have survived. That there
are not more extant need not be taken as surprising.

We do not know how explicit and imperative the imperial injunction was, nor whether it had required that
there should be an inscriptional memorial of the worship.

It is difficult to decide from this single instance how strong or sincere was the belief at Claros
in the universality of cult. Perhaps the prophet was
less exhibiting his belief in the truth of all religions than "hedging his bets" in dealing with an
emperor whose reactions were unaccountable. The sudden spread of the influence of the Clarian Apollo in
the western empire shows no signs of having continued
after the one impulse initiated by Caracalla.

The connection of Apollo with the sun in popular
worship is best illustrated by an inscription of a
very rustic kind on an altar in the backward region of
Yelinez-Serai (the upper Tembris valley) in Northern
Phrygia. (27) The enquirers were a local family of
private individuals who had asked for a method to
ensure prosperity for the crops. The response was:-

> "Set up for me in this place an altar for all to
> see, facing towards the rays of the far-seeing
> sun, and perform lawful sacrifices on it each
> month, in order that having become your protect-
> or, I may make things seasonable. For it is I
> who am the provider of fruits to mortals whom-
> soever I wish to preserve and to whom I know how
> to keep bringing good repute."

The wording of this answer is awkward and peculiar. This may be partly the fault of an ill-educated
stone mason, but ultimately it must go back to the
Thespiodos or Prophet at Claros. So probably it is a
production of the late third century when the oracle
was in decline. It may have been only at that stage
that the idea of equating Apollo with the sun was
accepted there. Possibly this identification had been
adopted more quickly and easily at Didyma, where the
early form of the legend of Branchus had recognised
Apollo as the sun-god. If the same belief had existed
at Claros in pre-hellenic times, as is quite possible
it had been blotted out by the traditions which connected Mopsus with the Epic Cycle. But as we shall
see in a later example the equation of Apollo with
the sun may have come not through mythology but
through the developments of philosophic theology.

One notes that this oracle contains a strong
assertion of Apollo's function as the god who provides
crops. This would have been to the classical world
an unfamiliar concept of his field of activity. It is

therefore perhaps significant that it recurs again in another response connected with the worship of the Sun. This is preserved as a somewhat fragmentary verse inscription from Nicomedia, which L. Robert plausibly claims for Claros. (28) Like that which we have just considered, its wording is somewhat clumsy, suggesting a late date. Its first lines were addressed to the city magistrate and advised sacrifice to the sun, the moon and the winds. A dozen lines from the middle are lost, but the last two lines indicate that the purpose was to guarantee a fruitful harvest.

> "For thus, as I bid, when you ply these things, citizens, as helpers of prosperity you will reap the crop bountifully."

This time one cannot say that Apollo and the sun are equated but the worship of the sun and the moon may be meant to parallel Apollo and Artemis. Also the promise of fertile harvests is linked with the fulfilment of those oracular commands.

By the end of the second century A.D. Claros may have been more conspicuous than Didyma for producing theological oracles, particularly those that expounded a syncretistic view of the government of the universe. At Didyma, as we have seen, this was combined with a new willingness to give recognition to the God of the Jews, and this tendency is even more clearly shown in a response quoted by Macrobius. Someone had asked the Clarian Apollo "Which of the gods is he to be regarded who is called Iao?" (i.e. Johovah or Yahweh). (29) The reply was:-

> "Men who have learned sacred mysteries should keep them hidden in secrecy. But if indeed you have small intelligence and a feeble brain, observe that Iao is the god above all gods. In winter he is Hades, at the beginning of the spring Zeus, the Sun in summer and in the autumn delicate Iao."

The oracle begins with a rather curious and paradoxical address to the un-named enquirer. He is warned of the ban against revealing doctrines learnt in religious mysteries. But Apollo does not therefore refuse to answer the question. Instead he explains scornfully that the truth should be obvious even to one of low intelligence. The revelation is that Iao is the same god who takes various forms throughout the four seasons - Hades, the god of the underworld in winter, Zeus in spring, the Sun, probably identified as Apollo, in summer and Dionysus in autumn. This last identification is probably the meaning of "delicate Iao". To modern thought "delicate" or "dainty" would seem a most inappropriate description of Jehovah, but to the Greek it was otherwise. From an early stage in their contact with the Jews they had accepted that the god of the temple at Jerusalem was Bacchus. This was linked with such notions as that the Holy of Holies contained a golden vine. Hence Jehovah could well acquire the epithet appropriate to the Hellenistic concept of the god of wine, and autumn might seem his proper season.

As Nock observes "this notion of a sovereignty of a supreme Being of whom the other deities are only functions derives from philosophy and exhibits itself with eclat in the Middle Platonic school of the second century A.D." It is no doubt from some such philosophical sources that the priestly authorities at Claros derived their inspiration.

This version of the belief in a supreme god as well as connecting with philosophy also has links with the mystery religions. To them the concept of the deity Aion - the ruler of time and eternity - was central, and here the picture of Iao as immanent in the cycle of the seasons is very expressive of this approach. It has also been suggested that the choice of the particular deities for the different seasons was guided by a wish to combine the prominent sects of the Eastern Empire. On this interpretation Zeus stood for the old Hellenic religion, Hades for Osiris and the cult of the Egyptian gods, the Sun for Persia and Zoroastrianism, and Iao for the Hebrew faith. At any rate the attempt to create by a process of syncretism a universal theology is clear and earnest.

The response from Macrobius appeared to attempt to preserve the persons of the conventional gods as to some extent dominant. But an even more complex and elaborate example, which raises difficult questions of historicity and interpretation shows a more mystical concept of the supreme deity. In its fullest form it is found in the Tübingen Theosophy where it is introduced with the heading: "One Theophilus by name enquired of Apollo whether you are God or another, and he replied with this oracle". There follow sixteen hexameters of very abstruse poetry. There would be no great justification for assigning this to Claros in particular any more than various other Apolline oracles in that corpus, if it were not that Lactantius in his "Religious Education" quotes the last three lines. He introduces them with the words:- "Apollo... replying from Colophon (whither I suppose he had emigrated from

Delphi induced by the charm of Asia) to some one who
asked him who or what ultimately God was replied in
twenty-one verses of which this is the principium." (30)
It is natural to accept this as proving at least
that Lactantius knew a version of the oracle which is
preserved for us in the Tübingen Theosophy and assigned it to Apollo Clarius. But some controversial problems remain. For instance, Lactantius mentions twenty-
one verses, while the Tübingen text contains only sixteen. It is easy of course to conjecture a lacuna of
five lines hidden in this copy, and it has been usual
to place it just before the last three lines quoted
by Lactantius. Again, the fact that Lactantius chose
to describe his quotation as the principium of the
response raises difficulties. If the word was used in
its simplest meaning and should be translated "beginning", one would have to suppose that the version
which Lactantius knew was very different from that of
the Tübingen text, being not only five lines longer,
but also starting with the last lines of the Tübingen
version. But Buresch suggested that "principium"
should instead be translated "main point", and this
suits the context in Lactantius, who did not want to
quote in extenso this lengthy oracle, but wished to
deal precisely with the idea contained in the last
three lines, which are the real answer to the enquiry.
The text then runs:

"There is a burning which has occupied a vessel
above the heavens aloft - infinitely in motion, a
boundless eternity (Aion). He is not within the
grasp of the blessed gods, unless the Mighty
Father should plan his purposes so that he might
himself be looked upon. Where he is, neither
does the upper air bear stars with their kindly
light, nor is the moon with its pale light be-
held. No god meets him on his path, and even I
myself do not grasp him and shed on him my rays
as I whirl in the upper air. But God is in form
the vast channel of a torch moving in a spinning
motion, and with a whistling sound. But if one
touched that heavenly fire, one could not divide
one's heart to understand it. For it does not
admit division, but is in incessant occupation.
Eternity (Aion) is united with Eternities by God
himself. ...Self-begotten, self-taught, without
mother, without stumbling, not giving place for
a name by word, dwelling in fire - that is God;
and we his ministering messengers are but a tiny
part of God."

This impressive production contains many of the inner features of contemporary philosophy and mysticism. But before it is considered further, a new piec of evidence needs to be added to the picture. In 197 George Bean published for the first time a legible text of an inscription of Oenoanda in Northern Lycia, and this was identified by Louis Robert as commencing with the three lines which Lactantius quoted from the Clarian oracle. Unfortunately, the setting and there fore the probable date and circumstances of the inscription were somewhat misunderstood, leading to fur ther dubious deductions. A. S. Hall, working on the Oenoanda Survey, now appears to have established that it is part of a shrine of the Most High God (Theos Hypsistos) founded in the latter half of the third century A.D. (31) The inscription was cut on an alta shaped design carved out of a block in what had been the Hellenistic wall of the city, which went out of use when the circuit of the fortifications had been considerably reduced (c.260 A.D?). This stretch of wall, when given up by the city, became available for worship. The choice of this spot in the wall, and th deity to whom it was dedicated were influenced by the fact, as Hall observed, that it is the first place in Oenoanda to be struck by the rays of the rising sun.

The text which Bean disclosed corresponds to the quotation in Lactantius, except that there was one interesting difference in reading. God was described as "not giving place to a name, but of many names". Clearly this part of the Oenoanda text is likely to b the original version, which would be quite acceptable to pagan thought. The lines in Lactantius and the Tübingen Theosophy had been amended so as to suit Christian thought and exclude the idea that any of th names of the pagan gods could have been appropriately applied to the supreme deity.

The remainder of the Oenoanda inscription continues in a different form and with different content; not as a direct oracular response, but as a third-person paraphrase in hexameter verse. "To those who enquire this concerning God - who he originally is - he replied: "God is the all-seeing upper air (Aither). To whom looking at dawn, pray as you gaze to the sunrise."

This second half of the inscription is evidently a kind of charter and justification for this place of worship. That it was a place of worship is demonstrated by another inscription lower down on the same stretch of wall which consists of a dedication of a lamp in accordance with a vow to the Most High God from a woman. This was inscribed on a similarly car-

ved altar design and was provided with a niche to hold
the lamp. Evidently the shrine did not belong to an
official cult of the city of Oenoanda, but to some
small community of citizens.

The oracular inscription seems to consist of two
parts which probably did not originally belong together. In fact, they contain a theological inconsistency. In the Tübingen text God is clearly stated to be
beyond the upper air (Aither): in the Oenoanda inscription he is identified with the upper air itself.
But those responsible for the Oenoanda inscription
may not have been aware of the inconsistency if they
had simply encountered the three lines as a quotation
in some literary source. Both parts of their inscription seem to be taken from some religious anthology
and neither of them as inscribed is a complete and
direct response given to the inscribers. Instead they
have, as it were, dedicated the site by putting up two
scriptural texts, one describing the nature of God and
the other prescribing worship at such a place. Only
the former need be attributed to Apollo Clarius on the
authority of Lactantius. The latter half may report
an enquiry and response at Claros on some other occasion, but it might have been from any other oracle-
centre.

If we revert to the full text of the oracular
response as given in the Tübingen Theosophy, the
concept of God is the quintessence of Greek mysticism.
The supreme deity is no longer, as in the Macrobius
oracle, manifested in a series of conventional gods
and even identified with one of them. Instead he is
above and beyond them and so superior to them that
they cannot even see him, unless his will agrees. He
is identified with fire, but, though this is not stated, this is obviously not the terrestrial element, but
the Primal Fire, which is described in the Chaldaean
Oracles as the energy of the Supreme God. In fact,
this response contains such echoes of the phraseology
and ideas of the Chaldaean Oracles that one cannot
suppose that it was produced before they had been
published and had had time to influence contemporary
theology. This suggests a date for the response not
earlier than the beginning of the third century
A.D. (32)

The history of our texts may then have run as
follows:- the question was put to Apollo at Claros
by a private individual soon after 200 A.D. (33) The
reply ran to twenty-one hexameter verses, of which
sixteen are preserved in approximately the correct
form in the Tübingen Theosophy. But a comparison
between that text and the Oenoanda inscription shows

the occurrence of one alteration attributable to
Christian influence and there may be more latent. This
particular change was already introduced before the
time of Lactantius. No doubt the response was reproduced in the collections of Porphyry and Cornelius
Labeo. It seems to have been from the latter, directl
or indirectly, that St. Augustine acquired his knowledge of the final lines. (34) But the text may have
suffered a further mutilation before it was reproduced
in the Tübingen Theosophy. Five lines were omitted,
probably where the lacuna has been proposed after line
13. These missing verses may have expanded further on
the subject of the nature of God in some way inconsistent with the Christian doctrine. The anonymous com-
piler of the Tübingen Theosophy was evidently intending to create a corpus of pagan oracles which could
be shown to be more or less consistent with Christian
theology, and may therefore have chosen to omit any
offending lines.

To the Christian reader the response was interesting for its detailed and intense description of a
transcendental deity far above all the pagan gods, bu
even more for its outspoken admission that these paga
gods were mere servants of the supreme God. The word
used is "angels" (angeloi), but it is probably better
translated as "messengers" or "ministers". For the
priestly official who composed the poem, the word
would not have the special signficance of the Christian use of "angels",though this is exactly what both
Lactantius and St. Augustine read into it. To them
Apollo Clarius was a demon, who to deceive his worshippers posed as an angel.

Even if we put aside this Christian gloss on the
passage, it is sufficiently remarkable that the proph
et should first put into the mouth of Apollo a passag
identifying him with the sun and then end by making
him describe himself as "a tiny part of God". In the
classical period it might not have been suitable for
Apollo to claim the position of king among the gods.
That title belonged to Zeus, and the Pythian Apollo
had been content to be accepted as the mouthpiece of
Zeus. But there had been a great change and development of ideas on the nature of deity owing to the influence of philosophy. Already early in the second
century A.D. Plutarch, while sincerely devoted to the
Pythian Apollo, was prepared in his dialogues to
represent a group of learned men at Delphi discussing
whether the failure of oracles could among other
reasons be due to the death or departure of the super
natural beings who had operated them. This response
of the Clarian Apollo at last follows this view to

its logical conclusion and makes the oracle itself declare that it is not the word of God himself, but of one of his humble servants.

It is tantalising that we cannot date with any precision these later responses of Claros. Only the oracle given to Caracalla, if correctly attributed, has a precise date. The prescriptions against the plague probably belong to the years after 166 A.D. But the other cult instructions are very uncertain in chronology. It would possibly be wrong to suppose that the theosophical responses must stand later in time and development than such more simply pagan instruction as the response from Yelinez Serai. One should perhaps instead picture the prophets as capable of replying in the same period on different levels of sophistication according to the type of their enquirers and the nature of their questions. To the simple peasant with a need for guidance and reassurance a plain command to establish a traditional kind of cult might be what was needed. But if a philosophical scholar came with a direct problem in theology the prophet deployed all his knowledge of contemporary mysticism.

The final stages of the history of Claros are completely obscure. One gathers from Louis Robert that the inscriptional evidence for the practice of proskynemata continued into the first half of the third century A.D. but no further. (35) Unlike Didyma there is no indication that the sanctuary was involved in such physical dangers as the Gothic raids, nor does the oracle appear to have been concerned in Diocletian's final struggle with Christianity or Julian's attempted revival of paganism. It may be significant in this connection that the remains of the temple show such little evidence of deliberate destruction by human hands. Both Delphi and Didyma exhibit the signs of an intentional demolition of the structure concerned with the production of oracles. But there is no great indication of vandalism at Claros. The underground passages remained intact with even such furniture as the marble bench for the enquirers and the stone omphalos still in position. Even the cult statues were not demolished. Much of the Apollo is missing, but, as it was held together by wooden tenons, it is impossible to tell whether it was systematically dismembered or simply collapsed through neglect and was later pillaged. It was evidently an earthquake during the Middle Ages that produced the main destruction on the site.

The very philosophic and cultured tone of the last response which we have considered may give a clue to the true personal feelings and belief of the final

prophets.   If so, would it be reasonable to suppose
that their relations with the Christians when they
came to power   may have been dignified and resigned?
Picard records the evidence for a large Byzantine
church and monastery in the plain of the Ales near
Claros. (36)   So there may have been no lack of Chris
tian neighbours.   But the end of the sanctuary of
Apollo seems to have been peaceful, and the alluvial
soil of the river valley closed quietly over it till
it was to be rediscovered after some sixteen centurie

PART III

Chapter Ten

OTHER APOLLINE ORACLES

Didyma and Claros are the two oracles of Apollo in Asia for which the largest amount of literary evidence is extant. Also they are the only two where excavation has been carried out with systematic thoroughness. For no others are both sources of evidence available in adequate quantity. In two instances, Gryneion and Patara, ancient authors supply a number of references, and inscriptional texts, found elsewhere, prove that they had an active existence as oracle-centres. On one site, Hierapolis (Pamukkale), a find of local inscriptions suggests the presence of an Apolline sanctuary with a practice of prophecy, but literary evidence is lacking. Otherwise, there are a number of places in Asia Minor where ancient texts or inscriptions indicate the presence of an oracular cult of Apollo, but with such limited information about it that there is little scope for discussion.

AEOLIS, THE TROAD AND NORTHERN ASIA MINOR

Gryneion reminds one somewhat of Claros. It and Notion both appear in Herodotus' lists of the twelve Aeolian cities. While Notion lay to the south, Gryneion was situated northward on the shore of the bay of Elaia, halfway between that town and Myrina. Its typical position on a small peninsula suggests that it was one of the original colonies, but it cannot be traced in history till the early years of the fifth century, when it was under Persian domination. After the battle of Marathon, Darius rewarded Gongylus, who had betrayed his native city of Eretria to the Persians, by giving him a small fief consisting of Myrina and Gryneion on the coast and Gambrion inland. He cannot have held it for long; for the coast was liberated after 479 B.C., and Gryneion was included

as a separate community in the Delian League. Its
tribute was assessed at a sixth of a talent annually,
compared with the third of a talent paid by Notion,
but later the amount was doubled, putting on the same
footing the two Aeolic cities with famous Apolline
sanctuaries. By the end of the Peloponnesian war at
latest Gryneion had fallen again into Persian hands,
and a descendant of the original Eretrian dynast named
Gongylus had re-established his claim, and held
Myrina and Gryneion. But after 399 B.C. no more is
heard of him. In 335 B.C. in the preliminary raiding
before Alexander's expedition Parmenio captured
Gryneion by storm and enslaved the inhabitants. So
evidently at that time it had been held in the Persian
interest. The city must have suffered severely, but
as it continued to issue coins in the third century it
still survived and remained an independent community.
By the end of the Hellenistic period at latest it had
become incorporated in the territory of Myrina. (1)

In none of these references to Gryneion in history is there any allusion to it as an oracle-centre.
For that aspect we must consult the geographers.
Strabo briefly notes in a gazetteer of the coast that
after Myrina and the Harbour of the Achaeans is "a
small town Gryneion and a sanctuary of Apollo and an
ancient oracle and a costly temple of white marble".
The picture is filled out a little more by Pausanias
who in a digression mentions "Gryneion, where is the
fairest grove consecrated to Apollo and consisting of
trees both fruit-bearing and those that do not bear
fruit, all those that provide some enjoyment in scent
or sight". This enthusiastic description was probably
based on the personal experience of a visit by the
guide-book writer. (2)

Strabo's description of the oracle as "ancient"
would imply that it had been active in the archaic
period, but he may have been drawing conclusions from
the existence of a mythological background to
Gryneion. For this we must turn to the poets and their
commentators. Vergil in the sixth Eclogue is cele-
brating his patron, Cornelius Gallus, the politician
and poet. He describes how the Muses bestow on Gallus
a gift of pipes "with which the origin of the Gryneion
grove is to be told that there may be no wood on which
Apollo boasts more". In other words, Vergil forecasts
that his patron will produce one of those _epyllia_
(miniature epics), which were the new fashion in Roman
poetry, on the subject of the foundation of the
Gryneian oracle-centre. There is no evidence that this
forecast was ever fulfilled. But of course Gallus
was not intending to write an entirely original poem.

He meant to reproduce in Latin verse a theme already
handled in Greek poetry. Servius is probably right
in supposing that the intended model was Euphorion of
Chalcis, the inventor of the _epyllion_. He had written
a poem in which the contest in prophecy between
Calchas and Mopsus was transferred from Claros to the
sacred grove at Gryneion, and the subject of the test
was appropriately the number of fruits on a tree. Why
Euphorion chose to set his scene in Gryneion cannot
be proved. It is unlikely that he had any ancient
authority for the transfer, as otherwise there is no
evidence connecting Mopsus with this sanctuary. It
may have been simply a wish to produce a variation on
the Hesiodic treatment. But also it might have been
that he wished to appeal to a patron, and, as we shall
see, the dynasty of Pergamum was connected with
Gryneion, which was much the nearest Apolline oracle-
centre to their capital. Euphorion ended his days in
Syria as librarian of King Antiochus III, but he may
very well earlier have courted the favour of the
Attalids. (3)

Servius reproduces the foundation legend of
Gryneion, which also presumably comes from Euphorion.
It was named after Grynus, the son of Eurypylus and
grandson of Telephus. When he became king, he was
challenged by his neighbours and summoned to his help
from Epirus Pergamus the son of Neoptolemus and
Andromache. This alliance achieved victory, and
Grynus founded two cities, Pergamum in honour of his
ally and Gryneion named after himself, in accordance
with an oracle of Apollo. This response was, as one
may suppose, the first prophecy of the god on the new
site calling for establishment of the temple. Anyway,
the legend, linking Pergamum and Gryneion in foundation was evidently a fabrication of the period of the
Attalids.

Another legend of the death of Calchas is told
in the same scholium by Servius. Calchas was planting
vines when a neighbouring prophet, as he passed by,
told him that he was making a mistake, for it was
fated that he would not taste the new wine from them.
But when the work was finished and the vintage was
done Calchas called to a feast his neighbours, including the prophet. Then he set the wine before them and
said he would pour a libation to the gods from it, and
not only drink of it himself, but also share it with
his guests. When the prophet, unperturbed, repeated
his original forecast, Calchas was seized with scorn
and began to laugh so immoderately that his breath
was choked, the cup fell from his hand, and he died
with the wine untasted. Nominally this story could be

regarded as a fulfilment of the oracle that Calchas
would die when he met a better prophet than himself.
But actually there is no contest in prophecy involved
The planter of the vineyard is simply a misguided
sceptic, and the motto of the tale is: "There's many
a slip twixt the cup and the lip ".

The story can be traced back to Aristotle's
Samian Constitution, where it was told of Ancaeus, th
son of Poseidon and Astypalaea - obviously a mythical
personage. The warning it put into the mouth, not of
a neighbouring prophet, but on one of his own slaves.
Again as with the contest of Calchas and Mopsus, it
appears that some Hellenistic author has transferred
to Gryneion with some modifications a legend belongin
elsewhere. This all suggests that by the 3rd century
B.C. when the Attalid dynasty gave it some importance
Gryneion, unlike Claros, had no genuine legends datin
from the archaic period.

Servius may have found this latter tale somewher
in Varro. For he goes on immediately to cite from him a
account of a practice at Gryneion which showed that
the place was regarded ritually as an asylum. If any
one entered the sacred territory in chains or fetters
these were stripped from him and nailed to a tree.
Elsewhere also Servius records a quite different derivation for Gryneion. It was called after an Amazon,
Gryne, whom Apollo met and outraged there - an unusua
legend which Lyne thinks would more suit the style of
Euphorion than those which we have already discussed. (4)

The limited number of mentions of Gryneion in
inscriptions from neighbouring sites fit into the pic
ture derived from literary sources. For instance, th
well-known agreement between Eumenes I and his mercen
aries was to be set up in the sanctuary; which suggests a link with the dynasty even at this early date
But also neighbouring city-states, such as Smyrna,
used it for the same purpose. (5)

This small amount of evidence would perhaps suggest that there was a handsome and important sanctuar
of Apollo at Gryneion by the third century B.C. at
least, but that its activity as an oracle-centre migh
be legendary. Such was the position when in 1954
George Bean published an inscription which he had
found in Caunus in Caria. This was an official recor
of an enquiry at Gryneion in the Hellenistic period.
"In the priesthood of Eunomus, the son of Leonidas,
Menodorus the son of Sosicles, of the Imbrian district
was sent to Gryneion and brought back an oracle. Wit
good luck the people of Caunus enquires what deities
they should appease so that their crops should be fin

and bountiful." The god replied: "When you honour
Phoebus, the son of Leto, and Zeus the ancestral god
you are fixing your fame for ever with bands that
cannot be loosed..." (6)

The text of the response itself is uncertain as
it has been restored conjecturally, but it is clear
enough that it consisted of at least two hexameter
verses: possibly more if the text continued in the
lost lower portion of the stone. Apollo gave clear
enough instructions that the Caunians should worship
him and Zeus, but may have continued with the metaphorical phrases expected of oracles. On the strength
of the script Bean would date the enquiry to the first
century B.C., probably before Caunus was given to
Rhodes by Sulla (c. 85 B.C.). At any rate suddenly
like a spotlight on a darkened stage there emerges the
sight of a city enquiring at Gryneion and being answered in such a typical fashion as to suggest that,
though this is the solitary piece of evidence, actually
a regular business of oracular consultation was in
operation at Gryneion throughout the Hellenistic period. Ecstatic prophecy seems implied, but whether by
a male prophet is not indicated. There is no need to
suppose that the enquiry and response should be taken
otherwise than their superficial meaning suggests.
Caunus had experienced a bad harvest or two and felt
the need for divine help to overcome what was possibly
the result of divine displeasure. Apollo reassuringly
suggested some traditional cults as a safe recourse.
Why the city of Caunus should have thought it advisable
to consult a centre as distant as Gryneion cannot be
explained.

In the Imperial Roman period the name of Gryneion
occurs as an oracle in two literary contexts, but with
no suggestion that the centre was actually active.
Vergil makes Aeneas cite it together with Patara as
the source of divine commands that he should settle in
Italy. Philostratus, when telling a legend about the
head of Orpheus prophesying, groups Gryneion with
Claros as one of the places which suffered by this
miraculous competition. The only factual reference is
in Aelius Aristides who gives a vivid description of a
journey on which he stopped there and sacrificed to
Apollo. But he makes no mention of an oracle or consultation. It is impossible to draw any conclusions
from this on the question whether it continued to
function at this time. (7)

The site of the town of Gryneion has been convincingly identified on a small peninsula projecting
into the bay of Elaia. But no remains of the temple
have been found. A platform which held a Byzantine

building might represent the place, but only excavation could establish the fact. It looks as though the marble temple which Strabo praised may have been bodily romoved in the Byzantine period to provide building material elsewhere. (8)

Besides Notion and Gryneion, one other colony of the Aeolians possessed an Apolline oracle. This was the rather insignificant town of Aigai some distance inland to the south west of Gryneion. According to Bean the temple is 45 minutes walk from the town. So excavation might confirm that the shrine was pre-hellenic and related to Aigai like Claros to Notion. Apollo there had the title Chresterios ("god of oracles"); so he must have given responses, but there is no literary evidence to fill out the picture. Two inscriptions contain the title: one is a dedication from Philetairos, the son of Attalus I, and younger brother of Eumenes II, which shows that about 200 B.C., the Attalids must have patronised the shrine; the other is a dedication in Greek and Latin in which the people of Aigai expressed their gratitude for "having been saved by Publius Servilius Isauricus the proconsul" (46-44 B.C.). Evidently, he must have conferred some considerable benefaction on the town. One is reminded of his successor, Sextus Appuleius, the second founder of Colophon. (9)

From Gryneion northward throughout the Troad is a region much devoted to the worship of Apollo. As Strabo says in another connection, "Along the whole of this coast as far as Tenedos Apollo is highly honoured, being called Sminthian or Cillaean or Gryneian or by some other appellation." (10) No records, literary or epigraphic, of any particular enquiries in the historic period at any of these centres have survived, but sometimes there is a legend about a consultation, in which case not surprisingly it is linked to the mythical traditions of Troy. While such stories are pure inventions, they would not be attached to particular temples, if they had never acted as oracle-centres.

The most important of these sanctuaries was that of Apollo Smintheus at Chryse. This was situated in a grove in the territory of the small town of Hamaxitos. The site was found by Spratt in the mid-nineteenth century, and an Ionic temple of middle Hellenistic date was partly excavated by Pullan. Since then the site was lost, only to be rediscovered in recent years. Though Strabo rejected the identification, one can suppose that this was the shrine of Chryses, the priest of Apollo, whom Agamemnon spurns in the first lines of the _Iliad_. Homer does not des-

cribe him as a prophet. Pausanias tells that there was
a tomb of the Sibyl Herophile in the grove, near a
statue of Hermes and a spring of the nymphs. When
Spratt visited the place, he saw "two springs of ex-
cellent water...near the site of the temple, one of
which issues from a small cavern". (11) This suggests
a setting for divination like those known elsewhere.
So it is not surprising to find a legend of a mythical
consultation. Ovid in the Fasti tells that when king
Ilus had just founded Ilion, the image of the Pallad-
ium fell from heaven on Mount Ida. Apollo Smintheus
was consulted and prophesied, that so long as it was
kept within it, the city would be preserved. The legend in some form can be traced back to the Epic cycle,
but Ovid appears to be the only author who assigns the
prophecy to a particular oracle-centre. It is impossible to tell whether he invented this detail.
Such a proceeding would be quite in keeping with his
practice. Alternatively he may have taken over the
attribution from some lost Hellenistic poet. (12)
     A more reliable, but indirect piece of evidence
that divination was practised at the Smintheion can
be extracted from Menander the rhetorician. (13)   In
the third century A.D. he composed a textbook on orat-
ory with fully worked-out examples. The specimen of
an epideictic oration is on the subject of Apollo
Smintheus and is evidently imagined as delivered to
the people of Alexandria Troas, which by that period
had taken over the territory of the shrine. According
to him Apollo after his birth in Lycia came first to
found the Sminthian oracle-centre. There he first
"moved the tripod", and the other oracle-centres of
the Greek world were all derived from it. The point
is repeated later in the speech where Menander devotes
separate sections to each of Apollo's main activities.
He claims that this is the greatest and specially
chosen function of the god, and that but for it the
world would be uninhabited for the lack of the colonies which had been established from Delphi and Didyma.
The credit for this blessing all belonged to the
Sminthian shrine as the first oracle. At this place
Menander interpolates what was meant to be a paren-
thetical instruction to the pupil:- "in this section
insert anything you may learn from traditions that the
god had performed from oracular responses." It is
unfortunate that the teacher did not trouble to give
us any of these examples himself. So we remain unin-
formed about actual responses of Apollo Smintheus.
But while the claim to historical precedence over
other oracle-centres can be discounted as the bombast
typical of a panegyric, the existence of a practice of

divination on the site can be taken as established.

Neither Ovid nor Menander mention what was the remarkable feature of Apollo Smintheus. Traditionally his title was derived from "sminthos", said to be a word meaning 'mouse', and he was credited with having earned it through overcoming plagues of field-mice. (14 But also the mouse was his sacred animal, and white mice lived in holes under his altar. Probably Menander felt that this was too trivial and vulgar a subject to introduce into his high-flown oration. Instead he inserted a quite irrelevant purple patch on Apollo's slaying of Python at Parnassus. But one may wonder whether the mice did not actually play some part in the act of divination. Pliny described the mouse as "a creature which must be taken seriously in portents". So it may be significant that Aelian also states that in the temple of Apollo Smintheus there was a mouse (presumably a carved figure) beside the tripod. He and Menander both refer to tripods in the temple, and it is possible that they are suggesting some use of that apparatus in the same way as at Delphi. But the existing evidence does not carry us further. (14)

Other Apolline sanctuaries in the neighbourhood of the Troad also are described as oracle-centres or have some implied connection with divination. Strabo mentions such a sanctuary of Apollo Actaios and Artemis in the plain of Adrasteia between Priapus and Parion. It had been wiped out in the fourth century B.C. when the fittings and stonework were removed to Parion where they were used in the construction of a famous altar designed by Hermocreon. A similar destruction, Strabo also adds, had overtaken another oracle-centre at Zeleia. In the case of the Actaean Apollo we have from another source a legend connecting it with the fall of Troy. Apollo of Priapus had warned Ilus not to settle on the Mount of Ate, which was said to have been the original name of the hill of Ilion. (15)

For one Apolline sanctuary there is only legendary evidence. This was at Thymbra just outside Ilion on the landward side. It is mainly known as the scene where Troilus was ambushed by Achilles. But it was also the place where Helenus and Cassandra as children received the gift of prophecy according to one story. When they were sleeping in the temples of Apollo and Artemis snakes licked their ears. Folklore recorded elsewhere that this was the way in which Melampus had received his power to understand the speech of birds. So it is a primitive motif. But whether it can really be used as evidence for a former oracle-centre at Thymbra is doubtful. (16)

There are also two places in the Troad associated with the Sibyl; Marpessos, her birthplace, and Gergis, which, like the sanctuary of Apollo Smintheus, claimed to possess her tomb. Unlike the Sibyl of Cumae in the Aeneid, there is no suggestion in our sources that this Sibyl could be consulted in the manner of the Pythia. She was a prophetess of doom uttering spontaneous forecasts of disasters. So the existence of her tomb in the sanctuary of the Gergithian Apollo cannot in itself prove that it was a place of oracular enquiry. (17)

The one other doubtful instance lying in this direction is an unspecified sanctuary of Apollo visited by Aelius Aristides on the way between Pergamum and Cyzicus. As it contained a "diviner" (mantis) it may have been an oracle-centre, but Aristides does not actually describe it as such. (18)

Chalcedon, opposite Byzantium, had several connections with prophecy. The local Apollo, as at Aigai, had the title Chresterios ('God of oracles'), and L. Robert has called attention to the recurrence of the omphalos on its coins and the importance of the prophetes among its magistrates. One may also perhaps detect the influence of the cult behind the fictitious attempt to derive the name of Chalcedon from a legendary son of Calchas, the Homeric prophet. He would have provided suitable antecedents for the oracle.

A pair of Hellenistic inscriptions show that the god could look after his own city's interests. He had issued a response authorising that the territory of Chalcedon should be 'sacred and inviolate', and this claim of asylia was recognised by Phocaea and Tenedos. Also the Delphic oracle gave its approval. But Apollo Chresterios could also be consulted by enquirers from a considerable distance. An inscription of 250 B.C. or a little later found at Istrus (Constanza) records a decree appointing a commission to be sent to Chalcedon to enquire about the acceptance of the cult of Serapis in the city. It is interesting that the Istrians, though a colony from Miletus, did not feel obliged to consult the Apollo of Didyma on such religious matters, but could go to the nearer oracle-centre on the Bosphorus.

These are the only certain instances of the consultation of Apollo Chresterios, but an oracle, which Zosimus assigns to the Sibyl or to Phaennis the Chaonian, may probably be interpreted as two responses in hexameters delivered by the Apollo of Chalcedon at the time of the third century Gallic invasion. All these instances belong to the third century B.C., and one might rashly suppose that it was the only period

of the oracle's activity. But it probably had a con-
tinuous career, and may, like Didyma and Claros, have
flowered again in the second century A.D. At least,
the author of the Anaplus of the Bosphorus, probably
writing shortly before Severus' siege of Byzantium
(195 A.D.) mentions the sanctuary enthusiastically as
'an oracle-centre not inferior to any of the chief
ones'.

The sanctuary was also connected with two instances of spurious prophecy. Alexander of Abonuteichos claimed to have dug up in the oldest precinct
of Apollo in the city bronze tablets which foretold
that Asclepius with his father Apollo would visit
Pontus. Two centuries later in the reign of Valens a
fraud of the same kind was repeated. An inscription
in hexameter verse referring in obviously apocalyptic
terms to contemporary events was said to have been
found on a marble block while it was being removed
from Chalcedon for use in Constantinople. One can
suppose that the tradition persisted that it was an
appropriate place for prophetic revelations. (19)

PHRYGIA AND THE MAEANDER VALLEY

So far we have surveyed the Apolline oracle-centres
the parts of Asia Minor touched by the original Hellenic migrations or by the colonisations of the archaic
period. But there is some evidence, though limited,
for other centres in the interior of the continent,
where the Greeks did not penetrate as settlers till
the Hellenistic age, but probably found already before
them sanctuaries with prophetic traditions linked with
local gods, whom they identified as Apollo. Such a
site was at Hierapolis (Pamukkale) in Phrygia, famous
among ancient authors as the scene of a Charoneion -
a natural source of toxic vapour. This was visited in
the imperial period by travellers, and was made a kind
of tourist attraction. We have accounts from two
visitors covering a lapse of two centuries. Strabo
and Dio Cassius both were allowed to test the toxic
power of the source by throwing small birds into the
vapour. Also they both reported that the only human
beings who could safely encounter the gas were the
Galli, the eunuch priests of Cybele. But though these
put on an act of venturing into the vapour to impress
the tourists, neither Strabo nor Dio record that the
place was dedicated to Cybele or any other deity. At
the end of the fifth century A.D., when these practices had long ceased and the natural aperture had been
to some extent built over, Damascius the philosopher

together with a colleague, Dorus, ventured successfully into the place. He described it as "a way down
under the temple of Apollo". (20)

The Italian excavators in 1963 have found remains
exactly corresponding to Damascius' account: a temple
erected in the early third century A.D. on late Hellenistic foundations with under one side an arched doorway leading into a chamber, below which flowed a stream
emitting poisonous fumes through an aperture. Built
into the walls of the temple were reused stones with
two sets of inscriptions which point to the previous
existence in Hierapolis of an Apolline oracle-
centre. (21)

One inscription is dated by Pugliese Carratelli to
the Hellenistic period (second to first century B.C.).
It is an example of the ready-made responses designed
for use by drawing lots, which are a special feature
of Southwest Asia Minor. Twenty-four sentences each
contained in a single hexameter are arranged with
their initial letters in the order of the Greek alphabet like an acrostic. As Kaibel originally conjectured, the enquirer would draw from a vessel a lot
marked with one of the letters of the alphabet, and
then by consulting the tablet he could read the response appropriate to his circumstances. The sentences
are typically vague, suggesting success or failure,
sometimes in metaphorical phrases. It is interesting,
however, to notice that in two instances the title
Kareios is used, which was also applied to Apollo as
the local god in the Clarian oracle already discussed.
Under sigma the sentence reads: "The king of the
Immortals will save you by the oracles of Kareios";
and under omega: "To whom the god is well disposed,
Kareios has assigned his fortune". This document,
then, indicates the existence of an active oracular
centre of Apollo Kareios at Hierapolis in the late
Hellenistic period. Whether other procedures besides
the use of the lot were employed then cannot be
proved. (22)

At least two centuries later in the Hadrianic
period several oracular responses in hexameters were
inscribed on a block later built into the northeast
corner of the cella of Apollo's temple. The prefatory
heading of the series stated that a Hieropolitan,
whose name cannot be restored, "inscribed for his own
sake the oracles in accordance with the command of the
founder-god Apollo". Though evidently intended to
explain the document, this leaves some points unclear.
The reference to a 'command' could imply that the
writer had consulted an Apolline oracle and received
a response containing this order, but it might equally

refer to some less definite form of divine communication, such as a dream or an omen. Also one may ask
which were 'the oracles'. The plural suggests that the
heading covered not merely the long response about a
remedy for the plague, attributable to Apollo Clarios,
but also the three other texts found in association
with it, even though in somewhat different lettering.
They are all in hexameters and have no introductory
phrases addressing the enquirer or describing the
subject of the enquiry. (23)

The first seems to be in response to a prophet,
who may have asked about his rights to perquisites
from offerings. It begins abruptly:-

> "Take possession of the thigh (of the victim).
> By the voice of the intelligent god you speak
> divine matters and you yourself hear holy
> commands."

The next ten lines are fragmentary and unintelligible,
except for some tantalising phrases:- "by the madness
and violence of the Immortals"..."laid low"... "of
torchbearing women". (Possibly there may be another
response also concealed in this passage.)

The second answer seems to be addressed to some
magistrate or some person enquiring about them and
recommends that their judgements should be somewhat
mitigated:-

> "Altogether sound are the plans and thoughts of
> the kings who are nurtured by Zeus, and, when
> they take care, they have enjoyed the advantage
> of their second thoughts. By decree on the
> judgement seat the wise one relaxed his bitter
> interpretation... for thus you will not miss
> those things which the god is urging on you, and
> from a fear of god you will hit the mark, a fear
> which will not harm you at all, but in a more
> timely way..."

In the middle of a third response is a sentence
containing an address to Hierapolis by that name. It
proves that the city was the enquirer in this instance,
but also the informal way in which it is addressed would
suit the supposition that this is the utterance of a
local oracle. The Hierapolitans had been enquiring
about some "testing of the waters" - perhaps not
because of drought, which would be an unlikely trouble
at this place, but rather some question of pollution.
Apollo curiously seems to begin by warning against the
danger of a god trying to be too clever.

It cannot be proved that these responses are the utterances of Apollo Kareios, but it seems likely that it is so. In style they show some resemblance to each other and are distinctly different in tone from any of the replies preserved from Claros or Didyma. The god is more informal and inclined to talk round the subject of the question put to him. If so, we may suppose that there was a local tradition of divination at Hierapolis stretching down from pre-Hellenic times. The very fact that the Greek settlers called it "Sacred City" shows that it was a holy place before they came. The cult-titles of the god - Kareios in earlier periods, Lairbenos in later - go back to native sources. What had been the relation between the two remains obscure. But the very nature of the place with its copious streams impregnated with chemicals and emitting powerful gases would suggest to the primitive mind the presence of a supernatural power at work. (24)

Whether the Charoneion played any part in the divination is hard to decide. Our literary sources do not suggest it, but they do not mention prophecy at all. Yet at another Charoneion in the Maeander valley divination of a limited scope again took place. This was at Athymbra in the territory of Nysa, where there was a cavern consecrated, not to Apollo, but to Pluto and Persephone. A healing cult was practised, whose priests slept in the cave, which was regarded as deadly to unauthorised visitors. This procedure of incubation produced revelations of cures for those who consulted the shrine. (25) The toxic aperture at Hierapolis would not lend itself easily to such a method of divination. But the fact that it was provided with an arched entrance in its final phase shows that it was meant to be approached, under whatever conditions of caution. Hierapolis in these ways is a revelation how much beyond our literary evidence the less familiar sites of Asia Minor may conceal.

A settlement of similar name, Hieracome ("Sacred Village"), in the Maeander valley, south of Tralles, contained another oracle-centre of Apollo, whose features are only known from a couple of sentences in Livy. "There is a venerable (augustum) shrine of Apollo and an oracle; the prophets are said to give responses in poetry of some elegance." This indicates a site with the traditions of other Asian sanctuaries, but until there is successful excavation, no knowledge of its local characteristics is available. (26)

CARIA, LYCIA AND SOUTHEAST ASIA MINOR

Apart from the Maeander valley there are a number of
places in Southern Asia Minor where there were oracle-
centres of Apollo or shrines associated with Apolline
divination whose traditions evidently reached back to
native origins. In Caria the most notable was
Telmessus, a community of villages grouped round a
sanctuary of Apollo, which was controlled by an hereditary clan and possessed consecrated land. It was
situated on the peninsula of Myndus in what at least
by imperial times was the territory of Halicarnassus.
From coins and inscriptions it is clear that the god
was called Apollo Telmesseus and that he was the
ancestor of a family which traced its line back to
his son Telmessus. But there does not appear to have
been an oracle-centre of the ordinary sort at Telmessus; instead the inhabitants all claimed to have an
hereditary gift of divination. As Arrian describes
it: "the Telmessians are wise in expounding things
divine, and by birth there is given to them, men,
women and children the gift of prophecy." Arrian
illustrates this by a legendary tale about Gordius the
Phrygian and how he won the kingship for his son by
the help of his wife, a Telmessian diviner. The reputation went back to the archaic period at least as
is indicated by two stories told by Herodotus of
Lydian kings consulting the Telmessians about the interpretation of ominous happenings. In the classical
period they were well enough known to the Athenians
for Aristophanes to write a comedy on them. The
surviving fragments do not give enough to reconstruct
the plot, but in one a character can be detected asking the Telmessians what course of action to take in
view of one of their predictions:- "Well then, whenever these things come, what ought I to do, Telemes-
sians?" The most famous member of the clan was
Aristandros, who accompanied Alexander from the beginning of his expedition and is repeatedly reported
as interpreting omens which the king encountered.
Their fame continued into the Hellenistic period, to
which may belong a legend which links the origins of
the two great families of diviners, the Galeotae of
Sicily and the Telmessians of Caria. The eponymous
ancestors, Galeotes and Telmessus, were said to have
consulted Zeus of Dodona at the same time, and to
have been sent by the oracle west and east respectively to
found their cults of Apollo. To Cicero Telmessus was
"a city in which the teaching (<u>disciplina</u>) of the
haruspices (diviners) excels", and to Pliny it was
<u>urbs religios issima</u> and a stage in the spread of

magic from the east to the west. But there is no sign
that it took part in the "flowering of the oracles" in
the second century A.D. (27)

Generally, one may say that the Telmessians may
represent the rudimentary state from which such an
oracle-centre as Branchidae, also in Caria, developed,
but in their case the prophetic cult remained at the
elementary stage of interpreting omens instead of
progressing towards an organised institution for
ascertaining and enunciating the god's will.

In Lycia the Apolline oracle at Patara has much
the same kind of evidence for its existence as that
for Gryneion:- legends recorded in the Vergilian
commentaries, casual mentions in the geographers and
other authors and a few epigraphic documents from
elsewhere which confirm its functioning. But besides
these sources there is one important reference in
Herodotus, which casts light on its operations in the
fifth century. He is describing the temple of Bel
in Babylon, which he had evidently visited in his
travels. On the topmost storey of the Ziggurat "is
a large shrine in which lies a big bed well furnished
with a golden table standing besides it. There is no
image erected in it anywhere, and no mortal man rests
on the bed, but only a woman of the local people,
whomsoever the god shall choose from them all, as the
Chaldaeans say, who are priests of the god. They
also say, what I do not believe, that the god himself
is regularly accustomed to enter the shrine and sleep
on the bed in the same fashion as the Egyptian Thebes,
as the Egyptians tell. For there too a woman goes to
bed in the temple of the Theban Zeus (Amun-Ra), and
both women are said to have no intercourse with any
men. Just as also in Patara of Lycia the woman who is
the prophetic mouthpiece of the god whenever the oracle is functioning - for there is not an oracle at all
times there - whenever it is functioning, then she is
shut in for the night together with him in the
shrine. " (28)

This passage has been quoted in full to convey
the feeling of strangeness which Herodotus evidently
experienced in face of these exotic practices. His
Ionic rationalism rejected the notion that the god
came down regularly to sleep with his human consort
in the shrine at Babylon or Egyptian Thebes, but in
both places which he had visited he knew of the
actual practice of providing a bed for the god and a
chosen female partner. So he cited what one can take
to have been the only parallel instance known to him
from a land near to Greece - Patara in Lycia. While
he does not say so, he could probably have visited

the place on one of his voyages to the East, for it
was a well-known port of call. On the other hand, he
describes the procedure so carefully though briefly,
that he assumes that it is unfamiliar to his audience.
In this respect, he writes very differently from
elsewhere when he refers to the procedure at Delphi in
such a way as to imply that every Greek was familiar
with it. (29)

In designating the woman concerned in the procedure at Patara Herodotus uses the term which elsewhere he applies to the Pythia (promantis). The
implication is that she was the mouthpiece of the god,
but not necessarily the same person who conveyed the
response to the people. The description of her as
"shut in with" does seem to involve Herodotus in an
admission that she encountered the god in the sanctuary by night, but he avoids or at least omits any
suggestion that in the Lycian example there was sexual intercourse between Apollo and his female mouthpiece. It could be open for one to believe, for
instance, that the promantis slept in the temple so
as to receive divine revelations in dreams, or even
that the experience in itself of sleeping in the
temple was regarded as inspiring the promantis in the
replies which she would utter the next day.

Herodotus elsewhere indicates his knowledge of a
link between Lycia and Greece in the cult of Apollo.
When discussing the tombs of the Hyperborean maidens
on Delos he mentions that their names occurred in a
hymn sung by the Delian women, and that this and the
other ancient hymns sung on Delos were composed by
Olen, who had come from Lycia. This Lycian hymn-
writer is probably a legendary figure. A Delphic
tradition cited by Pausanias made him the first prophet there and the first composer of the hexameter, but
a Hyperborean, not a Lycian. (30) This divergence of
tradition accords with the fact that Delphi in the
archaic and classical periods was markedly at variance
with Delos. However, since Herodotus already in the
fifth century knew of Olen on Delian authority as a
Lycian, evidently the Delian priesthood had early
recognised Lycia as an important centre of Apollo's
worship. This association is all the more remarkable
as both places claimed the title of birthplace of
Apollo. Yet in one way they appear to have arrived at
a happy compromise. By the Hellenistic period at
least, if not much earlier, it was believed that, when
Apollo was absent from Delos in winter, he was resid-
ent at Patara in Lycia. According to our late commentaries on Vergil he spent the six winter months in
Lycia giving oracles, and then returned for the six

summer months to Delos. The god's spring epiphany
and the festival devoted to it were made the subject
of a famous simile in the Aeneid. Also the link between the two places inspired Horace with his address
to Apollo as the god of Delos and Patara, which forms
the climax of the fourth ode of book three. The
seasonal character of the cult of Apollo in Lycia had
already been suggested long before by Herodotus in his
emphatic statement that the oracle did not function
all the time in Patara, but teasingly he does not make
clear during what periods it was active, nor whether in
the fifth century the intervals were associated with
his presence in Delos. The interesting point is that,
where Delphic theology used the mythical land of the
Hyperboreans as the winter resort of Apollo, the
Delian tradition substituted the actual oracle-centre
of Patara. Earlier scholars would have been inclined
to read into this legend evidence that the cult of
Apollo originated in Lycia and was diffused from
there. But a recent find of a bi-lingual inscription
gives the Lycian form of the god's name and demonstrates that it is quite different from "Apollo" and
cannot have supplied that nomenclature to the
Greeks. (31)

Another tradition about Patara links it with
Delphi, but in a way that can hardly have commended
itself to the Delphian priesthood. The legend, which
must be Hellenistic in date, set out to provide a
Greek derivation for Patara and also to claim for the
Lycians the credit for founding the Pythian sanctuary. "Some say that in the temple of Apollo (at
Delphi) stood an altar inscribed (in Greek) "To the
Ancestral" (Patriou) "Apollo," because Lycadius, the
son of Apollo and a nymph, Lycia, when he had reached
maturity, first named the district in which he had
been born Lycia after his mother, and then founded a
city in it (dedicated) to Apollo and consecrated lots
and a tripod, and that it might bear witness that
Apollo was his father he named it Patara. When he
was travelling from there to Italy, he was the victim
of a shipwreck, and is said to have been received on
a dolphin's back. When brought to land near Mount
Parnassus, he founded a temple dedicated to his
father Apollo and called the place Delphi after the
dolphin." (32)

The legend manages to combine a series of ety-
mologies, deriving Patara from the word for "father",
Delphi from a story of a rescue by a dolphin (delphis)
reminiscent of Taras, Phalanthus or Arion of Methymna,
and Lycia from the name of a local nymph. The tale
how the Delphic temple was founded by Lycadius, a

Lycian, seems to be modelled on another tradition tha
the founder was Eicadius, a Cretan. To derive the
origin of the Pythian sanctuary from Crete was only a
rationalising version of the original legend told in
the Homeric hymn. But to assign it to a Lycian and
represent it as subsequent to the foundation of Patar
as temple and oracle has no ancient authority elsewhere. It can best be interpreted as a piece of Lyci
nationalism produced at some time in the Hellenistic
period when the prestige of Delphi had sunk so low
that this almost impudent fiction could be circulated
It presents a notable contrast to the legends connect
ing Didyma and Claros with Delphi. Those sanctuaries
in the archaic period or the late fourth century were
glad enough to link their founders with the Delphic
oracle and thereby strengthen their reputation in the
Greek world.

There were also other quite different legends to
explain the derivation of Patara. Hecataeus had the
usual genealogical explanation. It was named after
Patarus, the son of Apollo and Lycia, the daughter of
Xanthus. She was probably to be thought of as a
nymph, the daughter of the local river. This may all
be simply Greek mythological invention, but, if the
prophets at Patara were an hereditary priesthood, the
may well have claimed descent from the native god
identified as Apollo. An alternative version of the
genealogical myth gave a somewhat hostile picture of
the foundation. Patarus and Xanthus, the sons of
Lapeon, after making a profitable living from piracy,
settled in Lycia. The elder founded the city of
Xanthus, the younger that of Patara, naming them afte
themselves. (33)

Neither genealogical story refers to the oracle
as such, but Alexander Polyhistor, the erudite schola
of the mid-first century B.C., produced another derivation for Patara, which at least linked it closely
with Apolline cult practice. "A maiden of Salace in
Ophionis was carrying offerings to Apollo in a vessel
(patara). These consisted of lyres, bows and arrows,
made of pastry, ... She set down the vessel to rest o
the road, and a gust of wind hurled it into the sea.
The girl went home weeping, and the vessel was carrie
(by the current) to the peninsula of Lycia. There an
exile from Salace happened to find it. He burnt all
the pastries in it (as an offering) and dedicated the
peninsula to Apollo. The place was named Patara afte
the vessel (patara) which is translated 'hamper'
(kiste) in Greek." This myth is somewhat obscure.
For instance the place-names have not been identified
Salace was presumably some town in a district Ophioni

on the Asia Minor coast, but its whereabouts are lost.
The derivation of Patara from a native name for a hamper is probably erroneous, but it may have a substratum
of fact in that there had been a cult practice of
burning an offering to Apollo of pastry models of
objects associated with him such as harps and bows and
arrows. (34)

So far as our ancient authorities show, only at
one point did the oracle of Patara infiltrate Greek
mythology. This was in claiming that Telephus had
consulted the Lycian shrine instead of Delphi, after
he had received his incurable wound in conflict with
Achilles. The legend is not Homeric; it appeared first
in the Cypria, but received its classic expression in
the lost "Telephus" of Euripides, where the famous
reply - "he who wounded shall heal" - was probably
credited to the Pythia. The attribution to Delphi also
occurs in some later sources. The alternative attribution to Patara was based on a claim by the local
priesthood. In Pausanias' day at least they "showed
in the temple of Apollo at Patara a mixing-bowl which
they said was a dedication of Telephus and the work
of Hephaestus". The Lycian version of his cure seems
to have ignored the epic legend, for there was a spring
of Telephus seven stades (i.e. less than a mile) from
Patara, which was said to be muddied because there he
had washed away his wound. This tradition can be
traced back to the fourth century B.C. Similarly,
already in the third century it was recorded that in
the temple of Athena at Lindos on Rhodes was a bowl
with a gold boss inscribed "Telephus to Athena as an
atonement, in accordance with the words of the Lycian
Apollo". These legends all fit with the strongly nat-
ionalistic feeling of the Lycians towards Greek mythology. The whole complex connection of Telephus with
Apollo of Patara was evidently developed before the
rise of the Pergamene dynasty who claimed him as an
ancestor. Pergamum even at its greatest extent never
held power over Lycia. (35)

Apart from this legend there are no literary
sources for consultations at Patara. Prose writers of
various periods show knowledge of the oracle's existence, but the only instance worth quoting is from the
geographer, Pomponius Mela. He writes of Patara:-
"The temple of Apollo has made it famous, for once it
was the equal of Delphi in wealth and in credibility
of its oracle." This is probably based on some late
Hellenistic source, and sounds rather exaggerated,
particularly in the suggestion that Apollo Patareus
could have been in any way the equal of Apollo Pythius
in the value of his dedications. But the notable point

is that Mela implies that by his time at least the oracle was in decline or even had ceased. (36) That it did suffer a period of silence is proved by explicit reference to the fact in a Lycian inscription. These are two entries in a list of benefactions given by Oproimas, a local millionaire, to various cities in Lycia. The main occasion was an earthquake which laid waste the district in 141 A.D., but also there are records of "another 20,000 denarii to the people of Patara for the worship of the Augusti and in respect of their ancient and infallible oracle..." and "to the people of Patara to the account of Apollo the ancestral god, since his oracle which had been silent for a time has begun again to prophesy - 20,000 denarii". (37)

The situation which can be deduced from these records is quite in accordance with the general pattern of oracular history which we have already noted. Didyma appeared to show a considerable revival of activity from Hadrian's reign; Claros, which seemed to have sunk to very dubious practices, underwent a great reformation which coincided with a benefaction from the same emperor. So it would be quite plausible to suppose that the oracle of Patara had relapsed into silence, but in accordance with the new tendency of the age was revived by a timely benefaction in the mid-second century A.D. How long it had been silent remains quite uncertain. Mela, writing about 40 A.D. had treated it as already in decline at least, but it is impossible to prove whether he was simply reproducing an earlier source or describing contemporary conditions. The only evidence bearing on the matter is another Lycian inscription, which can with some degree of conjecture be identified as containing the text of an actual response of Apollo of Patara. (38)

This inscription from the town of Sidyma in Western Lycia appears to be a transcript of a speech in honour of the place. It is not dated in the surviving text. The editors suggest the time of Commodus on the grounds of the lettering. Evidently from its style and content it belongs to the period of the Second Sophistic movement. In the course of his address the anonymous orator mentions the priestess-ship of Artemis - the chief local deity. "Previously women were chosen priestesses, but later in accordance with an enquiry and an oracle of the god virgins were selected up to the present day. For a memorial and for an act of piety and for the glory of the goddess of the marriages producing female children, which we have enjoyed through the goddess when worshipped, I recall the oracle which was issued one hundred and twenty nine years before concerning the virgin priestess, inscribed by them as it was written." (The orator then quotes the document verbatim.) "In the federal priesthood of Artemeus and the urban priest hood of Telesinus, on the 26th of the month Loos, we, Eupolemus, the son of Aristonymus, and Ptolemaeus, the son of Aristonymus, Calabatianoi, deliver to the councillors (prytaneis) for you the oracle, which was issued, of which a copy is written below:- (39)

> "Receive clearly kinsman city, the good prophecies of Phoebus, how it shall be expedient for your land and all its inhabitants in the matter of your enquiry. But give heed to what the god Phoebus has assigned you:- by maiden skills to perform the priestly honours. For this is, indeed it is, pleasing to the divine daughter of Leto, not to bring near to her halls a priestess whom you choose to summon from the marriage bed to the unwedded shrines, but a young virgin, spotless, untouched. Choose that she be appointed over the rites, and let the temple under her be always kept holy, in order that whatsoever selection you make men may honour it in the rolling years to come. These things the king himself, the far-darter, reveals are blessed and his sister the huntress, the nourisher of hounds, whom together with Phoebus [you should worship...]" "

The text breaks off at this point, which must have been almost the end of the response. The name of the oracular shrine which was consulted is not stated by the orator, who evidently assumed that his audience would recognise it at once. This might be taken to mean that it was the local shrine, and in fact an inscription of the second century A.D. shows that at Sidyma there was an official described as "the prophet for life of the guiding gods Artemis and Apollo". (40) There might have been facilities for consulting the city's deities. But the text of the response excludes this assumption. Sidyma's oracle would not have addressed the enquirers as "kindred city" or refer to "your land". These are the expressions of a response from outside Sidyma, but also they would come very appropriately from the mouth of a prophet in the federal capital. The fact that the document is dated by the priesthood of the federation proves, if necessary, that the Lycian League was in being and Sidyma a member of it at the time of the enquiry.

It can best be supposed then that this is a response of Apollo Patareus. There is no occasion to

doubt its authenticity. In the second century A.D.
the orator had evidently obtained from the city records this genuine text of an oracle delivered 129
years earlier - the precision of the figure is significant. In form the response is a typical enough
example written in hexameters. It shows no great
effort to achieve epic style. Also one feature is re
markable. Apollo is always referred to in the third
person, and there is no use of the first person. Thus
the prophet claims to deliver the thoughts of Apollo
but does not by his expression imply that the god has
taken possession of him and spoken directly through
his mouth. If the prophecy was elicited by enthusias
tic inspiration, this fact is not conveyed in the
paraphrase. Here also the phrase used twice in the
document may be significant - "the response issued"
(ekpesonta or ekpeptokota). This verb would be literally appropriate if the response had "fallen out"
like a lot out of some vessel, but the text is too
elaborate and specific to have been a ready-made
answer written in advance of the enquiry. The phrase
however, may be intended to convey the idea that the
response was composed in this form by the prophet aft
the general sense had been elicited in some other way
Incidentally one of the few inscriptions from Patara
is an honorary decree for "Polyperchon, the son of
Polyperchon, high priest for life of Germanicus
Caesar and prophet of the ancestral Apollo and ex-
priest of the god". So, if Herodotus' description ca
be taken to prove that the oracle throughout its history had a woman as promantis, this inscription shows
that in the reign of Tiberius at least, and probably
at other periods, there was also a prophetes. (41)
     The date of the response can only be fixed very
approximately, as the oration in which it is quoted i
only vaguely datable. The editors assign it to the
reign of Commodus. So if one took 180 A.D. as a
starting point and counted backwards 129 years inclus
ively, one reaches 52 A.D. But obviously the date of
the inscription could be twenty years earlier or later
and the date of the consultation would shift accordingly. This is teasing because, as we have seen,
there is evidence that after an interval of silence
the oracle of Patara had been revived in 142 A.D.
approximately. The enquiry from Sidyma presumably fe
before this gap; but when remains quite uncertain. I
would be tempting to try to connect this silence of
the oracle with some political event in the history
of the Lycian League, such as the loss of its freedom
under Vespasian or earlier in 43 A.D. under Claudius.
But it is by no means certain that a political disast

of this sort would have immediate consequences in religious practice.

The subject of the enquiry and its treatment have interesting parallels in the enquiry at Didyma about the appointment of a married woman as priestess of Athena Polias in Miletus. (42) It dated from the latter part of the second century A.D., while the oracle from Apollo Patareus was probably Julio-Claudian in date. The Lycian response, though somewhat wordy, has none of the rather fantastic literary allusions of the Didymaean response. Also while Didyma had conceded the point and allowed the appointment of a married woman, Patara had adhered to the strictest interpretation of the rules and insisted that the priestesses of Artemis in Sidyma must be virgin and remain unmarried for life. These contrasting features, however, probably less imply anything with regard to the local practices of the oracles rather than illustrate the differences between the two periods. In the late second century responses were likely to be more fulsome in style, and the need to relax regulations so as to facilitate the finding of candidates for office was becoming pressing.

Patara in history and procedure can only be outlined in this very sketchy way owing to our lack of evidence. This is all the more tantalising since it is probable that excavation could provide much information. The site of Patara, which is easily identified, is extensive and mostly buried under sand. (43) The exact location of the temple of Apollo is not yet fixed, but probably the building itself could be found and unearthed, giving evidence of the history of the cult from its plan and from the inscriptions which would emerge. One point is notable in anticipation; the site is naturally waterless and had to be supplied by aqueducts. It would be unique among Apolline sanctuaries if there was no sacred spring in the precinct.

Elsewhere in Lycia was an Apolline oracle depending entirely on a fountain for its functioning. It was near Cyaneae and was consecrated to Apollo under the native cult-title of Thyrxeus. Our only information comes from a single reference in Pausanias. He describes at length an oracle-centre of Demeter at Patrae in Achaia where enquirers lowered a mirror on a string till it just touched the surface of the water in a sacred spring. After praying and offering incense they looked at the image in the mirror for the revelation. Pausanias is explicit that it could only be consulted about those who were ill, but it was infallible in showing them either alive or dead. He follows this up by referring briefly to the Apolline oracle-centre at Cyaneae where "when anyone has looked into the spring, in a like way he can behold all things that he wishes". This has been interpreted as naivety on the part of Pausanias, but probably he did not mean that the enquirer could see his every wish, but that at Cyaneae, unlike Patrae, the enquiry was not confined to the outcome of an illness. Also he does not suggest that in the Lycian sanctuary any apparatus was used. The enquirer appears to have gazed directly into the sacred spring, instead of into a mirror. But in default of more evidence this variant on catoptromancy cannot be followed further. (44)

The last incomplete sentence of the response from Sidyma associated Apollo and Artemis as revealing the correct rules about the appointment of priestesses. But this need not be taken as showing that Artemis was actually in partnership with Apollo in issuing oracles at Patara. It is probably only a reference to the circumstance that in this instance Apollo was expressing Artemis' views about the priestess. However, as we have noticed, in Sidyma itself an official was described as "the prophet for life of Artemis and Apollo". So such an association of the two deities must be regarded as possible. There was another oracle-centre in Southern Asia Minor where the only way to reconcile our evidence is on the supposition that both Apollo and Artemis were concerned in giving responses.

Strabo ends his account of Cilicia with the sentence: "In Cilicia is also the temple and oracle of Artemis Sarpedonia, and the responses are uttered by persons who are divinely inspired." This statement is strange, as never elsewhere in our literary authorities is Artemis mentioned as delivering responses on her own. We have seen already the temple of Apollo Actaios and Artemis in the plain of Adrasteia, which is the only other place where she is even associated with Apollo in an oracular sanctuary, again on the authority of Strabo. In contrast to Strabo's statement about Artemis Sarpedonia, our other sources refer over a period of four centuries to an oracle-centre of Apollo Sarpedonios at Seleuceia in Cilicia, which is cited for responses in hexameters of the style usually attributed to ecstatic prophecy. The city of Seleuceia had been founded by Seleucus Nicator near the mouth of the river Calycadnus in Rough Cilicia. As Apollo was the patron and ancestral god of the Seleucid dynasty, it would be appropriate for him to be the chief deity of the colony. But the use of the uniquely strange epithet Sarpedonios suggests that the site may have had an earlier cult of a hero whom the Greeks had identified with the famous leader of the Lycians in the Trojan war. There is, as we shall see, a curious confirmation of this theory from a late source. (45)

The earliest evidence of the oracle occurs in Diodorus Siculus, who tells that Alexander Balas, king of Syria (154-145 B.C.), shortly before his death had comsulted Apollo Sarpedonios, and had been warned to be on his guard against the place which bore the "two-shaped" one. The interpretation of this riddling prophecy was revealed when Alexander was killed at Abai in Arabia where a hermaphrodite had been born. Diodorus gives a long and detailed account of this woman, who in maturity had undergone a spontaneous sex-change to masculinity. Prophecies of the deaths of kings or tyrants are a favourite feature in Greek myths, and the usual pattern consists of an obscurely worded warning which is only understood after the event. The use in this instance of a specific word "two-shaped" suggests that Diodorus is paraphrasing a verse response, perhaps in iambics, which was supposed to have been delivered by a prophet in ecstasy. Whether there is a factual basis to some part of the story - for instance, the case of the hermaphrodite, which is described in great circumstantial detail - is beyond proof. (46)

Apollo Sarpedonios reappears at the time when Zenobia and the people of Palmyra were challenging the supremacy of the Roman emperor. Zosimus narrates that they "asked the oracle whether they would secure the hegemony of the East, and the god replied:-

"Go forth from my halls, baneful deceiving men, who cause pain to the glorious tribe of the immortal gods."

But when some persons enquired concerning the expedition of Aurelian against the Palmyrenes, the god responded:-

"A hawk inflicting a chilly groan on cowering doves, one against many, but they shudder at the slayer." "(47)

These vivid and colourful hexameters containing two unique poetic words are doubtless authentic specimens of the contemporary propaganda used by Aurelian's side against the Palmyrenes. Whether they really originated in the sanctuary at Seleuceia and were delivered on the occasions stated may be more

questionable. But obviously in these instances as in
the warning to Alexander Balas the legend would not
have been invented if there had been no oracle-centre
of Apollo Sarpedonios whose priests spoke in verse
under his inspiration.

How Strabo came to ascribe this oracle-centre to
Artemis instead of to Apollo is hard to decide. It
may be a mere slip on his part, or more likely it may
point to a combined cult of Apollo and Artemis, which
Strabo ascribed to the goddess, while our other sources only mentioned the god. Curiously in this instan
ce, the continuance of oracular practice on the site
can be traced into the Christian period. Basil,
bishop of Seleuceia in the fifth century, described
the contemporary cult of St. Thekla at her tomb in hi
see. The saint gave responses to enquirers, healed
the sick, sanctioned marriages and bestowed fruitful-
ness on fields and meadows. Basil recognised that
these functions were a continuation of the activities
of Apollo and even went so far as to trace the tradition back to a tomb of Sarpedon, the hero, whose
place had been usurped by Apollo and subsequently
filled by St. Thekla. Modern scholars without the
help of the bishop's evidence would have made just thi
conjecture to explain the strange epithet "Sarpedonios'
Basil does not mention Artemis in this connection, bu
one may wonder whether St. Thekla found it easier to
replace her pagan predecessor if there had been a
goddess as well as a god worshipped in the sanctuary
at Seleuceia. (48)

If we continue eastward again from Rough Cilicia
to the Cilician plain, the evidence for Apolline
oracles ceases. This is not to be explained by a lac
of worship of Apollo. He was for instance the chief
god of Tarsus. But there is no evidence that he
answered enquiries. The chief oracle-centres of the
Cilician plain were operated in the name of heroes -
Mopsus and Amphilochus, whom we have already encountered in the legends of Claros. They had issued responses from the archaic period, and Amphilochus at
least appears to have had a flowering in the second
century A.D. These cults suggest a parallel with
Sarpedon at Seleuceia. There Apollo appears to have
succeeded in intruding on the sanctuary of a local
hero, but at Mallus Amphilochus maintained his independence. It may be an echo of this struggle between
rival cults which produced the legend already known
to Hesiod that Apollo had slain Amphilochus at Soloi.

In traversing Southern Asia Minor from Caria to
Cilicia we have so far omitted one Apolline oracle-
centre where the method of procedure was unique and

so peculiar as to attract notice in antiquity to what was otherwise a very minor place. At Sura on the Lycian coast, southwest of Myra, a spring of fresh water came up through the sand in the shallows, producing a whirlpool (Dinos), which gave its name to the place. The local conditions made it a favourite spot for fish, and they were used for the purpose of divination. Beside the shore was a temple of Apollo with a grove, whose priest presided over the consultation. The enquirer offered a sacrifice of a calf, and after the meat had been cooked, ten pieces of it were threaded on to each of two wooden skewers (the appearance must have resembled shish kebab). Carrying these skewers the enquirer proceeded to the shore and threw them into the whirlpool, while the priest sat by in silence to watch for the result. Some descriptions stress the importance of the size of the fish that come to the bait and the variety of the species. "Whenever the prophet announces the kinds of fishes, the enquirer receives accordingly from the priest the oracle on the subject about which he prayed. There are revealed grey-green fish and sea-perch, and sometimes porpoises and saw-fish, and also many fishes which are not otherwise seen and are peculiar in appearance" (Polycharmus). Other descriptions lay emphasis on the behaviour of the fish. "The sea perch in a body swim to it and eat the meat like banqueters invited to a feast, and those who made the sacrifice rejoice...but if the fish with their tails cast the offering out on the land, as if they despised it and regarded it polluted, then that is believed to signify the wrath of the god" (Aelian). (49)

There is no serious inconsistency in the various accounts of the procedure. At most the different pictures are derived from different occasions, perhaps over a number of centuries. Also the authors obviously tended to make the most of the peculiar and picturesque features of the ceremony, but this does not destroy the clear evidence for the practice. In Hierapolis the presence of one strange natural phenomenon - the emission of toxic vapour - was made the occasion for a cult with divination in the name of Apollo. So also at Sura another natural marvel - the occurrence of a spring below tide-level - became the site of a cult and an Apolline oracle-centre. Ordinarily Apollo was not a god of fishes, but in the Aegean he was in some places associated with dolphins. However there is no link indicated between Apollo Delphinios and the Apollo of Sura. It is more likely that in Lycia and Phrygia when Greeks first encountered a peculiar oracle-centre they identified the local god with Apollo. (50)

EPILOGUE

The evidence for Apolline oracles in Asia Minor,
whether from material remains or literary sources, is
so patchy and incomplete, that one cannot expect to
draw up a long list of positive conclusions. Some
points in common, however, tend to emerge and are
worth stating briefly.

The cult which was paid to Apollo by the Hellenes
appears to have been practised on the same sites,
whether to a god of the same name or not, in pre-Hellenic times in such places as Didyma, Claros, Hierapolis, Telmessus, Patara and Seleuceia. In many
instances the oracle-centre was in a sanctuary which
was later incorporated in the territory of a city-
state - Didyma by Miletus, Claros by Notion and later
by Colophon, Hieracome by Tralles, Telmessus by
Halicarnassus and so forth. On other occasions a
Hellenistic polis was founded directly on the site,
such as Hierapolis and Seleuceia. Possibly in some
instances the Apolline sanctuary was established as
part of the foundation of a Greek colony. Apollo
Chresterios at Chalcedon is a likely example. At
Aigai the sanctuary is so far from the town that it
probably existed previously, but there and at Gryneio
excavation is needed to elucidate the facts.

Thus the typical Apolline temple in Asia Minor
was not on the Acropolis of a Greek city, but lay in
open country. Homer's picture of Apollo rescuing
Aeneas from battle and placing him "in holy Pergamon,
where his temple was built... in the mighty adyton...
is dramatically effective, but one may doubt whether
it had any basis in the topographical facts (Il. 5,
445). Much more typical was the sanctuary at Thymbra
in the Trojan plain, whose existence is implied in
the Epic Cycle and archaic art. It goes along with
this normal situation in the country that the feature
attributed in common to the largest number of Apollin

198

oracle-centres is a sacred grove (alsos). At Didyma
it consisted of bay-trees, which grew inside and outside the sanctuary, and was believed to have been
planted by Apollo. At Claros Nicander attributes the
planting of ash-trees to the god as a protection
against venomous reptiles, but this special feature
does not presumably exclude the presence of the usual
sacred bay. One may even wonder whether the fig-tree
whose fruit was the subject of the contest between
Calchas and Mopsus was not part of the grove. At
Gryneion Pausanias had particularly admired the fairest alsos, "consisting of trees both fruit-bearing
and those that do not bear fruit, all those that provide some enjoyment in scent or sight". There was
also a sacred grove in the sanctuary of the Sminthian
Apollo and even the fish-oracle at Sura had one on the
seashore. Perhaps the only place where it is hard to
believe that one existed is at Hierapolis, where the
temple was built on a rock-slope beside a mephitic
stream.

The importance of the sacred grove in the cult
is perhaps derived from oriental connections, but it
was also reproduced at Delphi, whose alsos is often
mentioned by ancient authors. Also it reminds one of
the letter of King Darius to Gadates, which we have
cited before. In it the Great King mentioned the
sacred gardeners of Apollo, though what Ionian sanctuary employed their services is left uncertain.

In view of the need for a grove it is not surprising that an Apolline oracle-centre also usually
had a sacred spring. A regular source of water would
be necessary for cultivation. But actually evidence
shows that at Didyma and Claros the fountain was the
source of inspiration. In Lycia at Cyaneae the ref-
lections of the water gave omens and at Sura the eddy
produced by a submarine spring was used in divination
by means of fish. All these examples make one suspect
that the vapours emitted by the water at Hierapolis
were used in prophecy, though evidence is lacking; or
again the fountain in the grove of Apollo Smintheus
beside the Sibyl's tomb may have had oracular functions.

Divination is such a typical function of Apollo,
associated with him in the earliest mentions of him
in the Iliad and the Odyssey, that one might expect
that it would be practised in any of his sanctuaries,
but actually our evidence shows it only in a limited
number of places. One cannot exclude the possibility
that in any Apolline shrine the god might be consulted
for local purposes, but the successful activities of
a few centres, such as Didyma and Claros, appear to

have drawn to themselves much of the business. Hierapolis, while it seems to have had an oracle of its
own, consulted Claros about the plague. Also Laodicea
with a distinguished sanctuary of the Pythian Apollo
frequently sent embassies to pay their respects
(proskynemata) to the Clarian. Rhodes had a great
temple of Apollo, but dispatched enquiries to Didyma.
More excavation would probably reveal some oracle-
centres at present unknown, but might also produce
further evidence for consultation of the well-known
centres.

At Didyma and Claros the vehicles of prophecy
were originally male prophets of hereditary families.
At Didyma the family tie continued unbroken till the
Ionian revolt. At Claros it may have lapsed much
earlier, but the tradition that the prophet must be a
man persisted, whereas in Didyma after the revival,
though the post of male prophet continued as an annual office, the mouthpiece of the god was a woman on
the analogy of the Pythia. For other oracle-centres
our evidence is tormentingly ambiguous. When Livy
wrote of the "seers" (vates) at Hieracome and Strabo
of the "inspired" (entheoi) at Seleuceia, the words
they chose were indeterminate in sex. At Telmessus
the hereditary gift of prophecy was shared by all
members of the community. But one may be justified in
arguing that in spite of the local practice of a female
promantis at Patara, male prophets of Apollo were
normal in Asia Minor.

Lot oracles also were generally known in Asia
Minor, but certainly at Didyma and Claros the highest
form of divination was ecstatic prophecy. If one
could also argue that wherever verse was used as a
medium ecstasy was present, then this was also practised in Gryneion, Hierapolis, Hieracome, Seleuceia
and Patara. But in the case of Patara we have noted
in the one example identified a failure of Apollo to
speak in his own person, which may suggest a different
procedure from the others. More difficult still is
the problem that the only authentic examples of any
archaic responses - three from Didyma before 500 B.C.-
all appear in prose, though two are introduced by the
phrase:- "the God said". One might expect that one
of the Branchidae speaking in the name of Apollo in a
sanctuary with Asian origins would utter his revelations in verse like an Old Testament prophet. But actually on our present evidence it would be possible to
argue that the use of hexameter verse for oracles was
another instance where a practice originating in Delphi was imitated later throughout the Hellenic world.

If one tries to assess the part played by the

Epilogue

Apolline oracles of Asia Minor in Greek culture, the question is one which is difficult to answer for any of these centres. Delphi figures prominently throughout all Greek literature, but the factual evidence for enquiries and responses is very limited. Dodona has only a scattered number of literary references, but by a fortunate chance its peculiar method of divination led to the preservation on lead tablets of a considerable cross-section of enquiries. The Asian oracles suffer generally from the loss of those Ionian historians and Hellenistic antiquarians who would give us much literary evidence. Inscriptional sources and citations in literature are largely confined to the period of late flowering in the second and third centuries A.D. Evidently the Branchidae had supported Milesian colonisation, and the restored oracle was used to endorse the city's policy and flatter its patrons, the Seleucids. But one cannot visit the vast and imposing mass of the temple at Didyma or the smaller but complex building at Claros without receiving the conviction that from the Hellenistic period at least these institutions fulfilled an important and satisfying purpose not only for the political and sacral enquiry, but also for the private individual with his personal needs.

As is usual with our sources the evidence for private enquirers is mostly about folk such as Rufinus or Poplas, evidently of high social standing and scarcely typical examples. The circus performer, Appheion, and the team of builders from the theatre at Miletus are perhaps our only instance of plebeians consulting Apollo, but one must imagine that over the centuries there were thousands of them. The human nature of the enquiries is well brought out, even among the religious questions, by such instances as Alexandra the priestess with her nervous feelings of anxiety and inadequacy, or Damianus the prophet with his enthusiastic devotion to his ancestral goddess. But the greatest demonstration of the close and important relationship between Apolline oracle-centres and Greek civilisation is the way in which the enquiries change in character over the years. The archaic enquirer at Branchidae asked about the justification for the practice of piracy, and was referred by Apollo to the traditional customs of the city-state. The enquirer of the Imperial age asked about the immortality of the soul or the nature of the supreme God, and the prophets of Didyma and Claros guided by contemporary philosophy tried to rise to the exposition of such exalted themes. That in the end they failed to satisfy the new yearnings of their age was scarcely their fault.

Epilogue

They had been part of a system which had for centuries adapted itself to meet the requirements of successive generations, till at last it was to be superseded by a different form of revelation.

APPENDIX 1. DIDYMA AND CLAROS. THE SOURCES OF THE RESPONSES AND SUPPLEMENTARY MATERIAL.

(i) THE ARCHAIC PERIOD

For the archaic period the only dependable sources of verbatim texts are three boustrophedon inscriptions, one from Didyma and two from Miletus (pp. 28-30 supra). The literary sources are (1) Herodotus 1,158-9 (pp. 15-18 supra) who does not report it in direct speech, though the enquiries and responses in substance are historically correct. (2) Demon, the atthidographer and paroemiographer explained the proverbial saying "Of old the Milesians were bold " as a response of the Didymaean Apollo (F. Gr. Hist. 327 f 16 = Sch Ar. Pl. 1002 and cf. D.S. 10.25, Zen. 5, 80 and Apostol. 13, 85 Also quoted without interpretation in Philostr. V., 22, 526), given before the Ionian revolt. The iambic line is imitated in Ar. V. 1060 and is quoted in Ar. Pl. 1002. So it was evidently familiar in Athens by the last quarter of the fifth century at least. Aristotle, presumably in the "Constitution of Miletus", used it as evidence for the decline of the city due to luxury (fr. 557 (Rose) = Ath. 12, 523F). But the scholiast on the Plutus also assigns the verse to Anacreon (fr. 81, no. 426, Page). If correct, this would make it virtually impossible for it to have originated as an oracular response at the time of the Ionian revolt. Hence the scholiast gives an alternative version attributing the enquiry to Polycrates (the patron of Anacreon) when fighting some unspecified enemy. Yet again the scholiast to the Wasps cites Didymus as describing the line as a parody on a verse of Timocreon of Rhodes (fr. 7, no. 733, Page). It looks as though Didymus was trying to rescue Demon's version from its chronological difficulty by transferring the quotation to a poet writing after the Ionian revolt. Whether he had any justification for this statement is doubtful. The most

likely theory is that the iambic line was originally
a sixth century popular saying aimed at the Milesians
and that the attribution to Apollo of Didyma is fictitious. Demon does not make his account any more
convincing by his reference to a prophetis at Didyma,
evidently based on the contemporary procedure of the
revived oracle.

(3) Heraclides Ponticus (fr. 50, Wehrli = Ath. 12
524A) in a treatise "Concerning Justice" quotes two
hexameters which, unlike the iambic line in Demon, have
all the appearance of a verse response in Delphic
style, though the diction looks unlikely for the implied date in the mid sixth century. They were probably a concoction of Heraclides himself, who used
highly picturesque verse oracles elsewhere in his
dialogues, and also wrote a book on oracle-centres,
(Mueller, FHG, 2, 197). For a fuller discussion see
Parke, Hermathena, 120 (1976), 50-54.

There are no responses of the archaic period attributed to Claros either in literary or epigraphic
sources.

(ii) THE HELLENISTIC PERIOD

After the revival of the oracle at Didyma our literary
sources chiefly concern its relation with kings. The
first responses mentioned concerned Alexander (p. 36
supra) and later Seleucus I and Antiochus II (pp. 45-6 and
57 supra). The Seleucid connections are amply illustrated by inscriptions. Pseudo-Scymnus, 55 implies that
the dynasty of Nicomedes III of Bithynia had been
foretold by Apollo Didymeus. This has no inscriptional support. Inscriptions from Miletus and Didyma show
the city consulting the oracle on political and religious questions. Inscriptions from elsewhere add
little. A Cretan inscription shows Didyma authorising
an asylia (p. 60 supra), and Michel, Recueil, p. 346,
no. 467 (Fontenrose, no. 18) records Antiochus III as
citing an Apolline oracle in urging concord (homonoia
on Iasos. This Apollo referred to as "the founder of
the family of the king" may well be Didymeus.

Of private enquirers, Pseudo-Scymnus, (l.c. supra
claims the patronage of Apollo Didymeus for himself
and one inscription from Cos (Inscr. Cos. 60, Fontenrose, no. 22) records a dedication to Apollo Delius,
lord of Calymna, authorised by Didyma.

Claros in the Hellenistic period has only one
verse response quoted in a literary source (Paus. 7,
5, 3,; cf. supra. pp. 126-8).

Appendix 1. Didyma and Claros. The Sources of the
Responses and Supplementary Material

(iii) THE IMPERIAL PERIOD

Under the Roman empire the amount of verbatim texts of
oracular responses from both Didyma and Claros in-
creases considerably. The inscriptions with texts for
Didyma are nearly all from the sanctuary itself or
from the territory of Miletus; those for Claros are
never found there, but occur in the territory of the
various enquirers. These have mostly been discussed
in detail. One inscription from Cyzicus of early
imperial date refers to an official consultation of
Apollo Didymeus, but without stating either enquiry
or response (B. Mordtmann, _AM_. 6 (1881), 121 and 10
(1885), 202; H. Lechat, _BCH_. 13 (1889), 378; Fontenrose, No. 28).

Texts of responses recur casually in such authors
as Pausanias, Aelius Aristides, Lucian and others, but
there are two specific literary sources, which deserve
more detailed discussion:- the lost book of Porphyry
"Concerning the philosophy to be derived from Oracles"
and the so-called Tübingen Theosophy .

(1) Porphyry's treatise was written early in his
career before he came to Italy in 262 A.D. and met
Plotinus. This fact is important as giving a _terminus
ante quem_, for Porphyry never dates the responses.
For his philosophical enquiry he also was not concerned to state what oracle-centre was the source. Actually he twice attributes them to Didyma and one other
instance by its content can plausibly be assigned to
it (supra pp. 88-92). The main evidence for his work
is found in the quotations in Eusebius' _Praeparatio
Evangelica_. But also further responses cited in
Lactantius and St. Augustine probably are derived
directly or indirectly from the same source. In
theory it should be possible for some of these verses
to be already centuries old when Porphyry quoted them,
but actually what he required were the rather verbose
utterances dealing with theological questions which
were typical of the period after 150 A.D. He shows
no sign of having obtained them by direct enquiry, but
probably assembled them from previous publications.

None of the citations of Porphyry in Eusebius are
attributed to Claros. But a Roman, Cornelius Labeo,
who has been identified as a pupil of his, is cited
by Macrobius for a book "Concerning the Clarian
Apollo" (cf. supra p. 160). He is also known for a
commentary on Vergil and appears to have written in
the last quarter of the third century. Perhaps he
deliberately filled a gap in the documentation left by
his teacher.

(2) The other special collection of oracular

responses is the so-called Tübingen Theosophy, which
is a surviving extract from an eleven volume work on
Christian doctrine and apologetics. A shorter selection from the same source preserved in manuscripts in
Florence and Naples was first published by G. Wolf in
his edition of Porphyrii De Philosophia ex Oraculis
Haurienda (Berlin, 1856, reprinted Hildesheim, 1962),
pp. 229-240. The much more comprehensive collection
from Tübingen was published in 1889 by K. Buresch,
Klaros, Untersuchungen zum Altertumswesen (Leipzig)
and H. Erbse Fragmente Griechischer Theosophien
(Hamburg, 1941). The original maker of the collection
was a Christian, who probably worked about the last
quarter of the fifth century A.D. His purpose appears
to have been to assemble responses from pagan oracles
which could be interpreted in agreement with Christian
theology. It is not possible on our limited evidence
to decide how strictly sincere this editor was in the
handling of his material. Mostly the responses are
not assigned to particular oracle-centres. So these
attributions have to be based on a limited number of
instances on external evidence or else made by conjecture. Also the enquirers are mostly not named or
have such dubious names as Theophilus. But two enquiries are assigned to one Poplas. Louis Robert
(CRAI. 1968/69, 513) has pointed out that this is a
rare form of name native to Asia Minor, and has identified him with Aelianus Poplas, who had a most prominent official career in Miletus under the reign of
Elegabalus (date, M. Jessop Price Num. Chr. 11 (1971)
131 and C. J. Howgego, N. Chr. 14 (1981), 148; career
Did. II, no. 363, 277, 179 and 241). The extracts
run:-

> "To a certain Poplas by name who had asked if it
> was expedient for him to send concerning money
> to the emperor for his advancement, the reply
> was as follows:-

> "...and this is very expedient for you to do for
> favours, while you pray to the immortal eye of
> all-seeing Zeus, and from your native country to
> the city of the imperial land dispatch a mission
> providing the trust of the famous embassy" "

(Wolff, no. 7; Buresch and Erbse, no. 22).

> "Another time this Poplas was grieved, since
> affairs went contrary to him and his property
> dwindled and his body was not well. So he sough
> to learn from whom he could find help,

Appendix 1. Didyma and Claros. The Sources of the
Responses and Supplementary Information

and the oracle ran:-

"Appease the glorious eye of Zeus who gives
livelihood." "

(Wolff, No. 8; Buresch and Erbse, no. 23).

The former response seems to be the latter part
of one of those verbose utterances of the period; the
latter is a complete one line reply, such as Didyma
used to private enquiries. Aelianus Poplas was the
only individual with that cognomen known to us who
could have been involved in such high questions as
official embassies to Rome.

The editor of the Theosophy seems to have been
interested in these extracts because of the phrases
about the eye of Zeus, which he must have felt could
be compared with Christian belief in the eye of God.
He followed with another example:-

"To a certain Stratonicus, who had seen a dream
concerning the years of his life and enquired
if he should trust it, the oracle replied:-

"Still a long time is assigned to you; but
reverence the eye of life-giving Zeus, with gentle sacrifices." "

(Wolff, no. 9; Buresch and Erbse, no. 24, who follow
the Tübingen Ms. in ending the second line with the
words - Ζηνὸς πανδερκέος ἄφθιτον ὄμμα   as in line
2 of no. 22. Wolff, following the other mss reads
Διὸς ὄμμα θυηπολίαις ἀγανῇσιν   which is preferable.
Cf. Hom. Il 9, 499). The name Stratonicus is too
frequent to be used as evidence, but Robert may be
right in conjecturing that this response also is
Didymaean (CRAI. 1968/69, 587). For Apollo Didymeus
asked to confirm dreams cf. supra p. 29 and p.240,
and for "The eye of Serapis" cf. supra p.78.

One further enquiry and response in the Theosophy
can be ascribed to Apollo of Didyma on the strength of
its citation under that attribution in Lactantius
(Buresch and Erbse, no. 37; Lact. Inst. Div. 7, 13, 5;
L. Robert, CRAI. 1968/69, 589 and cf. supra p.91).
Only Lactantius gives the name of the enquirer (Polit-
es) and of the oracle-centre. Wolff (Porphyrii de
Philosophia, p. 177) conjectures that Porphyry is
Lactantius' ultimate source.

I have omitted as not properly attributable to
Didyma the hexameter verse:-

Appendix 1. Didyma and Claros. The Sources of the
Responses and Supplementary Information

"The song was mine, but divine Homer wrote it
down."

(Anth. Pal. 9, 455 and Anth. Plan. 1, 67. Cf. Philostr.
Her. 19,2). This is cited in a slightly variant form
in Synesius, Dion. 15. But I am not satisfied that
the form of reference to Pytho and Didyma in the previous sentence proves that Synesius thought it was
derived from Didyma.

I would suggest instead identifying as Didymaean
the two hexameters which Socrates quotes in his
Ecclesiastical History (3, 23). Without naming the
oracle-centre he states that the response was given
to the Rhodians, when they were involved in a disaster. It enjoins that Attis, identified with Adonis and
Dionysus, should be appeased. Socrates follows with
two further examples of oracles enjoining cults both
of which he attributes to the Pythia (Parke and
Wormell, D.O. 2, no, 88 and 509). For Apollo Didymeus
and Rhodes, see p.111.

Also a fragmentary oracle from Didyma occurs in
Iamblichus, Letter to Dexippus about Dialectic (Stob.
II, p. 19):-

"neither a swift-flying arrow nor a lyre nor a
ship nor anything else would ever be of worth
without intelligent use."

The sentence is in prose but shows clear traces of
being paraphrased from hexameter verse. It is not
cited in the current lists of Didymaean responses.

One conjecturally identified Clarian response is
worth mention. L. Robert (Laodicée, p. 337) claims for
this oracle-centre the two hexameter lines read by
A. Körte on a building block at Aizanoi in Phrygia
(Ath. Mitt. 25 (1900), 398). As Robert points out
there is much evidence for proskynemata from Aizanoi
at Claros. But the content of the response is interesting. It was set up as a reply to the question
whether a certain Demetrius was to continue as priest
of the founder (the hero Euphorbus?):-

"Up, with swift hand busily seize the net's
catch. For it will give a close-packed haul to
whom I bring it."

This highly metaphorical reply, which can only by a
great stretch of interpretation be treated as relevant
to the enquiry at once suggests the examples quoted
by Oenomaus (cf. supra p. 2-3). Körte remarks on the
fineness of the script which he assigned to the second

Appendix 1. Didyma and Claros. The Sources of the
Responses and Supplementary Information

century A.D. So it can plausibly be identified as
another example of the set verse used by the Clarian
<u>prophetes</u> before the Hadrian revival.

APPENDIX II. THE FUNCTIONING OF THE ORACLES AT DIDYMA
AND CLAROS.

(i)   DIDYMA

The only description of the functioning of the oracles
at Didyma is found in Iamblichus, writing about the
end of the third century A.D.   The oracle was still in
operation at that date, but Iamblichus will not have
derived his knowledge from direct personal enquiry,
but from literary sources now lost.   The context de-
termines the rather strange form of the description.
Iamblichus was writing a controversial defence of
ritual magic directed against his teacher, Porphyry,
and assumed the literary disguise of an Egyptian
priest ("Reply of Abammon to Porphyry's Letter to
Anebo" - commonly called the De Mysteriis).   In handling the question of the functioning of oracles and
the material source of their inspiration his object
was to exhibit knowledge derived from wide reading,
but not to cast off the pseudonym and mask of Abammon.
So he makes statements without citing his Greek authorities and avoids direct naming of Greek gods and
individuals.   Also in stressing the spiritual aspects
of ecstatic divination he lays more emphasis on the
preliminary rites of preparation than other authors.
    His description is as follows:-

> "The woman at Branchidae who is a singer of
> prophecies, either when holding a rod which was
> originally handed over by some god, is filled
> with the divine radiance, or sitting on an axon
> she foretells the future, or dampening her feet
> or the hem of her robe with water or breathing
> from the water, she receives the god; from all
> these (methods) after being suitably prepared for
> the reception she has her share of him from with-
> out.   This is made clear by the multitude of the
> sacrifices and the rule of complete chastity and

Appendix II. The Functioning of the Oracles at Didyma and Claros.

> all the other things which are done in a manner worthy of the gods before prophesying - the baths of the prophetess and her fasting for three whole days and her living in the adyton when she is held both by the (sacred) light and rejoices in it for long." (Iamblichus, de Myst. 3,11).

Leaving aside for the moment the preliminary ritual, Iamblichus distinguishes four different methods of inspiration, and I would take it as probable that he had assembled them from four different sources.

(1) Iamblichus alludes to the legend that Apollo gave Branchus a wreath and a staff of bay, thus conferring on him the gift of prophecy (Varro ap. sch. Stat. Theb. 8, 198 and p. 5 supra); writing as an Egyptian priest he omits both Greek names. Wreaths of bay are so usual in Apolline worship that no conclusions can be drawn from them, but the gift of a rod of bay as conveying inspiration has a striking parallel in Hesiod's account of his own inspiration by the Muses (Th. 22-34 with West's notes). They met him, when he was shepherding on Mount Helicon, and "plucking it gave me as a staff (skeptron) a branch of thriving bay, and they breathed a song into me so that I should tell in verse what shall be and what was before". As West points out, Hesiod draws no distinction in subject matter between the gift of prophecy and the gift of poetry. This staff (skeptron) but without any suggestion of conveying inspiration, also appears in the Iliad (1, 234 etc) as the symbol of the person holding the right to address the gathering and therefore also of heralds (Il. 7, 277, cf. 1. 15). Rhapsodes later are described as holding a rod (rhabdos).

The myth of Branchus may have been modelled on Hesiod's story, but more probably they are both independent, but parallel legends. Elsewhere also Branchus uses a branch of bay like a magic wand to dispel the plague (p. 5-6 supra). This is quite unlike the usual spirit and practice of Apolline or even of Olympian cult. Hermes is the only Hellenic god who regularly carries a magic wand (the kerykeion: see F. J. M. De Waele, The magic staff or rod in Graeco-Roman antiquity, 1927, pp. 44 ff.).

Iamblichus implies that the prophetis in Didyma in his day might have been inspired by holding Branchus' sacred rod (rhabdos). If what purported to be such an object was used by the Branchidae, as is possible, it is most unlikely that it survived the Persian sack and the transportation to Bactria. Whether when the oracle was revived, a rod was included in the ritual, as a traditional feature may be doubted. More probably Iamblichus or his source knew of the legend of Branchus and arbitrarily transferred the same source of inspiration to the prophetis of late times.

Actually the Branchidae may have attributed their inspiration to other sources - as hereditary descent from the sun-god (cf. supra pp.3-4) or the loving kiss of Apollo as commemorated in the title Philesios (Conon, F. Gr. Hist. 26 f 1, 33, 4; Varro sp. Sch. Stat.Theb.3, 283; Pliny, HN. 34, 75; Macrob. Sat. 1, 17). Perhaps the first motif is pre-Hellenic and the second Hellenic in origin.

(2) The second method, "sitting on the axon" is a puzzle because the meaning of axon is by no means clear. Its only other occurrence in literature connected with divination is in Nonnus' Dionysiaca, where Cadmus is described as consulting the Pythian oracle (4, 259. Cf. Did, II, 217, 7, where the meaning turns on the restoration, p. 103 supra). The response is given to him by the Delphic tripod itself, which is described as the axon. This is not to be taken as genuine Delphic tradition or practice. Nonnus is partly indulging in fantasy and partly borrowing words and phrases from earlier literature, particularly from the Hellenistic poets. He had some authority, not known to us, for equating the function of the Delphic tripod and the Didymaean axon. There is good evidence for the belief that the Pythia derived inspiration from seating herself on the Delphic tripod (Parke and Wormell, D.O. 1, 25). So it would be reasonable for the Didymaean prophetis to be inspired by sitting on a quasi-tripod, called an axon. But what was it? The word literally means an "axle" or "pivot". So it suggests something containing a movable part. (For axones containing Solon's laws, i.e. wooden tablets hinged on a central stand, cf. P.J. Rhodes, commentary on Ath. Pol. 131-5.) Here we have to venture into the realm of conjecture. The two further methods of inspiration which Iamblichus mentions both concern proximity to water. May the axon have been a pivoted seat which would allow the prophetis to be swung out over the outflow of the sacred spring? It would have been possible, of course for the prophetis to wet her feet or the hem of her dress without being suspended in air, but the last-named method - receiving the vapour from the water - would undoubtedly be most effectively performed by being placed vertically over the spring. The word for receiving breath from the water is itself rather uncertain in meaning. Iamblichus quotes from Porphyry

Appendix II. The Functioning of the Oracles at Didyma and Claros.

(ad Ane . p. 3). So it must have been recognised as appropriate to the situation. But the root of the verb could mean any emanation from steam to water vapour. It is not likely that the prophetis was subjected to steam arising from a heated cauldron. More probably the spring was supposed to give forth an invisible breath which would inspire the prophetis, who inhaled it after suitable ritual preliminaries.

Here again it would be possible to draw analogies from the Pythia. When seated on the Delphic tripod she was over or in immediate proximity to a hole from which vapours were supposed to arise which inspired her, if she was in a proper state to receive them. So the functions of the axon and the sacred spring correspond exactly to the tripod and the mouth of the earth-oracle (stomion). For a recent description cf. G. Roux, Delphes, 109ff. On the other hand, there is a marked difference from Claros. Iamblichus never describes the prophetis as drinking from the sacred spring, while like other ancient authors he pictures the prophet at Claros as inspired by the actual draught of water. Again venturing into the realm of conjecture, can this be because the water at Claros was abundant, but at Didyma was scarce? The present state of the two sites would certainly suggest this picture. Even at the height of summer the chambers and passages of Claros are now so full of water as to make one wonder how the ancient priesthood controlled the supply. At Didyma on the contrary the floor of the adyton is normally dry. Of course there is some danger in supposing that the conditions were identical in antiquity. The water-table in both places may have shifted in opposite directions in the last two thousand years. But it is noteworthy that ancient tradition treated the Didymaean spring as having disappeared between 493 and 334 B.C., and again at the time of the Gothic invasions in the third century A.D. it was hailed as a miracle of Apollo that enough water could be found in the adyton to provide drinking for the local populace. If the sacred spring was often no more than a puddle, the practice may have been instituted that the prophetis need only have contact or near proximity to achieve inspiration.

The third and fourth methods depended on the use of water. Curiously enough, Iamblichus does not define this as the sacred spring in the adyton, but clearly this must be what is meant. The first reference to it, as we have seen (p. 36 supra) occurs in Callisthenes, when he records the re-emergence after Alexander had rescued Miletus from Persian control. It is treated as the miraculous revival of the oracle, and evidently it is implied that the spring played a major role in the functioning. But no details are given. One would naturally suppose on the analogy of Claros that in the archaic period the prophet had drunk inspiring draughts of water from the fountain. In the revival the authorities of Miletus, lacking a continuity of tradition with the Branchidae modelled their personnel and practice on Delphi (cf. supra pp. 41-2). At this time there is no statement that drinking sacred water played any important part in the ritual of the Pythia (Parke and Wormell, D.O. 1,27 ff.) So it is plausible that the Milesian restorers may have stressed other methods of contact with the sacred spring.

It may seem strange that four different descriptions of the prophetis' procedure should have been available to Iamblichus. But this raises the next question: how far did the enquirers at Didyma have access to the prophetis when she was in trance? At Delphi they were admitted to a room in the adyton, at least within earshot, and probably within sight of the Pythia. We have no literary evidence on the subject from Didyma, but the plan of the temple presents a very different picture. While at Delphi there was nothing to prevent the enquirer from proceeding direct from the entrance of the temple to the adyton, at Didyma, as we have seen, the pronaos ended in a blank wall with a great opening at a height of some five feet from the floor (p. 51 supra). It would have been possible to obtain access to the adyton by either of the two narrow sloping corridors, which lead down from the level of the pronaos. In fact it would be not unlike the system at Claros, if enquirers were led down to hear the oracle uttered. But this would be quite inconsistent with the striking feature of the great window opening. No ancient description of its use survives, but it has been generally supposed by modern scholars that, after the prophetis had spoken, the prophetes came to this elevated platform and delivered the responses to the enquirers waiting below in the pronaos. On this hypothesis enquirers were not admitted to the adyton, and it would suit with this that the methods of the prophetis were not known to the public.

Another unique feature at Didyma fits with this picture of the procedure. There was a building called the Chresmographeion ("oracle-writing place") put up in the third century B.C. (pp. 65 and 70 supra). Delphi contained no office of this kind. Scholars usually consider this building at Didyma from the point of view of the enquirer receiving the reply, and

Appendix II. The Functioning of the Oracles at Didyma and Claros

picture it as the place from which written answers were issued. This would not be inconsistent with the imagined ceremony of the prophet uttering Apollo's responses from the window opening. After hearing all the replies announced in succession, the enquirers could obtain copies of the individual answers from the Chresmographeion. But this was probably not its only function. The real importance of the office may have been that it was the place where the enquirer initiated his consultation by submitting his enquiry in writing. At Didyma this may have been particularly necessary because of the exclusion of the enquirer from the adyton. This had the effect that he was not able to control the form in which the question was put to the prophetis, whereas at Delphi he would have the satisfaction of being present in the adyton when the question was put. The best way to satisfy the enquirer that there had been no muddle during the secret happenings in the adyton at Didyma was for his question to be received in writing and ultimately to be returned with the official version of the answer appended. It may be because of this close linkage of question and answer in a written record that more often in the case of Didyma than of other oracular centres, when the god's reply was inscribed, it was preceded by a statement of the enquiry.

The special peculiarity at Didyma of the exclusion of the enquirer from the adyton and the ceremony of consultation is entirely involved in the structural plan of the building. This raises the question whether it was already foreseen and intended when the design of the temple was originally approved. Dr Voigtländer, Jungste Apollontempel, 33 has produced evidence to suggest that, when the walls of the adyton were first contructed, allowance had not been made for the great stairway to reach to such a height as it does at present. This implies that the original plan of the Hellenistic temple placed no obstacle in the way of the enquirer advancing through the pronaos and going straight down a staircase starting at the level of the pavement and ending on the floor of the adyton. Otherwise, the original restorers of the oracle had not thought of the practice of Didyma differing in this respect from Delphi. The exact date of the change in design is uncertain, but could well be before the mid-third century and be connected with the contemporary erection of the Chresmographeion. Also it was the time when Miletus might have been under political control of the Ptolemies. Can it be that the change in plan and procedure represented a turning

Appendix II. The Functioning of the Oracles at Didyma
and Claros

away from purely Hellenic practice and a deliberate
imitation of an Egyptian model? For an "audience-
window" (θυρίς), used for the transmission of petit-
ions to the Ptolemies or their high officials, see
Wilcken, Urkunden der Ptolemäerzeit, I, index. For
a more detailed discussion of this question see
H. W. Parke, JHS. 106 (1986).

Iamblichus does not mention how often a consultation took place, but his allusions to elaborate
preliminary exercises intended to fit the prophetis to
play her part in the rite implies that at the very
least it cannot have been more often than every fifth
day, and actually one may suppose that as at Delphi
the main consultation occurred once a month. There
is no evidence from Didyma to suggest that the rite
may have been suspended during the winter. At Delphi
this interruption was associated with the cult of
Dionysus, which took over the sanctuary for that period. But Dionysus has no special place at Didyma.

The preliminaries mentioned by Iamblichus are
only partly paralleled at Delphi. The total chastity
(if that is the meaning of Hagisteia) was required of
Pythia and prophetis alike. The baths are not mentioned at Delphi until in a source so late that it has
little value in itself, but purification by water was
so generally recognised there that it is unlikely that
the Pythia, at least in the fourth century B.C., had
no such practice, though it need not have been by
bathing in Castalia. There is some evidence that the
Pythia may have had a house in the extensive area of
the sanctuary, but nothing to suggest Iamblichus'
picture of the prophetis living in the adyton itself
(Parke and Wormell, D.O. 1, 34 and Parke, BCH. 102
(1978), 214). The nearest resemblance is at Patara,
where the promantis was shut into the temple at night,
when the oracle was functioning (p. 185 supra). How
it was done at Didyma is difficult to prove, but raises other hypothetical possibilities. The only buildings in the courtyard of the adyton for which the
German excavators could find evidence were the fountain head and the naiskos. This latter was clearly
designed as a shrine for the cult statue and not
meant primarily as a dwelling. It would not have been
physically impossible to put it to such a use, but it
seems undignified and improbable. On the other hand,
if the term adyton is taken in its literal meaning to
include all the parts of the temple not open normally
to the laity, the building at Didyma offers extensive
possibilities. Out of the great central room at the
top of the main staircase run two flights of stairs
in the thickness of the wall (cf. supra p. 52). Their

function was to give access to some space above the ceiling of the great central room. It has been suggested that they could be used to reach the front of the building, and that, as was found in other Asian temples, there were openings in the pediment, which could be the scene of ritual appearances or worship on an elevated level. For pedimental openings in the temple of Artemis at Ephesus, see Bluma L. Trell, N. Chr 4 (1964), 95 and R. Demangel, REG. 70 (1946), 144. We are in no position to exclude any such possibility, but also it might have been possible for the upper structures of the building to contain a suite of rooms for the use of the prophetis, while she was undergoing her ritual preliminaries. The three days' fasting which Iamblichus mentions has no parallel in the surviving accounts of the Pythia's preparations. But one must recall that Iamblichus wrote in the third century A.D., and some of his sources may have been near his own date. If so, it is not surprising if in the passing of centuries since Didyma first borrowed its ritual procedure from Delphi some elaborations of the original model had been introduced.

One of these was probably the use of choirs. Delphi was familiar with the singing of choral hymns to Apollo at festivals, but music and singing are not mentioned in connection with the consultation of the oracle. At Didyma, however, in the response in which Apollo rejected statues and expressed a wish for choral songs, he referred to them as being performed at the time of oracular enquiry (p. 103 supra). This would suit exactly again the structure of the temple. The grand staircase leading from the court of the adyton to the great central room and its window-opening is obviously designed for some majestic procession which would have most effect if accompanied by singing of hymns. Similarly also it is difficult to believe that the great window-opening was not designed to play its part in the ceremony. It should have remained closed by the leaves of a great door, or if that was impracticable, covered by a massive curtain, until the moment when the prophet was ready to appear. Vergil in his imaginary description of Aeneas consulting the Apolline oracle on Delos pictures in rhetorically heightened phrases the climax of just such an enquiry:-

> "Of a sudden everything seemed to tremble, the threshold and the bay-tree of the god, and all the mountain to move about them, and the tripod to bellow, as the adyton was laid open." (Aen. 3, 90).

217

Appendix II. The Functioning of the Oracles at Didyma and Claros

This was the effect which the consultation at Didyma aimed to produce.

In simpler terms one may picture that on the day of consultation the enquirers would gather in the pronaos. Already on the previous day they would have been required to submit their questions in writing to the secretaries at the Chresmographeion. For the three previous days also the prophetis had been undergoing her preliminary austerities. The main day of the consultation probably started early with the enquirers assembling in the pronaos soon after dawn. If we are right in the conjecture that the prophetis had slept in some room in the upper stories of the temple, the first act of the ritual may have been to escort her down the stairs into the central room and then to proceed down the grand staircase to the naiskos and the sacred spring. This ceremonial would be conducted by the prophetes, and he may have been accompanied throughout not merely by the minor officials, but also by a choir singing hymns. If at this point the central window was uncovered, the procession would be partly visible and fully audible to those standing in the pronaos. For the enquirers then an interval would elapse. The central window might be covered while the ritual in the adyton was performed. One imagines some worship before the cult image of Apollo. Sacrifices of animal victims would already have been made at the altar in front of the temple, but there might still be offerings to lay before the god and incense to burn. Then the prophetis would undergo the final process of inspiration at the sacred spring by one or more of the methods enumerated by Iamblichus. In a trance state she would reply to the questions put to her by the prophetes, and her answers would be arranged in the proper form of hexameters for public delivery. (It is better not to attempt to discuss the insoluble question how far the oracular responses were founded on actual utterances of the prophetis, and how far they were the composition of the prophetes and his staff, or again whether they were prepared to some extent in advance of the actual time of the trance.)

Meanwhile excitement will have been mounting among the enquirers in the pronaos. They could not see the procedure in the adyton, and it may have been shut off from them, if the window was closed. Perhaps at most some distant sounds of indistinguishable voices would drift through to the waiting crowd. At last the ritual of consulting Apollo would be over, and the prophetes would give the signal for the procession to re-form. The enquirers would hear the

Appendix II. The Functioning of the Oracles at Didyma and Claros

hymn commence in the distance and swell in volume as the choir mounted the staircase. The triple doorways at the top of the steps would make it possible to marshal the singers in two lines escorting on either side a line of officials culminating in the prophetes himself. As they stepped into the central room, the window would be flung open, and the prophetes would advance between the dividing lines to his position above the expectant crowd. One may surmise that the prophetis herself did not appear. After three days of fasting and the ordeal of the trance she would need to remain in the adyton below till she had recovered from her exhaustion. Meanwhile the prophetes delivered to the public the enquiries and the answers of Apollo. Then the window would be closed, and the gathering would disperse to collect the copies of their answers later from the Chresmographeion.

This description is largely based on hypothesis and is only offered exempli gratis. But something on these lines is required to fit with our literary and archaeological evidence. In this discussion attention has been focussed on the method of ecstatic prophecy, but at Didyma as at Delphi there may have been available to enquirers a cheaper and more frequent method of consultation by lot. The only evidence for it at Didyma is what can be extracted by conjecture from the knucklebone dedication (cf. p. 32 supra and for Delphi, Parke and Wormell, D.O. 1, 18).

(ii) CLAROS

Claros has the one point in common with Didyma that the procedure centred on a sacred spring which had been used for divination from pre-hellenic times. We are fortunate in having the description of its procedure recorded by Tacitus as well as several significant references in other authors. But it is best to begin again with Iamblichus, who this time gives a single account which corresponds closely with our other literary sources and the material remains:-

"The oracle at Colophon is agreed by all to function by means of water. For there is a spring in an underground building (oikos), and it is from that the prophet drinks. On certain appointed nights, when many religious rites have previously been performed, he drinks and utters the oracle, while he is no longer seen by the ambassadors who are present."

Iamblichus (3, 11) gives a more precise picture

219

Appendix II. The Functioning of the Oracles at Didyma and Claros

than Tacitus or Pliny who write of a grotto (specus; cf. supra pp. 137-8). Also the statement that the consultation took place on "certain appointed nights" is exactly confirmed by the allusion in Aristides to a "holy night" (cf. supra p. 147). The description of the prophet no longer seen by the ambassadors who are present fits closely with the procedure that the enquirers were admitted to sit on the benches in the outer room in the basement, while the prophet proceeded alone to the innermost chamber containing the spring. This account was obviously derived by Iamblichus from some author describing some official consultation from a city represented by a considerable delegation in the period after the Hadrianic revival.

Superficially, this description accords with Tacitus, but a closer examination may suggest some points of difference. Iamblichus and Tacitus agree that to achieve inspiration the prophet drank from a spring in the basement of the temple, but Tacitus gives no indication that the enquirers accompanied the prophet part way underground. In fact his description could imply the contrary. The prophet ascertains the names and number of enquirers before he leaves them, which suggests that he dealt with all the enquirers en bloc. The French excavators have not supplied an estimate of the number who could be accommodated on the marble benches in the basement, but it cannot have been many. Tacitus' description would fit better if the enquirers remained in the temple above, where obviously an indefinitely large number could be accommodated. This would explain why Tacitus omitted the sensational fact of the enquirers' underground pilgrimage.

Tacitus also wrote before the increase in personnel which accompanied the Hadrianic revival. To him the same priest (sacerdos) drinks the water and recites spontaneous verses. But as we have seen, (p. supra), the inscriptions from late in Hadrian's reign name three functioning officials: the priest (hiereus) the prophet and the singer of oracles (thespiodos) together with one or two secretaries. Of these the priest and the thespiodos were appointed for long periods or life: the prophet changed annually. The distribution of functions between these would seem to be that the priest was responsible for the performance of sacrifices and probably presided over all the ceremonies. The prophet drank the water and uttered the oracle. The thespiodos reproduced it in verse which he sang, while the secretaries kept a written record. This has been the usual hypothesis (e.g. Cagnat, IGRRP, 4, no. 1587 with notes). But L. Robert, though

Appendix II. The Functioning of the Oracles at Didyma
and Claros

originally following it (e.g. Anatolian Studies, 8
(1958), 59) has later argued that the thespiodos drank
the water and sang, while the prophet edited the prophecy (les redigeant): cf. La civilization grecque de
l'antiquité a nos jours, edited by Charles Delvoye and
Georges Roux (1967), p. 305. He argues that this
distribution of functions suits better with the annual
appointment of the prophet. Obviously some of the
complicated responses which are recorded for this
period would be unlikely to be produced and sung by
a novice, but might be possible for someone who had
developed such a technique over the years. But also it
would presumably be easier for him to produce them if
he was called on to versify and amplify some message,
which was first conveyed to him in prose. This process could have been spun out long enough to enable
him to produce his extempore versification. On the
other hypothesis, if the thespiodos within the holy
of holies uttered the response immediately in verse,
the function of the prophetes would seem to be superf-
luous. He might even be worse at intoning verse than
the experienced professional. Incidentally it is
perhaps worth giving some weight to Iamblichus' use of
the term prophetes. He quite correctly describes the
woman at Didyma as the prophetis. He does not mention
the thespiodos because he is exclusively interested
in the act of inspiration, just as he also does not
mention the prophetes at Didyma who had a similar
secondary function.

One may note the curious point that, beginning
with the first known thespiodos - Asclepiades the son
of Demophilus - it is recorded that he was a Heraclid
descended from Ardys (a king of the Lydian dynasty
before Gyges). Also a later thespiodos makes similar
claims. It is not clear whether the lineage was simply a distinction or whether it gave him some right to
the position (Picard, Ephèse, pp. 209-12). There was
a Mopsus or Moxos among the Lydian kings who seems to
have been the native counterpart of the Greek hero
(cf. Xanthus the Lydian ap. Ath. 8, 346D and Nic. Dam.
F. Gr. Hist. 90 f16). But these thespiodoi claimed
descent from a later member of the dynasty.

Here it is worthwhile to consider the practical
point that the system of basement passages could only
be made accessible safely to enquirers if there was
a good supply of official attendants familiar with the
route. Whether consultations took place by day or by
night, the labyrinth under the temple was not reached
by any external light. A narrow passage admitting
only a single line of persons at a time with a low
ceiling and half a dozen right angle turns calls for

the use of numbers of experienced staff equipped with torches or lamps. On the other hand it is unreasonable to suppose that such a complicated system was originally designed simply for the purpose of enablin the prophet alone to reach the sacred spring from the level of the temple-floor. It is probably not a mere accident of survival that the documents from Claros, at least as so far published, suggest that the Hellenistic period from 200 B.C. had a considerable establishment, and again from the time of Hadrian onward, but show little evidence for officials in the late Republican and Julio-Claudian periods. This may correctly illustrate the fluctuation in the numbers of staff at Claros. In the Hellenistic period the underground passages were designed to allow official embassies as separate bodies or individual enquirers at most in small groups into the subterranean chamber of enquiry. Such a procedure probably worked for som time, but after such events as the Pirates' raid or even the general decline in the late Hellenistic period, it had to be abandoned. Poverty and the growth of scepticism will have greatly reduced the number of official embassies, and the oracle with a skeleton staff will have tried to maintain its practice on the support of private enquirers dealt with as economically as possible.

The procedure of this period is illustrated not only by Tacitus' description, but also by the situation indicated by Oenomaus with his number of individuals consulting Apollo simultaneously. Again just as Tacitus states that the prophet answered the enquirer without having heard their questions and does not him self record Germanicus' enquiry, Oenomaus never state what he asked. In contrast the typical verse oracle of the post-Hadrian period contains an introductory address, which implies that the embassy has put a question in normal form and the theological responses are regularly preceded by a stated query.

All this points to a considerable development of procedure at Claros coinciding with the Hadrianic revival. The practice of taking sacred embassies, an other important enquirers at least, into the basement room was revived with some prestigious features. A date or dates in the month, perhaps the seventh or th twentieth - those numbers particularly associated wit Apollo - was declared the Holy Night for the purpose consultation, and the procedure was described as a Mystery. The enquirers would be required to satisfy the priests that they were not ritually impure and ma have been expected to undergo some mild requirements to abstain from certain food or drink and from sexua intercourse, to submit to lustration with holy water, and to repeat certain liturgic formulae after the priest. The ceremony itself in its reformed style must have been very impressive. Meeting in the temple in the dark and escorted by <u>mystagogoi</u> in batches down the steps and along the passages to the lamp-lit room, where they presented their enquiries and waited while the prophet went beyond them into the chamber containing the spring. His voice may have been heard indistinctly from within, and was taken up by the <u>thespiodos</u>, who chanted the response in verse. Then the first batch of enquirers would be ushered out through the opposite doorway and the alternative range of passages so as to make way for a new batch of enquirers. The most serious problem of subterranean traffic was presented by the stretch of corridor leading straight down the middle under the temple. It must have been necessary to ensure that no one entered this from the direction of the <u>pronaos</u> until all those coming from the inner room had passed through. Actually, if one approaches this passage from the <u>pronaos</u> by the northern flight of steps just before turning right to enter it there is a deep recess on the left which could have provided room for some official to stand and stop the movement along the central passage until he was certain it was clear.

There is no record of a separate <u>Chresmographeion</u> at Claros, but after the enquirers had emerged they must have been supplied with a copy of the <u>thespiodos'</u> poem, which had been taken down in shorthand by the secretaries. The texts which were inscribed in such places as Troketta and Pergamum were much too long to have been reproduced from memory after one hearing.

The changes of procedure and the introduction of special ritual for enquirers from the Hadrianic period onward may also have been accompanied by more stringent rules for the prophet. At least Iamblichus, who seems to be well informed about Claros, was prepared to give some details. He describes the condition of the prophet when inspired and also his preliminary regimen. "The prophet is not in his own control and does not follow at all, what he is saying or where he is, so that even after uttering the oracle he has difficulty in recovering himself. Also before drinking he fasts completely for a whole day and a night, and in certain sanctuaries untrodden by the populace he has retired by himself when he begins to be inspired, and by his retirement and abstention from human affairs he presents himself untarnished for the reception of the god."(<u>De Myst</u>. 3, 11).

It was the purpose of Iamblichus' argument to

stress the spiritual side of oracular inspiration, bu
we can take it that he was correct in the requirement
of a fast of twenty-four hours as a preliminary. Thi
was much less rigorous than the three days' fast impos
ed on the prophetess at Didyma. The retirement is
rather vaguely described and probably should be taken
as referring simply to the way in which the prophet
when seeking inspiration from Apollo went into the
farthest part of the <u>adyton</u>, which was not to be entered by others. The account of the trance-state
attained at the time of inspiration is vivid and may
correspond to an actual phenomenon: but whether on al
occasions it is impossible to tell.

It is not certain that the elaborate ceremonial
of the Holy Night with the Mystery and the undergroun
consultation entirely took the place of some simpler
form of oracular consultation. The very fact that th
records of enquiries by embassies from cities make
explicit mention of the initiation ceremony may indic
ate instead that it was possible to evoke a response
from Apollo without waiting for a special occasion an
undergoing an expensive ritual. Just as at Delphi it
seems to have been possible to obtain oracles by lots
drawn by the Pythia without waiting for the one day a
month when she went through the full ritual of the
tripod, so also one may suppose that at Claros there
were simpler day-time procedures more frequent than
the occurrence of the Holy Night.

These are the main points with regard to the pro
cedures of the oracles at Didyma and Claros which are
open to conjecture. It is interesting finally to observe that at Didyma, once the temple and its ritual
were restored again at the beginning of the Hellenistic epoch, the method and procedure, so far as our
evidence goes, continued basically unchanged till the
collapse of paganism. This, if fact, is attributable
to the greatness and stability of Miletus, with which
the sanctuary was so intimately linked. Claros, as
it would appear, had a more varied pattern of proceed
ing, which rose and fell in dignity and complexity
according to the alternating fortune of the sanctuary

(1)   Paus. 7, 2, 6.

(2)   The Clytiads and the Iamids, Parke, Oracles of
Zeus, 173ff. George Forrest reminds me of the
Kragalidai at Delphi, for whom see his article,
"The First Sacred War", BCH. 80 (1956) 45ff.
and Parke and Boardman, JHS. 77 (1957) 277f..
But none of these families ever gave their name
to their oracular site. At Claros in the second century A.D. the Thespiodos in two instances is described as a Heraclid, but it is not
clear that this gave an hereditary right, cf.
supra Appendix II p. 221.

(3)   The only occurrence of Didyma, Hdt. 6, 19, is
in a verbatim quotation of the Delphic oracle
(Parke and Wormell, D.O. 2, No. 84).

(4)   Conon, 33 (F. Gr. Hist. 26, 1. 33); Script.
Rer. Myth. ed. Bode (1834) p. 28. (Myth 1. 81);
Varro ap. Sch. Stat. Theb. 8, 198. For the
crude and unGreek character of this myth, cf.
the comment of Klees (Eigenart, p. 54) on the
prophetic dream in Persian contexts in Herodotus. Weizsacker (Roscher, s.n. Branchus),
followed by Escher (P.W.s.n. Branchos), refers
to Quintilian, 11, 3, 55, where a defect of
speech producing a tremolo is so called, and
suggests that "branchos" was a form of utterance used by prophets and therefore a title for
the prophets themselves. But there is no reference to prophets in Quintilian, and the reading is now discredited. Butler (Loeb) prefers
βρασμόν , and is followed by Winterbottom (OCT.).
I can only trace Branchus as a mythological
name in Apollodorus, Epit. 1, 3 - the father of
Cercyon,

(5)   The earliest reference to Branchus appears to
occur in Callimachus, fr. 229 (Pfeiffer) = P.

Oxy. 2172, 1-22, though the name itself canno
be restored in the fragment. There is, however, an allusion to him as descended on his
father's side from the family of Daitas and o
his mother's from the Lapiths. Strabo, 9, 3.9
when describing the tomb of Neoptolemus at
Delphi mentions that "Branchus who was in
charge of the sanctuary at Didyma" was a descendant (ἀπόγονος) of Machaereus, who slew
Neoptolemus. For Machaereus as a son of Daitas, see Asclepiades of Tragilus, F. Gr. Hist.
12 f.15 = Sch P.N. 7, 62. The legend of Smik
ros is found in Conon, 33 (F. Gr. Hist.26, 1,
33) and Varro ap. Sch. Stat. Theb. 8, 198.
The versions differ in that Varro describes
Smikros' father as 'Cius quidam decimus ab
Apolline" and the owner of the goats as "Patron". Also the goddess Leucothea does not
identify herself.

(6)   The fullest account surviving is in Varro ap.
Sch. Stat. Theb. 8, 198. Also Statius, Theb.
3, 478 with sch. References to Branchus as
the beloved of Apollo, often in association
with Hyacinthus or Admetus are frequent in
late romantic literature:- Longus, Daphnis
and Chloe, 4, 17, 6; Philostratus, Ep. 5, 8
and 57; Lucian, Domo, (10), 24, D. Deor. (79)
2. For two Pompeian wall paintings and a Hel
lenistic relief identified as representing
Branchus, P.W. 3, 814. For the rod in connec
tion with the functioning of the oracle, see
Appendix II, pp. 210-12 supra.

(7)   Callimachus, fr. 229. He described Apollo as
brought by a dolphin from Delos, Οἰκούσ]ιον εἰ
ἄστυ   . The use of periphrasis for Miletus
as George Huxley points out to me, may be
meant to suggest a pre-Ionian setting. Cf.
Nikainetos, fr. 1. (Powell) = Parthenius II.

(8)   Callimachus, fr. 194, 28. The reference to
the "sons of the Ionians" suggests here a
setting after the Ionian migration, but Callimachus need not be expected to have been his
torically consistent between one poem and
another.

(9)   Clem. Al. Str. 5, 8, 48, citing Apollodorus
of Corcyra. The words do not make a sentence
but are just a succession of nouns. Hesychiu
s. vv. gives explanations for the meanings of
some of them, which differ from Clement. See
L. & S. (9) s. vv. On the subject, Bentley,
Epist. ad Millium, 477ff. Lobeck, Aglaophamus,

1331.

(10)   Conon, 44 (F. Gr. Hist. 26), Wilamowitz, GGA.
176 (1914), 75.

(11)   Nicolaus of Damascus, F. Gr. Hist. 90 f.52.
Assesos, Hdt. 1, 19 and 22. Wilamowitz, GGA.
168 (1906), 640.

(12)   For a similar legend, cf. e.g. the aition for
the cult of Dionysus Aisymnetes at Patrae,
Paus. 7, 19, 49 and Parke and Wormell, D.O. 1,
333. For the Kabeiroi at Miletus and Didyma,
B. Hemberg, Die Kabiren, pp. 138 ff., 153 and
170. The decree of the proconsul Caecina
Paetus, Wiegand, Abh. Akad. Berlin. 1908, 26ff.
Forrest has called my attention to the family
of the Totteidai on Chios in the fourth century B.C., an island which also had a cult of
the Kabeiroi, B.S.A. 55. (1960), 172-189 and
Hemberg, op. cit. 140. The cult and the family name must have reached the island well
before that century.

(13)   Rehm, Milet, 3, no. 185. Note the problem of
Cyzicus, whose founder is described as Apollo
himself, but is not identified as Pythian
(Parke and Wormell, D.O. 2, no. 522). Was he
Apollo Didymeus? For the Milesian exile who
may have consulted Delphi, Parke and Wormell,
D.O. 1, 81, note 85.

(14)   Parke and Wormell, D.O. 1, 387ff., and 2,
no. 247 and 248. Dedication to Apollo of
Didyma, D.L. 1, 32; to Apollo Delphinios at
Miletus, D.L. 1, 28; to the Ismenian Apollo at
Thebes, Plu. Sol. 4, 3.

(15)   For the evidence on the Seven Wise Men and
further discussion, Parke and Wormell, D.O.
1, 388.

(16)   Hdt. 2, 159, 2. Dedications by Amasis in Lindos and Samos, Hdt. 2, 182.

(17)   Alyattes' invasions and reconciliation Hdt.
1, 17-23. Croesus' test, Hdt. 1, 46, 2.
Croesus' magnificent dedications, Hdt. 1, 92,
2; 5, 36, 3; 6, 19, 3. For a favourable view
of the historicity of Croesus' test, Klees,
Eigenart, 64ff. For a fuller discussion of
the relations of Croesus with Branchidae, see
Parke, G.R.B.S. 25 (1984).

(18)   Hdt. 1, 157-161. It is not clear what building the sparrows nested in. It might have
been in the outer wall of the new temple or in
the old sekos wall, if it was still standing.
If there was a new naiskos, Aristodicus would
not be likely to have had unrestricted access

to it. I find Truesdell S. Brown, <u>AJP</u>. 99 (1978), 64ff. unconvincing.

(19)   Cyrus' understanding with Miletus, Hdt. 1, 141, 4.

(20)   Cf. Appendix I, p. 204 supra.

(21)   Cf. Appendix I, p. 205 supra.

(22)   Hecataeus' advice, Hdt. 5, 36, 2 and 3.

(23)   Tacitus, <u>An</u>. 3, 63. The letter to Gadates, Meiggs-Lewis, no. 12. Delos, Hdt. 6, 97, 2. Burghard Fehr, <u>Marburger Winckelmannprogamm</u>, 1971/2, 51ff. Zur Geschichte des Apollonheiligtum von Didyma, argues on architectural grounds that Cyrus had largely subsidised the building of the late archaic temple. I do not find him convincing.

(24)   Parke and Wormell, <u>D.O</u>. 1, 141 (The response to Cnidus) and 158ff. (the response to Argos).

(25)   Hdt. 6, 18-21. Consistently with this destruction Herodotus writes of the oracle-centre elsewhere in the past tense (1, 157, 3 and cf. supra p.16). For a different version of the sacking of Branchidae by the Pérsians, cf. Callisthenes, <u>F</u>. <u>Gr</u>. <u>Hist</u>. 124 f 14 and pp. 36-9 supra.

(26)   The knuckle-bone dedications: <u>Délégation en Perse</u>, (Ministère de l'Instruction publique et des Beaux-Arts), Tome 7; Recherches Archéologiques, Deuxième série, (1905). Ed. J. de Morgan, p.155. Offrande à Apollon Didyméen. Par B. Haussoullier. Cf. supra. pp. 30-31.

PART 1, CHAPTER 2.

(1)   The most recent general survey of the archaeological evidence, K. Tuchelt, <u>Die archäischen Skulpturen von Didyma</u> (Istanbuler Forschungen, 27, Berlin, 1970). For subsequent reports, <u>Istanbuler Mitteilungen</u>, 21 (1971) and later.

(2)   Tuchelt, op. cit. and Naumann-Tuchelt, <u>Ist</u>. <u>Mitt</u>. 13/14, (1963/64), 15ff and 31ff.

(3)   Necho, p. 14 supra. Croesus, p. 15 supra. The dimensions at the top step of the Heraion of Rhoecus were 52m x 94.6m, and of the Artemisium 55.1m x 115.4m. The archaic Didymeion can only be measured inside the peristyle, where it was 20m x 70m (probably). As the east end is lost the exact length cannot be established. Cf. R. A. Tomlinson, <u>Greek Sanctuaries</u>, p. 125 and p. 129, and H. Berve and F. Gruben, <u>Greek Temples</u>, <u>Theatres and Shrines</u>.

(4)   Tuchelt, Die archäischen Skulpturen, p. 199
        argues for a naiskos of c.550 B.C. with a new
        mainland type of sloping tiled roof. See also
        Gruben, JDAI, 78 (1963), Das archaische Didy-
        meion, pp. 95ff.
(5)   Paus. 5, 13, 11. Tuchelt, op. cit. p. 305.
        B. Fehr, Marburger Winckelmannprogramm, 1971/
        72, 29, denies the identification and des-
        cribes it as a tholos.
(6)   Paus. 2, 10, 5, and 9, 10, 2.
(7)   Pliny, H.N. 34, 75. Of reproductions the most
        important is the relief of the imperial per-
        iod from the theatre at Miletus, R. Kekule von
        Stredonitz, Sitz, Berl. Akad. 1904, 786-801.
(8)   E. Bielefeld, Ist. Mitt. 12 (1962), 18-45,
        R. Ghirshman, Beiträge zum alten Geschichte
        und deren Nachleben, (Festschrift Altheim), 1
        (1969), 35, un précurseur urartien d'Apollon
        Philesios.
(9)   E. Simon, Charites: Studien zur Altertumswis-
        senschaft, ed. K. Schoenburg (Bonn, 1957),
        pp. 38-46. For Zeus with the deer associated
        in Caria, though not represented on the hand,
        see A. Laumonier, Cultes, 127-129 and for
        Apollo Philesios, 578ff.
(10)   Didyma, II, no. 11. Jeffery, LSAG, no 36. Cf.
        the reply of the Pythia: νόμῳ πόλεως   Parke
        and Wormell, D.O. 2, no. 135.
(11)   Milet, 3, no. 132, p. 276. Sokolowski, Asie
        Mineure, no. 42, p. 114, Jeffery, LSAG. no.
        39. May the fact that the Branchidae used
        prose, not verse, in ecstatic prophecy be be-
        cause their ancestors never acquired the tech-
        nique of Greek epic hexameters?
(12)   Milet, 3, no. 178, p. 397, Jeffery, LSAG, no.
        33. See Parke, Hermathena, 130/31 (1981), 99-
        112, Apollo and the Muses.
(13)   Hommel, Ist. Mitt. 7 (1957), 32-37.
(14)   Haussoullier in Délégation en Perse, 155,
        Jeffery, LSAG. no. 30. See p. 21   supra and
        p. 228 note. 26 . The source of the dedicat-
        ion (ἀπο λείο)is philologically more likely
        to mean "from a standing crop", but more
        plausibly "from booty". Haussoullier's compar-
        ison with the "golden harvests" dedicated by
        cities at Delphi is not relevant. For this
        and other astragaloi in Greek art, P. Perdriz-
        et, REG. 34 (1921), 64ff. and J. Six, JHS 13
        (1892/3), 134. At Tegea, IG. 5, 2, 125. At
        Olympia, the statue of Charis, Paus. 6, 14, 6.
        For actual astragaloi as offerings, perhaps

connected with divination, P. Amandry, L'antre
Corycien, II, BCH. Suppli. IX, 347-78. Ch.
Picard, REG. 42 (1929), 121, suggests a connection between the dedication at Didyma and
the method of divination used - an idea which
occurred independently to the present author.
See also Laumonier, Cultes, 572. For lot-
oracles see also p. 181 supra.

PART 1. CHAPTER 3.

(1) Hdt. 6, 19, 3ff. For archaeological evidence
of a deep burnt stratum at the temple, Hahland, JDAI, 79 (1964), p. 144.
(2) Hdt. 9, 104.$_3$
(3) Ditt. Syll. ^{3} 57.
(4) Apart from the negative argument of the silence of our authorities on the oracle at Didyma for the period 493-334 B.C., and Herodotus's use of the past tense, when writing of it
(1, 157, 3), there is the positive statement
of Callisthenes (F. Gr. Hist. 124 f.14), as
cited by Strabo (17, 1, 43), that the oracle
had ceased and the spring failed from the
sacking of the temple (cf. supra p. 36). The
German excavators have found fragmentary remains of architecture attributable to the fifth century and have been tempted to conjecture
a revival of the oracle before the time of
Alexander. Hahland, JDAI. 79 (1964), 146 for
restored altars; Knackfuss, Didyma, I, pp. 12
and 142ff. for a roofed building conjectured
from some of the material which Hahland assigned to altars. The latest reconstruction
is by W. Voigtländer, Ist. Forsch. 22 (1972),
93ff. He produced from the evidence a design
of both a well-house and a "cult room"; also
he argues with much special pleading for the
probability of a fifth-century revival of the
oracle. This takes no account of the point,
to which I would attach much importance, that
up to 494 B.C. the oracle at Didyma had not
been managed by the city of Miletus, but by
the family of the Branchidae operating in
territory controlled by the city. The removal of the Branchidae had created a complete
gap, which the city did not fill till 334 B.C.
It is possible, though the archaeological
evidence is not decisive, that a spring with
a well-house was restored in the fifth century. But it need not have been used for

oracular purposes, but only for other sacred use.

(5) On the fifth-century history of Miletus, J. P. Barron <u>JHS</u>. 82 (1962), 1, and for the latter part of the Peloponnesian war, H.W. Parke, <u>JHS</u>. 50 (1930), 45. Miletus and Cyrus, Xen. <u>An</u>. 1, 1, 7. Maussolus, Polyaen. 6, 8 and the evidence of coins, Hiller von Gaertringen, <u>P.W</u>. Miletus, 30, 1601.

(6) Ditt. <u>Syll</u>.³ 225. After 346 B.C. Delphi revived its traditions and foreign relations. Cf. Ditt. <u>Syll</u>.³ 292-5, the re-inscribed <u>promanteiai</u>, and the <u>Register of Pythian Victors</u>, edited by Aristotle and Callisthenes. (N. Robertson, <u>Cl.Qu</u>. 28 (1978), 54)

(7) Arr. <u>An</u>. 1, 18, 3. Alexander Stephanephoros, Rehm, <u>Milet</u>. 1, 3, 132.

(8) <u>F.Gr.Hist</u>. 124 f 14 (Str. 17, 1, 43). For the most recent discussion of these rather uncertain dates, A. B. Bosworth, <u>JHS</u>. 101 (1981), 17-40. Curtius places the Branchidae episode shortly before the capture of Bessus (summer, 329); Diodorus immediately after it.

(9) Additional references:- Str. 11, 11, 4 and 14, 1, 5. D.S. 16, list of contents, 20. Curtius Rufus, 7, 5, 28ff. Plu, <u>De sera numinis vindicta</u>, 12 (557C). Paus. 1, 16, 3 and 8, 46, 3. Aelian, fr. 54 (Suda, Βραγχίδαι)

(10) W. W. Tarn, <u>Alexander the Great</u>, 1, 67 and 2, 273 (Appendix 13). Most modern biographies of Alexander simply omit the episode. For a more detailed discussion in reference to Alexander, see Parke, <u>JHS</u>. 105 (1985)

(11) Cf. infra. p. 48

(12) Rehm, <u>Did</u>. II, p. 323b, and No. 273 (second century A.D., middle) and No. 235B ("Gaius, I greet the pretty little prophetess") - an obscure graffito of sarcastic intent. A recently discovered inscription (50-60 A.D?), W. Günther, <u>Ist. Mitt</u>. (1) 30 (1980), 170-75, no. 5 shows a <u>Hydrophoros</u> recording her great-grandmother and namesake 'the prophetis Tryphaena, whom the god appointed by oracle'; presumably a special case.

PART 1. CHAPTER 4

(1) Appian, 11 (<u>Syr</u>.) 56 and 63. Rejected by Wilamowitz, <u>GGA</u>. 168 (1906), 83. The Hellenistic period at Didyma is dealt with in detail by W. Günther, <u>Das Orakel von Didyma in hellen</u>-

istischer Zeit, eine Interpretation von Stein-
Urkunden, (Ist. Mitt.Beiheft 4, 1971). This
should be read in conjunction with the lengthy
criticism by J. Seibert, GGA. 226 (1974),
184ff. Günther rejects this response (p. 70):
Seibert accepts it (pp. 200-2). One of the
difficulties in treating it as authentic is
that Seleucus would not be likely to be in a
position to consult the oracle personally after
its revival, by which time he was probably at
a distance with Alexander. Seibert supposes
an enquiry by letter, which seems rather unlikely. He and Günther both appear to treat
the recurrence of the response at 63 as a
second issue, but this does not seem to be
Appian's meaning.

(2) D.S. 19, 90, 4. Wilamowitz also rejects it.
Günther, 70; Seibert, 202. Demetrius, Plu.
Demetr. 10, 3. Seleucus, 315-13 B.C., D.S. 19,
58, 5 and 68, 2ff; 75 2.

(3) Liban. Antiochicus, (11), 303. Günther, 70.
Justin, 15, 4, 8, connects the consecration of
Daphne with the legend of Apollo's begetting
of Seleucus. For the date of the Antiochicus,
see W. G. Liebeschuetz. Antioch, p. 137, n. 2.
Haussoullier, Études, 215, identifies the two
oracles, addressing Seleucus as king and enjoining on him the foundation of Daphne.

(4) For the latest discussion, see R. A. Hadley,
JHS. 94 (1974), 57.

(5) On the problem of the marriage of Seleucus and
Stratonice, Seibert, op. cit., 198-9.

(6) The decree for Antiochus, Ditt. OGI. 213, Did
II, 479, Günther, 29. The decree for Apame,
Did. II, 480. Günther, 21. Günther's datings
and readings of the inscriptions should be
corrected in view of Seibert's criticisms,
199-200. In describing the relations of the
Hellenistic kings to Didyma, Günther inter-
prets them largely by political motives, while
Seibert refuses to recognise any but religious
purposes. I am inclined rather to agree with
Günther, and do not find Seibert's analogies
from Samothrace and Delos valid, as Didyma,
unlike them, lay in the territory of a polis
of great strategic and economic importance.

(7) Pliny, HN. 6, 49. M. Cary and E. H. Warming-
ton, The Ancient Explorers, p. 135 (Penguin).
But for a later dating, Tarn, The Greeks in
Bactria and India, p. 83. Since I wrote this
L. Robert, BCH. 108 (1984) 167-72 has produced

an elegant argument in favour of the earlier dating.

(8) Did. II, 434-37. See Günther, p. 37, no. 70. These inscriptions were dated by Rehm c. 250 B.C., but L. Robert, Gnomon, 31 (1959), 669 and REG. 74 (1961), 232, no 637 has shown that they should be dated in the period 311-306 B.C.

(9) Kraus. Ist. Mitt. 11 (1961), 126 and Hahland, JDAI 79 (1964), 234. Voigtländer, Jungste Apollontempel, 34-43, the naiskos designed c. 300 and finished before 270 B.C. W. D. Heilmayer, Gnomon, 52 (1980), 741. L. Haselberger's discovery of architectural drawings on the adyton walls may alter the relative and absolute dating of parts of the building, Ist. Mitt. 30 (1980), 191-215 and 33(1983), 90-123.

(10) Vitruvius, 7, preface, 16. On the Artemisium Str. 14, 1, 22. The latest discussion of the Didymeion from the point of view of its decoration is W. Voigtländer, Jungste Apollontempel. He accepts Paeonius as the architect, but would date the production of the design unnecessarily before 334 B.C.

(11) Rehm, Milet. 1, no. 158, Ditt. OGI. 744. It may have been a thank-offering for the return of Canachus' statue as well as for contributions to the building of the temple.

(12) Paus. 1, 16, 3 and 8, 46, 3. The restoration of the Harmodius and Aristogeiton statues by Alexander. Arr. 3, 16, 8 and 7, 19, 2; Pausanias, 1, 8, 5, attributes the restoration to Antiochus.

(13) The Paean, Coll. Alex. p. 140. Justin, 15, 4, 3. For an earlier version of the anchor motif App. Syr. (11), 56. The anchor on coins, Hadley, JHS. 94 (1974), 60, who also discusses the whole subject there and in Historia, 18 (1969), 151. The later continuance of the tradition of Apollo as ancestor of the Seleucids is illustrated by Ditt. OGI. 212, 13 and 219, 26, and the regular coin type of Apollo seated beside the omphalos from Antiochus I. Euphorion, court poet of Antiochus III gave poetic form to the legend of Laodice (fr. 174 Coll. Alex. p. 58). For Didyma as the origin, Stähelin, P.W. Seleucus, col. 1211 and Bevan, The House of Seleucus, 1, 131, 1. See Rostovtzeff, SEHHW. 1, 476 for a curious tradition in Malalas that Seleucus I had a sister, Didymaia, whose sons, Nicanor and Nicomedes, were regents of the East.

(14) For descriptions of the building and its dimensions, see H. Knackfuss, Didyma, I, die Baubeschreibung (1939); A. Rehm, Die grossen Bauberichte von Didyma, Abh. Bayer. Akad. 1939 Roland Martin, Le Didymeion, La Civilization Grecque de l'Antiquité à nos Jours, (eds. Charles Delvoye and Georges Roux), 1967, 296ff., Fehr, Marburger Winehelmannprogramm, 1971/2, 15ff. argues on theoretical grounds that even the archaic temple had had a similar design. Voigtländer, Jungste Apollontempel that the original plan was altered in constuction about mid-third century.

(15) Knackfuss, Did. 1, 48, on the use of the staircases as service to the maintenance of the building. Contrast Rehm, Bauberichte, 9, to climb to the circuit walls and the front part of the building: cult purposes unknown. Günther, 98, n. 17.

(16) See Appendix II, p. 214 supra.

(17) C. C. van Essen, BCH. 70 (1946); 607. Notes sur le deuxième Didymeion. He attempts to define with dates the various stages of the construction. Voigtländer, Jungste Apollontempel, provides the most recent study of this question and of the relations of cult and construction.

(18) Lysimachus and Miletus, Ditt. Syll.^{3} 368. Seleucus' letter, Dittenberger, OGI. 214, Did. ii, 424, Welles, 5, Günther, 44. Seibert, 192 casts doubts on the political implications.

(19) Demetrius and Miletus, Plu. Demetr. 46, 2. The loan from Cnidus, Milet, III, 138.

(20) Ptolemy's acquisition of control in Miletus and the gift of land, Milet, 1, 3, 123, 38ff. and 139, 2. (Welles, no. 14); Günther, 51 with corrections in Seibert, 204. Seibert, 191 n. 10 casts doubts on this interpretation.

(21) Did. II, no. 426, 6-8.

(22) Timarchus, an Aetolian mercenary commander (Polyaen. 5, 25; Front. Str. 3, 2, 11). was presumably in the service of Ptolemy II, and is to be identified with the tyrant of Miletus of the same name (App. Syr. (11), 65). For his rebellion against Ptolemy II, Trogus, prol 26. The dates of these events are very uncertain, but Miletus appears to have been loyal to Ptolemy as late as 262/1 B.C. (Milet, 1, 3 139; Welles, no. 14), and to be restored to freedom in 259/8 B.C. (Ditt. OGI. 226, Did. I no. 358).

(23)   Callimachus, _Iambus_, IV, fr. 194 (Pfeiffer) and
        Branchus, fr. 229. See further Parke, _JHS_. 1986.

(24)   Parthenius, _Erot_. 1. For Aegeus, see Parke
        and Wormell, _D.O._ 1,300 and 2, no. 110. The
        cult legend, _D.S_. 5, 62. On Kastabos, J.M.
        Cook and W. H. Plommer, _The Sanctuary of_
        Hemithea at Kastabos, esp. 162-3. The shrine
        seems to have been rebuilt as a beautiful Ionic
        temple in the last years of the fourth cent-
        ury. Cook and Plommer do not notice the par-
        allel with the Aegeus legend. The difference
        was that Aethra had no sisters. So there was
        no question of rivalry in seduction.

(25)   Antiochus Theos, App. _Syr_. (11), 65. Seleucus
        II, Ditt. _OGI_. 227, _Did_. II, 493, Welles,
        no. 22, Günther, 66.

(26)   Ditt. _Syll_.^{3} 590. On the question of the early
        or late dating of the legend, Wilamowitz,
        Glaube, 1, 324 note 4; Rehm, _Bauberichte_, 7,
        note 2. There was otherwise no tradition about
        the conception of Apollo, but cf. Plu. fr. 157
        (Eus _P.E_. 5, 11).

(27)   On the _asylia_ of Miletus, Günther 81ff.,
        Seibert, 211. On _asylia_ in the Hellenistic
        period, Rostovtzeff, _SEHHW_. 1,200ff.

(28)   On the Zeus-Leto statuette, Naumann-Tuchelt,
        Ist. Mitt. 13/14 (1963/64) 57 and Taf. 23,
        1-4; Hahland, _JDAI_, 79 (1964), 162; Tuchelt,
        Die Archaischen Skulpturen, 192. For the
        statues of Zeus and Leto in the period of Dio-
        cletian, cf. supra. p. 98.

(29)   Delphi and Smyrna's _asylia_, Parke and Wormell,
        _D.O._ 1,371 and 2, no. 345. Delphi and Didyma
        on the _asylia_ of Teos, _Inscr. Cret_. 1, 19, 2.
        The practice may have begun in a rudimentary
        form when Cyzicus requested Delphi to declare
        their territory sacred (_hiera_) on account of
        the festival of the Soteria. The _Didymeia_,
        earliest reference as a local festival; _Did_.
        II, 479, 37 (the decree in honour of Antiochus
        300/299 B.C.); cf. supra, p. 47 . In Ditt.
        Syll.^{3} 590 for the first time the _Didymeia_
        is treated as a Panhellenic festival. The
        Milesian officials named seem to be active
        c. 200 B.C. So the institution of the Panhel-
        lenic _Didymeia_ is usually assigned to about
        that date, which is also the period of some
        victory dedications at Didyma. If the _asylia_
        was declared soon after 247 B.C., the interval
        of over forty years is hard to explain.

(30)   On the Hellenistic settlements of mercenaries,

(31)   Rostovtzeff, SEHHW.1, 149 and 500.
Milet, 1, 3, no. 33 and no. 36; also no. 37b,
34. Wilamowitz, GGA. 176 (1914), 102, and
SEG. 29 (1980), 1348 for proposed supplements.
Professor Errington has suggested to me the
point about the declining population of older
cities.

(32)   F. Sokolowski, Asie Mineure, no. 47; L. Robert,
CRAI. 1968, p. 593, note 6.

(33)   Agreement of Miletus and Magnesia, Milet, 1,
no. 148; Ditt. Syll.3 588; Günther, 92;
Wilamowitz, GGA. 176 (1914), 91.

(34)   Milet, 1, 3, no. 150; Ditt. Syll.3 683.

(35)   Timarchus and Heraclides, App. Syr.(11), 45.
Antiochus IV, Eumenes II and Miletus, Did. II,
488 and Hermann, Ist. Mitt. 15 (1965), 71ff;
Welles, 52; Ditt. OGI. 763. For rather dubious evidence of warm relations between Apollo
Didymeus and the dynasty of the Nicomedes of
Bithynia [Scymnus], 55ff.; not confirmed by
inscriptions at Didyma. The author also
claims the patronage of this Apollo for his
work.

(36)   On the economic state of Miletus at this time
Rostovtzeff, SEHHW. II, 665ff. The building
accounts from 232 B.C., Did. II no. 25ff. Rehm,
Bauberichte, passim.

(37)   Did. II, 32. For a German translation of this
and all the rest of the building accounts, see
Voigtländer, Jüngste Apollontempel, 144-159.
For the Chresmographeion, supra p. 70 and
Appendix II, p.214-9.

(38)   Did. II, 132. Rehm dates by the script to
late second century B.C., and notes the term
ἐπιστατῶν as indicating that Andronicus worked
in the period before Group V of the building
accounts (last years of the second century and
later). The title Asphaleios has a literary
tradition as old as the fifth century B.C.

(39)   Rostovtzeff, SEHHW. II, 825 for the economic
decline. The Pirates' sack, Plu. Pomp. 24.

(40)   Did II, 394 (Ptolemy XII, 54/3 B.C); Günther,
93, note 170. Did. II 218, 6 (Ptolemy XIII,
between 51 and 48 B.C). Voigtländer, Jüngste
Apollontempel, p. 9, and 91, note 250, main-
tains that the opening was too large for any
doors to be hung. Admittedly the term used
(θυρῶμα) could apply to the frame of the
doorway, but I prefer to follow Rehm and suppose that the ivory was to decorate two leaves
of the giant door, and not only the frame of

an empty opening.

PART 1. CHAPTER 5.

(1)   <u>Did</u>. II, 218, 11. 4-6 and <u>Milet</u>, 1, 3, 126, 1.
23.

(2)   The Prophets' House inscriptions, <u>Did</u>. II
pp. 155-168. Knackfuss's reconstruction, <u>Did</u>.
I, 150ff. For names of priests inscribed all
over the place, cf. Laumonier, <u>Cultes</u>, 372 at
Lagina, from the beginning of the first century.

(3)   Tac. <u>Ann</u>. 2, 63. Cf. supra p. 19. Caesar's
<u>asylia</u>, Did. II, 391 A II.

(4)   Suet. <u>Cal</u>. 21; D.C. 59, 28, 1; Zonaras, 11, 7.
The temple of Miletus, L. Robert, <u>Hellenica</u>, 7
(1949), 206ff. The craftsmen of Asia at Didyma, <u>Did</u>. II, 107.

(5)   <u>Did</u>. II, 237 II, and 268; <u>Milet</u>, 1, 3, 134.

(6)   <u>Did</u>. II, 55-57. For conjectures about Trajan
and Didyma, see, id. p. 198b. Prophetes, id.
no. 318. Stephanephoros, id. no. 293. Dio
Chr. 45, 4 with C. P. Jones, <u>Chiron</u>, 5 (1975),
403.

(7)   Hadrian Stephanephoros, <u>Did</u>. II, 306a; prophet, 494; his visit as an annual festival, 254,
10; his cult in Miletus, p. 224a.

(8)   E. R. Dodds, <u>Pagan and Christian in an Age of</u>
<u>Anxiety</u>, (1965). Tac. <u>Ann</u>. 4, 1 (deum ira in
rem Romanam); 16, 16 (ira illa numinum in res
Romanas); 6, 22 (astrology).

(9)   Of the extensive literature, see P. Grimal's
edition and Leon Herrmann, <u>Antiquité Classique,</u>
21 (1952), 16ff., D. Fehling, <u>Amor und Psyche</u>,
23ff. The only evidence for Apuleius in Asia
Minor is <u>De Mundo</u>, 327 (Hierapolis). Cf. 180
infra.

(10)   <u>Milet</u>, 1, 1, 9.

(11)   Wiegand, <u>SB</u>. <u>Berl</u>. <u>Akad</u>. 1904, 83; W. H. Buck-
ler, <u>Anatolian Studies</u>...Ramsay, 34ff; George
E. Bean, <u>Aegean Turkey</u>, 227; L. Robert, <u>CRAI</u>.
1968, p. 581 and note 4.

(12)   Wiegand, <u>SB</u>. <u>Berl</u>. <u>Akad</u>., 1906, 256. <u>Milet</u>, 1,
7, 205(a); Buckeler, <u>Rhein</u>. <u>Mus</u>. 61 (1906),
472; L. Robert, <u>Etudes Epigr. et Philol</u>. (1938)
106 and <u>CRAI</u>. 1968 578, who explains the use
of <u>Heros</u> of the deceased, and illustrates the
Asian practice of financing buildings from
testamentary dispositions.

(13)   Aelian, <u>Hist. An</u>. 7, 4 (Loeb: trans. A. F.

Scholfield). Sen. <u>Did</u>. 4, 31, 6. For Nemesis as goddess of contests, R. Wunsch, <u>Philol</u>. 53 (1894), 400-15.

(14) Wiegand, SB. Berl. Akad. 1906, 256. Milet, 1, 7, no. 205(b). For the identification of Carpus, L. Robert, <u>CRAI</u>. 1968, 876, citing Ditt <u>OGI</u>. no. 755 and 756.

(15) <u>Altertümer von Pergamum</u>, 8, 3, C. Habicht, Die Inschriften des Asclepeions, (1959), no. 2, p. 23. For Marcellus, see <u>The Suda</u>, s.n. For Rufinus, H. Hepding, <u>Philol</u>. 88 (1933), 90 ff. The prohibitions on burial within a city, Ulpisn, <u>Dig</u>. 47, 12 3 and <u>Hist. Aug</u>. Vita Pii 12, 3.

(16) Anth. <u>Pal 14</u>, 72. L. Robert, <u>CRAI</u>. 1968, 599. On oaths and oath ceremonies, J. Plescia <u>The Oath and Perjury in Ancient Greece</u>, (1970) 8ff. (not discussing this instance); Hom. Il. 3, 275.

(17) Rehm, <u>Did</u>. II, 496. I have translated the fuller text, which W. Peek, <u>ZPE</u>. 7 (1971), p. 207, no. 8, has produced, though it may be somewhat daring in its supplements. A. Balanza, Un Frammento degli Ἰωνικά de Paniassi? (<u>Studi Triestini in Antichita in onore di Luigia Achillea</u>, Stella, 1975) conjectures that the reference to Neleus with the peculiar epithet ἀκοντόδοκος comes from Panyassis. I owe this last reference to Professor G. Huxley See Val. Max. (Nepotianus) I, E3, 5, (Julius Paris) 1, 1, 5. and Lact. <u>Div. Inst</u>. 2, 17, 19 for a miraculous vengeance on Alexander's soldiers at the Milesian temple of Demeter. On <u>Epistaseis</u> see L. Robert. Hellenica XI - XII, 544, n. 5.

(18) Professor Wormell and I (<u>D.O</u>. I, 373 and II, no. 467) rather rashly identified this as a Delphic response on the theory that it came from the territory of Magnesia, a city much connected with the Delphic oracle. But we also pointed out Didyma as a possibility. Claros owing to the site and the metre is to be excluded. We now think Didyma much the most probable source, as it fits in style and method with other examples from there. See also Kern, <u>Inscr. Magn</u>. 228 and Rehm, <u>Did</u>. II, 501. Rehm strangely suggested that the reference was not to a eunuch, but to Hercules.

(19) P. Hermann, <u>Chiron</u>, 1 (1971), 291-98; R. Merkelbach, ZPE. 8 (1971), 93-5; T. Drew-Bear and W. D. Lebek, <u>GRBS</u>. 14 (1973), 65ff.

(20) See Appendix I, p. 206 supra.

(21)   Did. II. 277; L. Robert, CRAI. 1968, 586 and
Hellenica, XI-XII, 543.

(22)   Did. II, no. 278. For spontaneous addresses
by the Pythia, Parke and Wormell, D.O. II no.
71 with JHS. 82 (1962), 175 (Battus), no. 29
(Lycurgus), no. 8 (Cypselus) and no. 431
(Attalus).

(23)   Porphyrius Euseb. PE. 5, 6, 190b; Wolff, 129;
L. Robert, CRAI. 1968, 579. For the cult of
Pan in Asia Minor see K. Tuchelt, Ist. Mitt.
19/20 (1969/70), 223. For Porphyry as a
source, see Appendix I, p. 205-6 supra.

(24)   Ael. Hist. An. 13, 21. Cf. Did. II, 497, the
reference to Hamadryads in an oracular response, which was probably of a rather literary
character.

(25)   Porphyrius ap. Euseb. PE. 5, 7, 192a; Wolff,
p. 123.

(26)   See Appendix I, p. 207 supra.

(27)   Porphyrius ap. Euseb. PE. 5, 16, 204d; Wolff,
p. 172; Buresch, p. 41, n. 8; Haussoullier,
Milet-Didyma, no. xliii no. 1. Wolff argues
from the use of Phoebus in line 1 and the Sun
in line 7, that this response was uttered by
someone other than Apollo, and plumps for
Alexander of Abonuteichos, who was credited
with referring clients to Claros and Didyma,
(Lucien, Alex. (42), 29). But the reference
to "my voice" in the first sentence seems
sufficient use of the first person for the
practice of an Apolline oracle-centre. I take
the reference to the sun, not as implying an
identification with Apollo (though this would
be possible in responses of this period), but
simply as meaning, in contrast with the previous sentence, that these were the only
oracles not swallowed up subterraneously. The
style of this response is much more literary
than any attributed by Lucian to Alexander.
The adjective "Mycalean" applied to the prophetic spring at Didyma has no exact parallel.
Pausanias (5, 7, 5), as an analogy to the legend of Arethusa, states that the water of a
spring on Mount Mycale "went through the intervening sea and came up again by Branchidae,
beside the harbour called Panormus". This
folk-tale could be used to account for a
spring of fresh water on the sea shore, but
seems inappropriate to the sacred fountain at
Branchidae itself. This might be used as an
argument against the attribution of this res-

ponse to Didyma on the ground that it had
muddled the local legend. But in the century
after Pausanias the legend may have been transferred from Panormus to Didyma itself, or the
author could not resist the temptation to
work into his poem a picturesque adjective.
(28)   Fragmentary enquiries and responses from
Didyma, assignable to this period, but not
further discussed here are:- <u>Did</u>. II, 497
(parts of at least a score of hexameters with
references to such mythical beings as hamadryads); 500 (an enquiry about a dream and the
finding of a statue; cf. L. Robert, <u>CRAI</u>.
1968, p. 578 and <u>Hellenica</u>, XIII, 1<u>21-22</u>);
502 (the Philodionysoi enquiry about some
plans); 503 (probably a prophet or ex-prophet
enquiring); 505 (an enquiry about a dream or
vision connected with Artemis). An inscription on a re-used slab at Ephesus contains
seven fragmentary hexameters, evidently the
response from an oracle-centre. The original
editor (Joseph Keil. <u>Anz</u>. <u>Akad</u>. <u>Wion</u>, 1943,
7-53) conjectured that it was originally set
up at Claros and was transferred later as
building material to Ephesus. But L. Robert
(<u>Bull</u>. <u>Épigr</u>. 1946/47, 182 and <u>CRAI</u>, 1968,
p. 571) argues convincingly for Didyma as the
source of the response, and the stone as re-
used locally. The enquiry from a private individual was about the setting up on an altar
in the open air, and perhaps another indoors
with offerings of incense. The deity concerned may have been Eros.

PART 1. CHAPTER 6

(1)   Laumonier, <u>Cultes</u>, p. 390. The incompletion,
<u>Did</u>. I, 1, <u>p. 22</u>.
(2)   <u>CAH</u>. 12, 148 and 721; <u>Didyma</u>, II, p. 137ff.
(3)   <u>Did</u>. II, 159; <u>SEG</u>. 4 (<u>1929</u>), no. 467 (the
descriptive title is misleading). For Festus'
date, Rehm, <u>Philol</u>. 93 (1934), 74-84. L. Robert, <u>Hellenica</u>, 4, 25, 68 and 75. For a general discussion, Rehm, <u>Did</u>. II, p. 138 and for
the structural changes to make the temple de-
fensible, Knackfuss, <u>Did</u>. I, 1, p. 42. For a
note on such <u>Konkurrenzgedichte</u>, P. Fraser
Ptolemaic Alexandria, 11, 863, n. 427
(4)   <u>Did</u>. II, 89 and 90; Rehm, <u>Philol</u>. 93 (1934),
74-84.

(5)   Did. II, 504. L. Robert, Gnomon, 1959, 670 and
        CRAI. 1968, 583-4.
(6)   W. Günther, Ist. Mitt. 21 (1971), 97ff. Parad-
        ise, Ditt.³ Syll. 463, 8, Str. 14, 1, 5.
(7)   Did. II, 217; R. Harder, Navicula Chilonensis,
        Studia Felici Jacoby oblata (1956), 88-91;
        H. Hommel, Festscrift Friedrich Smend (1963),
        7-18 and IV Epigr. Kongress, Wien (1963), 140-
        156; W. Peek, ZPE. 7 (1971), 196ff., whose
        text I follow, though not always his inter-
        pretation.
(8)   Cf. supra. p. 5
(9)   Cf. Appendix II p. 210-13 supra.
(10)   Lactantius, Div. Inst. 4, 13, 11; G. Wolff,
        Porphyrii de Philosophia, 184, comparing with
        Augustine, CD. 19, 22.
(11)   Lactantius, De Ira, 23, 12; Augustine, C D.,
        19, 23; Wolff, Porphyrii de Philosophia, 142.
(12)   Nilsson, Gr. Rel. 2, 636ff.
(13)   Lactantius, De morte pers., 10, and Div. Inst.
        4, 27, 4   W. H. C. Frend, Martyrdom and
        Persecution in the Early Church (1965), 489ff.
        N. Baynes, CAH. 12, 663. Timothy D. Barnes,
        Constantine and Eusebius (Harvard 1981), 18,
        dates this episode to 299 A.D.
(14)   Lactantius, De morte pers. 11, 6.
(15)   Eusebius, Vita Const. 2, 50. Barnes, op. cit.
        211   R. Browning, The Emperor Julian, 13,
        assigns this as a response to the oracle of
        Apollo at Delphi and makes it offer an explan-
        ation for this oracle's silence, not its
        failure to give true replies.
(16)   Did. II, 306.
(17)   Sozomenus, Hist. Eccl. 1, 7, 2 (Hom. Il. 8,
        102-3). For examples from Delphi, cf. Parke
        and Wormell, D.O. 2, no. 343 and 464.
(18)   Eusebius, P.E. 4, 2, 10. The reference to
        Antioch in the same context is expanded in
        H.E. 9. 11, 6 which serves roughly to date the
        occasion.
(19)   Julian, 297C and Ep. 18, 451A. Cf. Wolff, De
        novissima oraculorum aetate, 46, and L. Rob-
        ert, CRAI. 1968, 581.
(20)   Sozomenus, Hist. Eccl. 20, 7.
(21)   Milet, 1, 6, no. 191, SEG. 1 (1923), no. 427
        and Did. II. 83.
(22)   See Parke and Wormell, D.O. 2, no. 600, for a
        corrupt version of a prophecy in hexameters
        given to encourage Julian. It might have been
        issued by Didyma, but as Ares is represented
        as speaking in the first person, this is doubtful.

PART II CHAPTER SEVEN

(1) Epic Cycle, Epigoni, fr. 4 (Sch. A. R. 1,308).
Parke and Wormell, D.O. 1, 51 and 369; 2, no.
20. For the dedication of Manto at Delphi,
cf. also D.S. 4, 66, 6; (where she is called
Daphne and remains at Delphi, acting as the
Sibyl). Apollod. 3, 7, 4; Paus. 7, 3, 1.

(2) The typical legend of the tithe, Parke and
Wormell, D.O. 1, 51. The motif of the "first
met", id, in the index. The motif of the unwilling or unexpected sending to found a colony, Magnesia, id, 1, 53, Croton 1, 69, Cyrene,
1, 74. The legend does not explain what
enquiry, if any, Rhacius was supposed to have
made.

(3) Paus. 7, 3, 1 and 9, 33, 3 (Parke and Wormell,
D.O. 2, no. 523).

(4) For other ancient derivations of Claros, (1)
from a hero, Claros, Theopompus, F. Gr. Hist.
133 f. 29 or (2) from the word for a lot
(cleros), because Apollo obtained the place
by lot, Nearchos, F. Gr. Hist. 26 f. 1, 6.
Both these are cited by the same scholiast on
A. R. 1,308, where the alternative form,
Lacius, in place of Rhacius is noted, and the
spring is said to be from the tears of Manto.
For derivations see also Sch. Nic. Ther. 958,
where Manto's husband is called Zograios and
Sch. Nic. Alex. 11, where he is described as
a Bacchiad. Roscher, s.n. Manto (p.2327),
emends to Branchid.

(5) This legend supplying an etymology for a place
name is a typical motif in connection with
colonies, but is not usual in Homer. This may
be the reason why T. W. Allen in his edition
of the Epic fragments stops his quotation of
the scholion at the mention of Manto weeping.
But there would have been no point in the
poet's recording this action without the etymology derived from it. For similar instances
where the Epic cycle uses motifs untypical of
Homer, cf. Jasper Griffin, JHS. 97 (1977),
39-53.

(6) Hesiod, fr. 278, M. and W. (Str. 14, 1, 27);
Apollod. Epit. 6, 3; Smyrn. 14, 360. The
rotten ships' timbers, Hom. Il. 2, 135 with
Sch. BT (Theopompus, F. Gr. Hist. 115 f 351).
The legend of Calchas coming to Claros was
told in the Nostoi in the Epic Cycle, but it
is only recorded there by Proclus, Chrest.

(Allen, p. 108, 22):- 'The company of Calchas, Leonteus and Polypoetes, when they had travelled on foot to Colophon, bury Teiresias, who had died there.' This sentence appears to be seriously corrupt, probably as a result of the original abridgement. Presumably by some confusion with Manto's father, Teiresias has been substituted for Calchas. If this hypothesis is not accepted, the only alternative would be to conjecture the existence of some lost version of the legend in which Teiresias, instead of dying in Boeotia, accompanied his daughter to Asia. But this would not explain why he should die just in time to be buried by the Greeks arriving from Troy, unless one is to introduce him instead of Calchas into some contest in divination.

(7)   Apollod. Epit. 6, 19 (where Amphilochus appears to be shipwrecked at Claros). Sch. Od. 13, 259 gives a different version in which Idomeneus is shipwrecked at Colophon with Calchas and Sthenelus.

(8)   Pherecydes, F. Gr. Hist. 3f 142 (Str. 14, 1, 27). For variations of the contest, Apollod. Epit. 6, 3-4, Tzetz. Lyc. 427 and 980. Immisch. Jahrb. f. cl. Phil. suppl. 17 (1889), 160ff. For the contest transferred to Cilicia, Soph. fr. 181 (Nauck), Str. 14, 1, 27. For a rationalised version, Conon, Narr. 6 (F. Gr. Hist. 26 f, 6).

(9)   For the Mycenaean tomb, see p. 124 and note 26 supra. There may have been other heroic claimants to Mycenaean tombs in the neighbourhood. For the tomb of Idomeneus at Claros, Lyc. Alex, 431 with the schol. and Servius, Aen. 3, 401. Picard, Ephèse, p. 107, plausibly connects this legend with the version of Rhacius' origin which made him Cretan.

(10)   For Mopsus the Lapith, see the references and discussion in Parke, Oracles of Zeus, p. 15 and note 33. For three holders of the name distinguished, Str. 9, 5, 22. For the two prophets confused, Seneca, Med. 654; Tertull. de Anim. 46; Cl. Alex. Str. 2, 108, 4; Amm. Marc. 14, 8, 3; Sch. Stat. Theb. 14, 521 - these references from Immisch, op. cit. 166, note 4. Of the other names in the genealogy Rhacius has no obvious derivation, but his father Lebes, means 'cauldron' - appropriate to an Apolline prophet through its association with the tripod.

(11)   G. L. Huxley, <u>Crete</u> <u>and</u> <u>the</u> <u>Luwians</u>, (Oxford) 1961, 47ff.

(12)   Callinus ap. Str. 14, 4, 3. Amphilochus in Pamphylia and as founder of Posideion, Hdt. 7, 91 and 3, 91. Coin of Aspendus with reference to Mopsus, <u>Num</u>. <u>Chr</u>. 11 (1971), 21 and 29, and L. Robert. <u>Hellenica</u>, 11-12 (1960), 177; minted c. 410-375 B.C. Amphilochus killed by Apollo at Soloi in Cilicia, Hesiod, fr. 168, Str. 14, 5, 17. Mopsus and his daughters as founders, Theopomp. <u>F</u>. <u>Gr</u>. <u>Hist</u>. 115 f 103, 15 (Phot, <u>Bibl</u>. 176, p. 120 a 14) Sch. Dion. Per. 850. His statue in Perge, Bean, <u>Turkey's</u> <u>Southern</u> <u>Coast</u>, 53. Cf. Hierapolis, supra p. 154.

(13)   Lyc. <u>Alex</u>. 439; Tzetz. sch. 440 and 444.

(14)   H. Th. Bossert, <u>RHA</u>. 9 (1949), 1-9. H. Goldman, <u>Tarsus</u>, 2, 205ff. G. L. Huxley, <u>The</u> <u>Early</u> <u>Ionians</u>, 20-21.

(15)   R. O. Faulkner, <u>CAH</u>. II^3, 2, 242. Cf. R. D. Barnett, <u>CAH</u>. II^3, 2, 364 and N. K. Sanders, <u>Sea Peoples</u>, 182-3.

(16)   The twelve Ionian cities, Hdt. 1, 142, 3-4.

The twelve Aeolian cities, Hdt. 1, 149, 1. Cf.

A. H. M. Jones, <u>Eastern</u> <u>Cities</u>, p. 28 and note I. J. M. Cook, <u>CAH</u>. II^3, 2, 782, assumes that Notion means "southern fort" of Colophon. For the situation of Colophon, see Leicester B. Holland, <u>Hesperia</u>, 13 (1944), 91ff.

(17)   Ar. <u>Pol</u>. 5, 1303 b 9.

(18)   Mimnermus, fr. 12, Str. 14, 1, 3-4 - Andraemon of Pylos as founder. Paus. 7, 3, 3 - Damasichthon and Promethos. No Apaturia, Hdt. 1, 147.

(19)   Gyges, Hdt. 1, 14, 4. Cavalry, Str. 14, 1, 28, where naval power also is mentioned without evidence. Landed property, Ar. <u>Pol</u>. 4, 1290 b 15, Siris, Str. 6, 1, 14, A. J. Graham, <u>JHS</u>. 91 (1971), 40, Dunbabin, <u>Western</u> <u>Greeks</u>, 34-5. Calchas, Lyc. 978 and 1074 with sch. Its other colony was Myrleia, unimportant until the Hellenistic period.

(20)   <u>Homeric</u> <u>Hymn</u>, 9, 3-7. The temple of Artemis, L. Robert, <u>A.S</u>. 1960, p. 21.

(21)   <u>Homeric</u> <u>Hymn</u>, 3, 40. Ananius, 4 (Arist. <u>Ran</u>. 659 with sch.).

(22)   Notion, Hecataeus, <u>F</u>. <u>Gr</u>. <u>Hist</u>. 1 f 233, where its description as a "Town of Ionia" is simply geographic: cf. Cybeleia similarly described, f 230. Separate assessment in tribute lists, <u>ATL</u>. s.nn., and for a new fragment of the

earliest list (454/3 B.C.), Meritt, <u>Hesperia</u>, 41 (1972), 410. The revolt, Meiggs-Lewis, no. 47. The Peloponnesian war, Th. 3, 34. Claros, Th. 3, 33, 2. Thrasyllus' expedition, X.<u>H</u>. 1, 2, 4; as a base, X.<u>H</u>. 1, 2, 11, and 5, 12-14. The decree of 403/2, Tod. 2, 97, 8.

(23)   Notion in the 4th cent., Theopompus, <u>F</u>. <u>Gr</u>. <u>Hist</u>. 115 f 118. J. G. Milne, <u>Kolophon and its Coinage</u>: <u>A Study</u> (Numismatic notes and monographs, no. 9, New York, 1941).

(24)   On the inscription, Meritt, AJP. 56 (1935) and L. Robert, <u>Rev</u>. de <u>Phil</u>. 10 (1936), 158ff.

(25)   R. Demangel and A. Laumonier, <u>BCH</u>. 47 (1923), 353ff., Fouilles de Notion.

(26)   Leicester B. Holland, <u>Hesperia</u>, 13 (1944), 91-171, Colophon, Lorimer, <u>Homer and the Monuments</u>, 106 and Coldstream, <u>Geometric Greece</u>, 97.

PART II. CHAPTER EIGHT

(1)   Page 123 supra and note 24.

(2)   Prepelaus, D.S. 20, 107. Lysimachus' colony, Paus. 1, 9, 7 and <u>CAH</u>. 7, 91. Phoenix, Paus 1. c. The <u>sympoliteia</u>, <u>BCH</u>. 39 (1915), 36. "The Colophonians who dwell in the old city" and "the Colophonians from the sea", Kern, <u>Inscr</u>. <u>Magn</u>., 53.

(3)   Buresch. p. 31.

(4)   Paus. 7, 5, 1. For Alexander's dream, but without the oracle, Aristid. 265, 5; 270, 15; 513, 10. For an emendation of the oracle's text, J. M. Cook, <u>Cl</u>. <u>Rev</u>. 11 (1961), 7. For a possible inscriptional text from Smyrna, <u>The Greek Inscriptions at Leiden</u>, (1958), no. 62. W. Peek, <u>ZPE</u>. 21 (1976), 145. For the coins <u>B.M</u>. <u>Cat</u>. <u>Ionia</u>, p. 279, no. 345, etc.

(5)   Str. 14, 1, 37. Aristides (513, 10) mentions Lysimachus in conjunction with Alexander. For a discussion, see C. J. Cadoux, <u>Ancient Smyrna</u>, 95ff., and J. M. Cook, <u>BSA</u>. 53/4 (1959), 34, who argues for a local tradition from Hellenistic times, referring to Pliny, <u>HN</u>. 5, 118. For the cult of Nemeseis, B. Schweitzer, <u>JDAI</u>. 46 (1931) 175-216. cf. Volkmann, <u>Arch</u>. <u>f</u>. <u>Rel</u>. 31 (1934), 75 and Paus. 9, 35, 6 for possible evidence for the cult in the archaic period.

(6)   For descriptions of the excavation and the temple, L. Robert, <u>Anatolian Studies</u>, 1 (1951) 17 ff.; 2 (1952) 17 ff.; 4 (1954) 15 ff.; 5

(1955) 16ff.; 6 (1956), 23ff,; 8 (1958) 28ff.;
10 (1960) 21 ff. Les Fouilles de Claros,
conférence donnée a l'université d'Ankara le
20 Octobre, 1953 (Limoges, 1954). Claros;
La civilization grecque de l'antiquite à nos
jours; edited by Charles Delvoye and Georges
Roux (Bruxelles, 1967) pp. 305-12. R. Martin
and H. Metzger, La Religion Grecque, (Paris,
1976), 53-61.

(7) Nicander, Theriaca, 957 ("snowy Claros");
Alexipharmaca, 9 ("sitting by the tripods").
For discussions of Nicander see O. Schneider,
Nicandrea, (1856); P. W. s.n. 10 and 11
(W. Kroll); A. S. F. Gow and A. E. Scholfield,
Nicander (1953). The Life of Aratus connects
Nicander with Ptolemy V (205-181 B.C.) and
there was another tradition that he was one of
the seven poets (the Pleiads) at the court of
Ptolemy II. For the coldness of the river
Ales, Paus. 7, 5, 10 and 8, 28, 3.

(8) Ditt. Syll.3 452.

(9) For Claros' freedom from reptiles, Nicander,
fr. 31 (Ael. NA, 10, 49). For ash trees as
an antidote to snake bites, Pliny, HN. 16, 64;
Diosc. 1, 80; Geop. 13, 8, 9.

(10) Ovid, Net. 11, 410ff. with Haupt's commentary
and [Probus] on Verg. G. 399. For a quite
different legend, Apollod. 1, 52. One may
compare how Apollonius built the legend of
Hemithea round Didyma, p. 56 supra.

(11) Immisch, Jahrb. f. cl. Phil. suppl. 17 p. 128;
Cagnat, IGRRP. No. 1655; Mutschmann, Rhein. Mus.
62 (1917), 150ff. Jacoby, F. Gr. Hist. 17 T.

(12) See L. Robert in La Civilization, cited in
note 6 above, cf. Tacitus, Ann. 2, 54, et ferme
Mileto accitus sacerdos.

(13) Colophon and Attalus I (Pol. 5, 77, 5 and the
decree in honour of his son Athenaeus, Picard,
Ephèse, p. 647). The statue of Antiochus L.
Robert, Les Fouilles, p. 13. The letter of
L. and P. Scipio, SEG. 1, 440. The Roman
legati give freedom from tribute to "Colophon-
is qui in Notio habitant" (Livy, 38, 39, 8,
based on Pol. 21, 46, 4, where the mss. give
simply "those who dwell in Notion").

(14) Th. Macridy-bey and Ch. Picard, BCH. 39 (1915)
pp. 33-52.

(15) Plu. Pomp. 24; cf. Cic. de imp. Cn. Pomp. 33.
Strabo (14, 1,27) writing originally before
7 B.C., treats of the oracle in the past tense

(16) L. Robert, Les Fouilles, pp. 16 and 20.

(17)   D. Magie, RRAM, p. 1580, where his proconsul-
        ship is dated after M. Tullius M. f. Cicero
        (29-28 B.C?) and before Paullus Fabius Maximus
        (10-9 B.C?). Pros. Imp. Rom. 961 does not
        recognise his Asian governorship. He triumph-
        ed from Spain in 26 B.C. and will have gone
        to Asia considerably later. See also, Syme,
        Roman Revolution, 378, etc., History in Ovid,
        152 and 159. K. Tuchelt, Frühe Denkmaler Roms
        in Kleinasien, I, 168. For this use of
        κτίστης , cf. L. Robert   Hellenica, 13 (1966),
        on MAMA, 8, 484 (Aphrodisias), 'au sens de
        'fondateur' par suito de construction d'édific-
        es'.
(18)   For the Augustan restoration, see L. Robert
        and L. Martin in the works cited in note 6,
        supra.   On the coinage, J. F. Milne,
        Kolophon and its Coinage, p. 82.
(19)   Claros is not mentioned in Catullus, Horace,
        Tibullus or Propertius. It is once used in the
        Aeneid as a synonym for Apollo ("tripodes
        Clarii". 3, 360). Ovid did not mention it in
        the Amores (published originally c. 16 B.C.).
        But in A.A. 2, 79 ("et Clario Delos amata
        deo"), completed by 1 B.C. Metamorphoses, 1,
        514 ("mihi Delphica tellus et Claros et Ten-
        edos Patareaque regia seruit") and 11, 410
        (the legend of Ceyx). Fasti, 1, 20 (written
        between 14 and 17 A.D.). For the problems of
        Ovid's dates, see Syme, History in Ovid esp.
        6-20 and 63.
(20)   Tac. Ann, 2, 54. Syme, Tacitus, 469-70. For
        a late literary reference to the prophet in-
        spired by drinking the water, Anacreontea, 12,
        5.
(21)   Pliny, HN. 2, 232. For the cave in the hill-
        side, cf. BCH. 39 (1915). 39-41 and Picard,
        Ephèse, 453 ff. Picard writes as though there
        was evidence of an oracle of Earth as Apollo's
        predecessor at Claros, as at Delphi.
(22)   See the descriptions cited in note 6, supra.
(23)   Paus. 8, 29, 3. The editors, Frazer and Hit-
        zig-Bluemner, dated the finding to the reign
        of Tiberius; Buresch (p.48) to the time of L.
        Verus (162-166 A.D.). Pausanias wrote c. 175
        A.D. Philostratus, Heroica. p. 288 gives a
        different version; "Aryandes, who some say was
        an Ethiopian, others an Indian, of 30 cubits
        lying in the land of the Assyrians not long
        ago the bank of the river Orontes disclosed
        when it was split." This is one of three

247

examples of giant's bones which Philostratus
apparently arranged in chronological order:-
the myth of Gyges, Aryandes and an example at
Sigeum found not fifty years before. The last
two are grouped by him as "in our time" in
contrast to Gyges. Presumably this did not
mean in Philostratus' lifetime, but merely not
in legendary periods. Hence the story of Aryandes
is not inconsistent with a date in Tiberius reign.
For the curious and ridiculous story that Tiberius
was responsible for giving the river the name Orontes, cf. Eustath. Dion. Per. 919. This may be an
echo of the work on the river's course in Tiberius'
reign. cf. also Pausanias of Antioch, F. Gr.
Hist. 854 f 10, 7.

(24)   Tac. Ann. 12, 22. Andresen conjectured 'orac-
ulum' in place of 'simulacrum', accepted by
Syme, Tacitus, 2, 470 and Koestermann in his
edition. This would imply an epistolary enquiry such as we have discussed (p. 135 supra)
in connection with Ovid. Fasti, 1, 20. But
the reference to 'magos' suggests the use of
magic incantation.

PART II CHAPTER NINE

(1)   P.W. 17, 2, col. 2250 (H. Mette). For a new
interpretation of the Jewish evidence, S. J.
Bastomsky, Apeiron, 8 (1974), 57.

(2)   Eus. P.E. 5, 22, 214A ff. Cf. Ch. Picard,
Aegyptus, 32 (1952), 3-9. For a similar response on an inscription, see Appendix I, p. 208.

(3)   Barnes, Constantine, 178. Julian, 188B,
199B ff. 209B ff.; Hesych. Mil. 15, 1 and 53,
15; Sud. Oi, 123 and   1142.

(4)   Parke and Wormell, D.O. 2, xi.

(5)   Dio Chr. 47, 5.

(6)   L. Robert, AS. 10 (1960), 21, that the dedicatory inscription is not earlier than Dec. 135
A.D. The benefaction from Hadrian and the
work of construction may have started some
years earlier. On the temples as incomplete,
Paus. 7, 5, 4.

(7)   Haussoullier, Rev. de Phil. 22 (1898) 259;
Cagnat, IGRRP. 4, no. 1586; Ditt. OGIS. no.
530, dated by the era of Amisos. This use of
the verb ἐμβατεύειν("make an entrance") is
special to Claros. But it was employed in the
previous century by St. Paul (Ep. Col. 2, 18)
of the worship of angels as a secret cult. For

a discussion see 'Conflict at Colophon', Sources For Biblical History, ed. F.O. Francis and W. A. Meeks, 4 (1978), 197. The great series of proskynemata from Laodicea with accompanying choirs started just before 128 A.D., L. Robert, Laodicée 299.

(8) Aristides, 15, p. 312, 5. Behr, p.62, dates to October, 147 A.D.

(9) Aristides, 15, p. 317, 20. Magie, RRAM 2, 1492 and 1584, dates Albus as proconsul 147/8 A.D.(?), Behr, p. 75 after September 149 A.D.

(10) Lucian, 42, 29 (Glycon's oracle) and for other references in conjunction with Delphi and Didyma, id, 8 and 43. Cf. also Philostr. VA. 4, 1; Clem. Al. Protr. 2, p. 4, Sylb.; Celsus ap. Orig. C. Cels. 7, 3; Him. Or. 60, 3 and 68, 8; Them. Or. 334a.

(11) The original outbreak, Amm. Marc. 23, 6, 24; Hist. Aug. Marcus, 13, 2 and Verus 8, 1. Later in 180 A.D. id, Marcus, 28, 4 and under Commodus, D.C. 72, 14, 3 and Herodian, 1. 12, 1. For an argument against the tradition of the plague, J. F. Gilliam, AJP. 82 (1961), 225.

(12) Buresch, pp. 10ff.; IGRRP. 4, no. 1498; Keil and von Premerstein, Denk. Wien. Akad. 53 (1910), 2, p. 8, no. 16.

(13) Kaibel, no. 1034; Weinreich, Ath. Mitt. 38 (1913), 64-72; Picard, BCH. 46 (1922), 190ff.; L. Robert, Hell. 9, 85.

(14) G. Pugliese Carratelli, Ann. Sc. Arch. Ath. 61-2 (1963/64), 351-70; H. Lloyd-Jones and M. L. West, Maia, 18 (1966), 263; M. L. West, ZPE. 1 (1967), 183.

(15) Lloyd-Jones, Maia. 18 (1966), 264, suggests that the wrath of Earth was because of Apollo's slaying of Python. It may be a confirmation of this conjecture that the myth had local associations with Hierapolis. See Leo Weber, Apollo Pythoktonos in phrygischen Hierapolis, Philologus, Beilage 69 (1910).

(16) Mopsus as son of Apollo, Apollod. Exc. Vat. 47; Conon, F. Gr. Hist. f 1, 6; Clem. Al. Str. 2, 109, 12 Dind. For proskynemata in accordance with an oracle (κατα χρησμόν cf. L. Robert, Laodicée, pp. 299ff.

(17) Kaibel, no. 1035; IGRRP. 4, no. 1360; Buresch, 70ff. The correct restoration of the preamble with a reference to initiation, which proves the attribution to Claros, was proposed by Ch.

Picard, BCH. 46 (1922), 190. L. Robert has often called attention to failures to note this fact, Bull. Épigr. 1952, 66 and 180; 1956, 27a; 1957, 401 and Laodicée, 305. W. Peek, ZPE. 21 (1976), 280.

(18) For a possible specimen of the hymns produced for this occasion, M. Fränkel, Inscr. Perg. no. 324. For the final prayer, cf. Soph. O.T. 194 and the popular saying jokingly parodied by Dio Chrysostom, 48, 5.

(19) IG. Bulg. 1, no. 224. Cf. L. Robert, Rev. Phil. 33 (1959) 190, and Laodicée, 305, note 4. For embassies to Claros, Picard, Ephèse, 303 and 694.

(20) G. Bean and Mitford, Denkschriften Akad. Wien. 85, p. 21, no. 26; L. Robert, Documents de l'Asie Mineure, 91-100. For a contemporary reward by Rome to a city that had repressed brigandage, F. Schindler, Die Inschriften von Bubon (Nord Lykiens), Oest. Akad. Wien. Sitz. 1972. no. 2.

(21) Cf. supra p. 101.

(22) IGRRP. 1, no. 767; Picard, Ephèse, 694 (after Hadrian in date).

(23) Paus. 2, 2, 8; Picard, Ephèse, 693, n.6.

(24) Eric Birley, Chiron 4 (1974), 511-13. ILS. 327 (Vercovicium, Corinium, Cuicul) with Année Épigraphique, Rev. Arch. 1929, no. 156, and R. Trouvenot, Bull. Arch. Com. des Travaux Historiques, 8 (1972), 221 (Volubilis), SEG, 26 (1976/7), no. 1290. The latest example is not included by Birley.

(25) Nock, 1, 165. Picard, Ephèse, 712ff. and Aegyptus, 32 (1952), 7, who appears partly to have based his belief in a corpus of Clarian oracles on the occurrence of the plural χρηζμους (sic) in the inscription from near Hadrianopolis - note 19 supra. But surely it is explained by the clumsy non-Hellenic style of the inscription? Birley does not mention either scholar. The theory of the 'ensemble d'oracle', seems to go back to Jules Toutain. Bulletin de la Societe nat, des Antiquaires de France, 1915, pp. 147-48 cited by Pierre Batiffol, Revue Biblique, 13 (1916), 172

(26) D.C. 77, 15, 5 (213 A.D.); 16, 8 (214 A.D.); Herodian, 4, 8, 15.

(27) A. Souter, Cl. Rev. 11 (1897), 31; A. Petrie in W. Ramsay, Studies in the History and Art of the Eastern Roman Provinces, 128 and 200.

(28) Kaibel, no. 1036; Merkelbach, ZPE. 18 (1975),

100 with a reference to L. Robert, Laodicée, 337, for attribution on the evidence of a proskynema.

(29) Macrob. Sat. 1, 18, 19. For Iao, cf. D.S. 1, 94, 2 and for the equation of Yahweh and Dionysus, Tac. Hist. 5,5, Val. Max. 1, 3, 2 and Plu. 4, 671C. On Labeo, whom Macrobius cites as his source, see Appendix I, p. 205 and W. Kroll, Rhein. Mus. 71 (1966) 309 and W. A. Baehrens, Hermes, 52 (1917), 39, and Cornelius Labeo atque eius commentarius Vergilianus (1918). For discussions see Picard, Éphèse, 718, Nock 1, 160 and R. Reitzenstein, Die Hellenistischen Mysterienreligionen³, (1927), 148 ff. S. Eitrem, Orakel und Mysterieu am Ausgang der Antike, Albae Vigiliae, 5 (Zürich, 1947), pp. 55-58). Nock following Jan read 'Iacchus' in place of 'Iao' in the last line on the theory that the supreme deity must be distinct from the gods of the seasons. But it is dangerous to try to tidy up the theology of oracles. Iao is both a god of a season and also the climax. Hence the curious order starting with winter.

(30) Wolff, 231 ff.; Buresch, 55 ff.; Lactantius, Inst. Div. 1, 71, 1 and 8. For a discussion, Nock, 1, 161. Lactantius continues with three short quotations from other Apolline responses, which do not occur elsewhere. But as he does not attribute them to Claros, I do not discuss them here.

(31) G. Bean, Journeys in Northern Lycia 1965-67, Oester. Akad. Wien. Denkschriften,104, p. 20, no. 37; L. Robert, CRAI. 1971, 597-619 and Bull. Épigr. 1974, no 555; M. Guarducci, Rendic. Acad. Lincei, 27 (1972), 335-347; A. S. Hall, ZPE. 32 (1978), 263, to whom I am greatly indebted for the use of his typescript and discussion on the problems of this inscription.

(32) For a discussion, C. Gallarotti, Philologus, 121 (1977), 95-105.

(33) Personally I find it too suspicious a coincidence that the enquirer had the appropriate name of Theophilus. Accidents of this sort occasionally occur in real life, but I suspect that the individual actually bore some pagan name, probably blatantly theophoric, and that the change to Theophilus was part of the Christian editing. Lactantius, who may have known the response before this process was

fully developed, gives no name.
(34)   Augustine, <u>C.D.</u> 9, 19.
(35)   L. Robert, <u>Les Fouilles</u>, 23.
(36)   Picard, <u>Ephèse</u>. 49

PART III CHAPTER TEN.

(1)   Hdt. 1, 149, using the form Gryneia, which is also cited by Stephanus Byzantinus from Hecataeus (<u>F. Gr. Hist</u>. 1 fr. 225). The dynasty of Gongylus, <u>X. H</u>. 3, 1, 6. In the Delian league, <u>ATL</u>. 1, 256. Parmenio, D.S. 17, 7, 9.

(2)   Str. 13, 3, 5, paraphrased by St. Byz. s.n. Paus. 1, 21, 7. A possible reference to the oracle-centre in Sappho, if the place-name is correct as a supplement, <u>Greek Lyric</u> 1, no. 99, ed. D. A. Campbell (<u>P. Oxy</u>. 2291). For the place without the oracle, Pliny, <u>HN</u>. 5, 121, and Scyl. 78.

(3)   Vergil, <u>Ecl</u>. 6, 72, with Servius' commentary (Euphorion, <u>Coll.Alex</u>. fr. 97). Another lost writer of the Hellenistic age was Hermeias, cited by Athenaeus (4, 149D) from the second book of his <u>Concerning the Gryneian Apollo</u> on the subject of a festival at Naucratis. G. Camasso, <u>P.d.P</u>.63 (1980), 256 ff. for an unconvincing attempt to show that the contest belongs to Gryneion.

(4)   Aristotle, fr. 571 (Rose), Servius on Vergil, <u>Aen</u>. 4, 345: on which see R.O.A.M. Lyne, <u>Cl.Qu</u>. 28 (1978), 186. For a somewhat different Ancaeus, Iamb. <u>VP</u>. 2.

(5)   Ditt. <u>OGI</u>. no. 266, 17 and 229, 85. For an inscription dedicated to Apollo Chresterios and wrongly assigned to Gryneion, id. 312, and note 9 infra. Beloch, <u>Gr. Ges</u>. 1^2, 140 had suggested that Gryneion was the federal temple of the Aeolians.

(6)   George Bean, <u>JHS</u>. 74 (1964), 85; H. Lloyd Jones, <u>JHS</u>. 75 (1955), 155; L. Robert, <u>Bull Épigr</u>. 1956, 274a and 1959, 401. R. Merkelbach, <u>ZPE</u>, 5 (1970), 45 with a different supplement.

(7)   Vergil, <u>Aen</u>. 5, 345, Aristides, 345, 15. Philostratus, <u>V.A</u>. 4, 14.

(8)   The earliest description is by Pottier and Reinach, <u>Rev. Arch</u>. 1 (1883), 351ff. For a recent one, George Bean, <u>Aegean Turkey</u>, (1966), p.111.

(9)   Hdt. 1, 149. <u>CIG</u>. 2, 3527 (from Cyriacus of

Ancona), BCH. 6, 205. IGRRP. 1177 and 1178,
Ditt. OGI. 312 and 450. L. Robert, Villes
d'Asie Mineure², p. 91, seems right in rejecting Keil and V. Premerstein, Erste Reise, 44,
n. 91 as attributable to Aigaī. On Aigai
generally see P.W. sn. and Bean in the Prince-
ton Encyclopedia.

(10) Str. 13, 2 5.

(11) For references to earlier exploration and a
modern description of the site, J. M. Cook,
The Troad, (1973), pp. 228ff. Str. 13, 1, 63.
Chryses, Iliad, 1, 11 (ἀρητῆρα) and 370
(ἱερεύς). The tomb of Herophile, Paus. 10,
12, 6.

(12) Ovid, Fasti, 6, 425ff.

(13) Menander Rhetor, Sminthiaca, (Spengel, 3,
437ff); ed. D. A. Russell and N. G. Wilson,
(1981), 207ff.

(14) For the derivation of Smintheus, Sch. A. Hom.
Il. 1, 39 and Frazer's note on Paus. 10, 12,
5; also A. Krappe, Cl. Phil. 36 (1941), 133-
141. For aetiological legends connected with
Delphi, Parke and Wormell, D.O. 2, no. 453 and
540. But for a Cretan derivation, Hsch.
Σμίνθος . A mouse beneath the cult-statue,
Str. 13, 1, 48 and by the tripod, Ael. NA. 12,
5. Mice in the sanctuary sacred, Heraclides
Ponticus ap. Str. l.c. and Ael. l.c. Mice
and divination, Pliny, HN. 8, 82.

(15) Str. 13, 1, 13, and 10, 5, 7. Hermocreon, P.W.
8, 890. Ilus described as enquiring of Apollo
Priepenaios - presumably the same, Hellanicus,
F. Gr. Hist. 4 f 25 (Sch. Lyc 29). Sch. Lyc.
29 also records a foundation legend of Ilion
involving Ilus and an oracle (unspecified).
Cf. Apollod, 3, 12, 3. I cannot trace any
consultation attributed to Zeleia.

(16) On Thymbra, see J. M. Cook, Troad, pp. 177 ff.
He seems right in maintaining that there was
no city of Thymbra only a sanctuary, whose
site on the plain of Troy cannot now be found.
For Helenus and Cassandra sleeping in the temple, Anticlides, F. Gr. Hist. 140 f 17 (Sch.
Hom. Il. 7, 44), Eustath. Il. 663, 40 and Hyg.
Fab. 93, where it is confused with the more
familiar story about Cassandra and the gift of
prophecy. For a discussion of this traditional way of receiving the power of divination,
Parke, Oracles of Zeus, 166.

(17) For Marpessos, see J. M. Cook, Troad, 281 ff.,
with references. For Gergis, Phlegon, F. Gr.

(18) Hist.275 f 2 (St. Byz. s.n.) and Cook, 347ff.
Aristid. Hieros Logos 5, p. 351, 7.

(19) L. Robert, A travers l'Asie Mineure (1980),
395, n.6. Hesychius Milesius, F. Gr. Hist.
390, p. 269, 24, Calchas. Head, HN^2. 512
(c.280 B.C.) SEG. 4 (1929) no. 720, decrees o
Phocaea and Tenedos. Ditt. Syll^3. 550
(Delphi), where the title given to the Apollo
of Chalcedon is Pythaios, as in the metropolis
Megara.   Did the Delphians wish to emphasise the Pythian connection? D. M. Pippidi,
Studii Classice, 6 (1964), 108, the Istrian
decree. Zosimus, 2, 37 and H. W. Parke,
Cl. Qu. 32 (1982), 441. Dionysius Byzantius
Anaplus Bosphori, ed. R. Güngerich, (Berlin,
1927), 35. Lucian, 42, 10, Alexander. Socrates Schol. H.E. 4, 8, the marble inscription

(20) The classic passages on Charoneia are Cic. de
Div. 1, 79, Pliny, HN 2, 207 and Iambl. Myst.
4, 1 (182, 9). Pease's notes on Cicero give
other references. Visitors to Hierapolis,
Str. 12, 8, 17 and 13, 4, 14 (where he calls
it a Plutonion) and D.C. 68, 27, 3. Strabo
was convinced from observing their expression
that the Galli did it by holding their breath
Also if Apuleius can be trusted, he visited
it (De Mundo, 327); he suggests that the Gall
did it by holding their faces upwards. Damascius ap. Phot. Bibl. 344 b 35. He went on
to dream about the Hilaria, i.e. the ritual
of Cybele.

(21) G. Carettoni, Scavo del tempio di Apollo a
Hierapolis (Rapporto preliminare), Ann. Sc.
Arch. Atene, 61-62 (1963/64), 411-433; J. M.
Cook and J. D. Blackman, Archaeological
Reports for 1970-71, 45-46: E. Akurgal,
Ancient Civilizations and Ruins of Turkey
(Istanbul, 1969), 177, and for a popular des-
cription with a reference to the gas as "prob
ably carbon dioxide", Sybille Haynes, Land of
the Chimaera (1974), 136.

(22) G. P. Carratelli, Ann. Sc. Arch. Atene, 61-62
(1963/64), 252-357 Χρησμοί di Apollo Kareios
e Apollo Klarios a Hierapolis in Frigia; H.
Lloyd-Jones and M. L. West, Maia, 18 (1966),
263-4; Oracles of Apollo Kareios; M. L. West,
ZPE. 1, (1967) 182-3; Oracles of Apollo Kareios, a revised text. M. Guarducci, RFIC, 102
(1978), 198 argues for an Antonine date for the
rostic inscription and offers new readings. The
standard discussions of alphabetic oracular tab

lets are F. Heinevetter, Wurfel- und Buchstaben-
orakel, (Breslau, 1911) and G. Bjorck, Symb.
Osl. 19 (1939), 86ff. Heidnische and Christ-
liche Orakel mit fertigen Antworten. Cf. Kaibel, Epigrammata, no. 1039 and 1040. For Apollo
Kareios, see also p. 153 supra.

(23) Carratelli, op. cit. 357-369; M. L. West, op.
cit. 186-7, who proposes "drought" as the subject of the third enquiry.   For the Clarian
oracle, cf. supra p. 153.

(24) Carratelli, op. cit. 370, makes some rather
conjectural suggestions about the relations of
the two Apolline cults.

(25) Athymbra (Nysa), Welles, no. 9, Seleucus and Antiochus confirm its sacred privileges. The Charoneion, Str. 14, 1, 43; Eustath. Dion. Per. 1153.
For a third Charoneion at Thymbria in the territory of Magnesia, Str. 14, 1, 11 and Laumonier,
Cultes, 536-7. There is no evidence at it for divination. The resemblance of names between Athymbra, this Thymbria and Thymbria in the Troad
(cf. supra p. 178) is teasing.

(26) Livy, 38, 43 describing the expedition of Cn.
Manlius against the Galatians.   It must be
distinguished from Hieracome in Lydia on the
river Hyllus, famous for its temple of the
Persian Artemis (P. W. s.n. Hierakome, the
only entry under that name.)   Bouché-Leclerq,
3, 259 also confuses it with Apollo of Hybla
and Hylae near Magnesia (cf. infra, note 49).
Lebas Waddington, no. 1652, Welles no. 69 is
a very fragmentary inscription from near
Tralles referring to Hieracome, but it does
not add to our knowledge of the oracle.

(27) Telmessus, A. H. M. Jones, Cities of the Eastern
Roman Provinces, 2 32 and Laumonier, Cultes, 610-
14; not to be confused with Telmessus in Lycia.
Arr. 2, 3; Hdt. 1, 78 and 84, Aristoph. fr. 518-541
(OCT). Aristandos, Arr. 1, 25, 8, etc. Galeotae
and Telmessians, St. Byz. s.n. Γαλεῶται and
Parke, Oracles of Zeus, 179. Cicero, de Div. 1, 41
and 42; Pliny, HN. 30, 1 Telmessos or Telmesseus
the prophet and his tomb in the sanctuary, Clem.
Alex. Protr. 3, 34, 215.   Telmessians as the in-
ventors of dream divination, Clem. Alex. Str.
1, 361 F.   Inscriptional evidence, J. L. Myr-
es, JHS. 14 (1894), 373 ff. and Ditt. Syll, 3
1044 with G. Daux's exposition, Rev. Phil. 15
(1941), 11ff.
Hdt. 1. 182.   This evidence for Patara is the
basic analogy for A. B. Cook's theory that the

Pythia was the bride of Apollo (Zeus, 2, 207). For the prophetis at Didyma shut into the Adyton before consultations, see Appendix II p. 211 supra, where Iamblichus carefully avoids any sexual implications.

(29) For Herodotus' treatment of Delphic procedure as known to everyone, 7, 111.

(30) Olen, Hdt. 4, 35, 3; Paus. 9, 27, 2 (a Lycian producing the oldest hymns for the Greeks) and 10, 5, 4 (a Hyperborean in the Delphic version). For the Hyperborean gifts interpreted as a link between Dodona and Delos and a sign of hostility between Delos and Delphi, Parke, Oracles of Zeus, appendix III, Delos, unlike Patara, had no importance as an oracle in the classical period.

(31) Vergil. Aen. 4, 143 with Servius' commentary; Horace, Odes, 3, 4, 65. For evidence for a consultation in summer at Patara, cf. infra note 39. For Apollo in Lycian, E. Laroche, CRAI, 1974, p. 121.

(32) Servius, Vergil, Aen. 3, 332 (Harvard edition) This gives both the Lycian legend and the Cretan version derived from Cornificius Longus, on whom see Elizabeth Rawson, Cl. Qu. 28 (1978), 192. The Harvard editors compare Servius, Aen. 12, 516. For the legendary connections of Didyma and Claros with Delphi, cf. supra p. 3 and p. 112. Patara, while apparently friendly with Delos, may have remained aloof from Delphi. It is perhaps significant that the one Lycian known to have consulted Delphi in the classical period was Arbinas, the dynast of Xanthus, who appears to have asserted his sovereignty in opposition to the original Lycian federation (Jean Bousquet, CRAI. 1975. 138f.).

(33) Hecataeus, F. Gr. Hist. 1 f 256. Pataros and Xanthos, Eustath. Dion Per. 129.

(34) Alexander Polyhistor, F. Gr. Hist. 273 f 131 (Steph. Byz. s.n. Πάταρα). For models in pastry attached to the eiresione at the Pyanepsia, Apollo's festival at Athens, Parke, Festivals, 76. Patara, here alleged to be a native word, strangely resembles the Latin patera, a flat dish used for offerings.

(35) The Cypria, Proclus, Chr. p. 194, 10 (Allen) merely κατα μαντεῖαν. For Euripides and later sources, see Parke and Wormell, D.O. 2, no. 198. Menaechmus, F. Gr. Hist. 131 f 11 (St. Byz. s.n. Τηλέφιος δῆμος). Paus 9, 41,

1. Xenagoras, F. Gr. Hist. 249 F4 (Tempel-
chronick v. Lindos, 13,8).

(36) Mela, 1, 82. Other references to the oracle-
centre, Lucian Bis. Ace. (29), 1, Philopseud.
(34), 38; Max. Tyr. 14, 1b; Paulus ex Lib.
Pomp. Festi. p. 106 (Lindsay). References to
the temple without the oracle D.S. 5, 56, 1;
Clem. Alex. Protr. 4, 41P; Sch. Lyc. 920.

(37) IGRRP. III, 739 and TAM. II, 905, xiii, 42
and xvii, 65.

(38) TAM. II, 1, 174, db, Benndorf, Reisen, 1,
75ff. no. 53. SEG. 6 (1932), no. 755 for an
improved reading in line 8. In view of the
complex problems about sources and dates it
is impossible to decide whether Oracula
Sibyllina, 3, 441 is a post eventum forecast
of the silencing of Patara or a hostile wish;
cf. 4,112 and for Colophon 3, 343 and 7.55.

(39) At this period the city of Sidyma used the
Macedonian calendar of months in which Loos
was equivalent to the Attic Hecatombaion, i.e.
the first month after the summer solstice.
This indicates that at this period it was
possible to consult the oracle in high summer.
This is inconsistent with the picture derived
from Servius, Ver. Aen. 4, 143 (cf. supra
p.186), that Apollo gave oracles in Patara in
winter and in Delos in summer. Perhaps the
practice varied at different periods. But
more likely Servius' picture is an imaginary
scheme, based on such facts as the Delian
spring festival and the intermittent times for
consultation at Patara, which may not have
fitted so neatly in actuality.

(40) IGRRP. III, 583.

(41) IGRRP. III, 680, TAM. II, 420.

(42) Cf. supra. p.130.

(43) On the topography and history of Patara, see
E. Kalinka, TAM. II, 141-7, and P. W. 18, 3,
2555ff. (G. Radke).

(44) Paus. 7, 21, 13: Bouché-Leclerq. 3, 257.

(45) Str. 14, 15, 19. For the foundation of Sel-
euceia, St. Byz s.n. (Alexander Polyhistor,
F. Gr. Hist. 273 f 132). Both Artemis and
Apollo appear on the local coins, Head, Hist.
Num.2 727.

(46) D.S. 32, 10

(47) Zosimus, 1, 57, 2. Date 270-71 A.D. For a
recent discussion of the historical context,
Fergus Millar, JRS. 61 (1971), 10.

(48) P.W. s.n. Sarpedon, (Zwicker). Basilius of

Seleuceia, Migne, <u>PG</u>. 85, 568 and 612b.   For
other discussions of the oracle-centre, Bouché
Leclerq. 3,258, n. 3; Picard, <u>Ephèse</u>, 398,
n. 2, and Laumonier, <u>Cultes</u>, 551, n. 7.   Socrates Schol. <u>Hist</u>. <u>Eccl</u>. 1, 18 refers to the
destruction by Constantius of an Apolline
temple in Cilicia, but its identification with
this is quite uncertain.

(49)   Polycharmus, <u>Lyciaca</u> and Artemidorus,
<u>Geographumena</u> ap. Ath. 8, 833D (probably both
Hellenistic authors); Ael. <u>Hist</u>. An 8, 5, and
12, 1. Plu. 6,976C and St. <u>Byz</u>. Σοῦρα .   The
site can be identified, though the spring is
now above sea-level, Bean, <u>Lycian Turkey</u>,
130ff., and Borchhardt, <u>Myra</u>,   76ff. with a
photograph of the remains of a late Hellenic
temple.

(50)   Pliny, <u>HN</u>. 31, 17, 22 describes briefly a
similar divination from the behaviour of fish
in the source of the River Limyra in Lycia,
whenever fed.   If he is not confusing the
site, this shows the use of freshwater fish
at an inland sanctuary, but it is not identified as Apolline.

      Other references to what have been taken
as Apolline oracles in Asia Minor, but which
are rejected in the present work:-

(1)   Apollo of Hybla: A consultation mentioned in
Menodotus, <u>Record of the notable things on
Samos</u>, (Ath. 15, 672E).   Wilamowitz, <u>GGA</u>.
1900, 573 n. 3 proposed to amend to Aulai and
identified it with the sanctuary of Apollo at
Hylai or Aulai, a mountain village near Magnesia on the Maeander, the site of an Apolline
cave (Paus. 10, 32, 6).   An ecstatic cult is
illustrated on the coins of Magnesia in the
reigns of Gordian and Otacilla.   But there is
no evidence for an oracle.   Picard, <u>Ephèse</u>,
462, would identify it with Hieracome.   But
all this association is denied by Laumonier,
<u>Cultes</u>, 704, who argues convincingly that
Hybla was on Samos.

(2)   D.L. 7. 21, the Delion in Sinope is given as
an alternative oracle-centre to Delphi as the
source of Diogenes' advice to counterfeit the
currency.   This could only be preferred on the
principle of <u>difficilior lectio</u>, which would
not apply plausibly in this case.

(3)   IGRRP. 4, 692, from Sebaste, describing the
foundation of the colony by Augustus, "when
the plans of Phoebus granted an oracle".

Cagnat supposed a Phrygian oracle-centre. Cf. W. Ramsay, _Cities_, II, no. 495, p. 603. But this vague poetic reference could as easily refer to a consultation by Augustus of the Sibylline Books - probably a legendary event.

(4)   SEG. 2, 710, a _lex sacra_ from Pednelissus in Pisidia concerning the admission by initiation of a priestess of an unspecified deity. As the priestess's title is Galato, the deity has been identified as Apollo (cf. the cult-title Calaxios). There is also a reference to a μάντις. But in spite of Nock, 1, 118, n. 290, the Apolline association is quite doubtful. Cf. Sokolowski, _Asie Mineure_, no. 79.

There are no doubt other casual references in inscriptions from Asia Minor to prophets or prophecy which the present writer has overlooked, but probably they would not add much to the picture of the Apolline oracle-centres.

SELECT BIBLIOGRAPHY

[The books chiefly cited with the abbreviations used.
Articles in periodicals are not included.]

Akurgal, Ekrem, Ancient civilizations and ruins of
    Turkey, Istanbul, 1969.
Barnes, Timothy, D., Constantine and Eusebius, Harvard,
    1981 [Barnes]
Bean, George E., Aegean Turkey, London 1966. Turkey's
    Southern Coast, London, 1968. Lycian Turkey,
    London, 1978.
Behr, C.A., Aelius Aristides and the Sacred Tales,
    Amsterdam, 1968 [Behr].
Benndorf, Otto, and Niemann, G., Reisen in Lykien und
    Karien, Vienna, 1884 [Benndorf, Reisen].
Borchhardt, J., Myra, eine lykische Metropole, (Istan-
    buler Forschungen 30), Berlin, 1975.
Bouché-Leclerq, A., Histoire de la divination dans
    l'antiquité, Paris, 1870-82 (Reprinted, Brussels,
    1963) [Bouché-Leclerq].
Buresch, K., Ἀπόλλων Κλάριος   Untersuchungen zum
    Orakelwesen des späteren Altertums, Leipzig, 1889
    [Buresch]
Cagnat, R., Inscriptiones Graecae ad res Romanas per-
    tinentes, Paris, 1911-1927 [IGRRP].
Collectanea Alexandria, ed. J. U. Powell, Oxford, 1925
    [Coll. Alex.]
Cook, John M., The Troad, an archaeological and top-
    ographical study, Oxford, 1973 [Cook, Troad].
Delvoye, Charles and Georges Roux (editors), La
    civilization de l'antiquité à nos jours, Brussels,
    1967. Martin, R. pp. 296 ff. Le Didymeion.
    Robert, L. pp. 305 ff. Claros.
Didyma, ed. T. Wiegand, Erster Teil, Knackfuss, H.,
    die Baubeschreibung Berlin, 1941 [Did. I].
    Zweiter Teil, Rehm, A., die Inscriften, Berlin,
    1958 [Did. II].

Select Bibliography

Dittenberger, W., Sylloge Inscriptionum Graecarum,
    Lipsiae, 1915-20 [Ditt. Syll.³] Orientis
    Graeci Inscriptiones Selectae, Lipsiae, 1903-5
    [Ditt. OGI.]
Dodds, E.R., Pagan and Christian in an age of anxiety,
    Cambridge, 1965.
Erbse, H., Fragmente de griechischer Theosophien,
    Hamburg, 1941 [Erbse].
Frend, W.H.C., Martyrdom and Persecution in the Early
    Church, Oxford, 1965.
Günther, Wolfgang, Das Orakel von Didyma in hellenist-
    ischer Zeit (Istanbuler Mitteilungen, Beiheft 4)
    Tübingen, 1971 [Günther].
Habicht, C., Altertümer von Pergamum, 8, 3, die In-
    scriften des Asclepieions, 1969.
Hausoullier, B., Études sur l'histoire de Milet et du
    Didymeion, Paris, 1902. [Haussoullier, Milet].
    Offrande à Apollon Didymeen, Délégation en Perse,
    Recherches archaeologiques, deuxième série, tome
    7, ed. J. de Morgan, Paris, 1905 [Haussoullier,
    Délégation en Perse].
Head, B.V., Historia Numorum², Oxford, 1911 [Head,
    Hist. Num.²].
Huxley, G.L., The early Ionians, London, 1966.
Jeffery, L.H., The local scripts of archaic Greece,
    Oxford, 1961. [Jeffery, LSAG.]
Jones, A.H.M., Cities of the Eastern Roman Provines²,
    Oxford, 1971 [Jones, Eastern Cities].
Kaibel, G., Epigrammata Graeca ex lapidibus conlecta,
    Berlin, 1878 [Kaibel].
Kern, O., Die Inscriften von Magnesia am Maeander,
    Berlin, 1910 [Kern, Inscr. Magn].
Klees, H., Die Eigenart des griechischen Glaubens an
    Orakel und Seher (Tübinger Beiträge zur Alter-
    tumswissenschaft, Heft 45) Stuttgart, 1965.
    [Klees, Eigenart].
Laumonier, A., Les cultes indigenes en Carie (Biblio-
    thèque des écoles francaises d'Athènes et de
    Rome, fascicule 188), Paris 1958 [Laumonier,
    Cultes].
Magie, D., Roman rule in Asia Minor to the end of the
    third century after Christ, Princeton, 1950
    [Magie, RRAM].
Martin, R. and Metzger, H., La religion grecque,
    Paris, 1976.
Meiggs, R. and Lewis, D., A selection of Greek histor-
    ical inscriptions to the end of the fifth century
    B.C., Oxford, 1969 [Meiggs-Lewis].
Milet. Ergebnisse der Ausgrabungen und Untersuchungen
    seit dem Jahre 1899, ed. T. Wiegand and others,
    Berlin, 1906 - [Milet].

261

Select Bibliography

Milne, J.G., Kolophon and its coinage : a study
    (Numismatic notes and monographs, no. 9), New
    York 1941.
Nilsson, M., Geschichte der griechische Religion²,
    Munich, 1955 [Nilsson, Gr. Rel.]
Nock, A.D., Essays on religion and the ancient world,
    Oxford, 1972 [Nock].
Parke, H.W. and Wormell, R.O.W., The Delphic Oracle,
    Oxford, 1956. [Parke and Wormell, D.O.]
Parke, H.W., The Oracles of Zeus. Oxford, 1967.
Pauly-Wissowa-Kroll, Real Encyclopädie der klassischen
    Altertamswissenschaft, Stuttgart, 1894- [PW.]
Picard, C., Ephèse et Claros, recherches sur les san-
    ctuaires et les cultes de l'Ionie du Nord, Paris,
    1922 [Picard, Ephèse].
Ramsay, W.M., Cities and Bishoprics of Phrygia, Ox-
    ford, 1895-7 [Ramsay, Cities]. Studies in the
    history and art of the Eastern Roman provinces,
    ed. W. M. Ramsay, Aberdeen, 1906. Anatolian
    studies presented to Sir William Mitchell Ramsay,
    Manchester, 1923.
Robert, L., Études épigraphiques et philologiques
    (Biblothèque de l'École des Hautes Études, fasc.
    272), Paris, 1938. Hellenica, recueil d'épig-
    raphie et de numismatique et d'antiquités grecq-
    ues, Limoges and Paris, 1940- [Robert, Hellenica].
    Les Fouilles de Claros, conférence donnée à
    l'Université d'Ankara le 26 Octobre, 1953, Lim-
    oges, 1954 [Robert, Les Fouilles]. Villes d'Asie
    Mineure, études de geographie ancienne,² Paris,
    1962. Documents d 'Asie Mineure meridionale :
    inscriptions, monnaies et geographié Hautes
    Études du Monde gréco-romains, ² Geneva and
    Paris, 1966. Laodicée du Lycus, La nymphée, by
    Des Gagniers, P. Devambez, etc. Univ. Laval,
    recherches archéologiques, série 1 : fouilles,
    1, Quebec and Paris, 1969. [Robert, Laodicée]
Roscher, W.H., Lexicon der griechischen und römischen
    Mythologie, Leipzig, 1884- [Roscher].
Rostovtzeff, M., The Social and Economic History of
    the Hellenistic World, Oxford, 1941 [Rostovtzeff,
    SEHHW]
Sokolowski, F., Lois sacrées de l'Asie Mineure (École
    francaise d'Athènes, travaux et mémoires 9),
    Paris, 1955. [Sokolowski, Asie Mineure].
Syme, R., The Roman Revolution, Oxford 1939. Tacitus,
    Oxford, 1958 History in Ovid, Oxford, 1978.
Tituli Asiae Minoris, ed. E. Kalinka, Vienna, 1901-
    1930 [TAM].
Tod, M.N., A Selection of Greek Historical Inscript-
    ions, Oxford, 1933-1948 [Tod].

262

Select Bibliography

Tuchelt, M.N., Die archischen Sculpturen von Didyma
      (Istanbuler Forschungen, 27), Berlin, 1970,
      [Tuchelt, Archischen Skulpturen]
Voigtländer, W., Der jüngste Apollontempel von Didyma;
      Geschichte seines Baudecors (Istanbuler Mitteil-
      ungen, Beiheft 14), Berlin, 1975.
Welles, C.B., Royal Correspondence in the Hellenic
      Period, New Haven 1954 [Welles].
von Wilamowitz-Moellendorff, U. Die Glaube der Hellen-
      en, Berlin, 1926-1932.
Wolff, G., De novissima oraculorum aetate. Berlin,
      1854 Porphyrii de Philosophia ex oraculis
      haurienda librorum reliquiae, Berlin, 1856
      [Wolff].

INDEX